THE NEW AVENGERS

SECRET INVASION BOOK 2

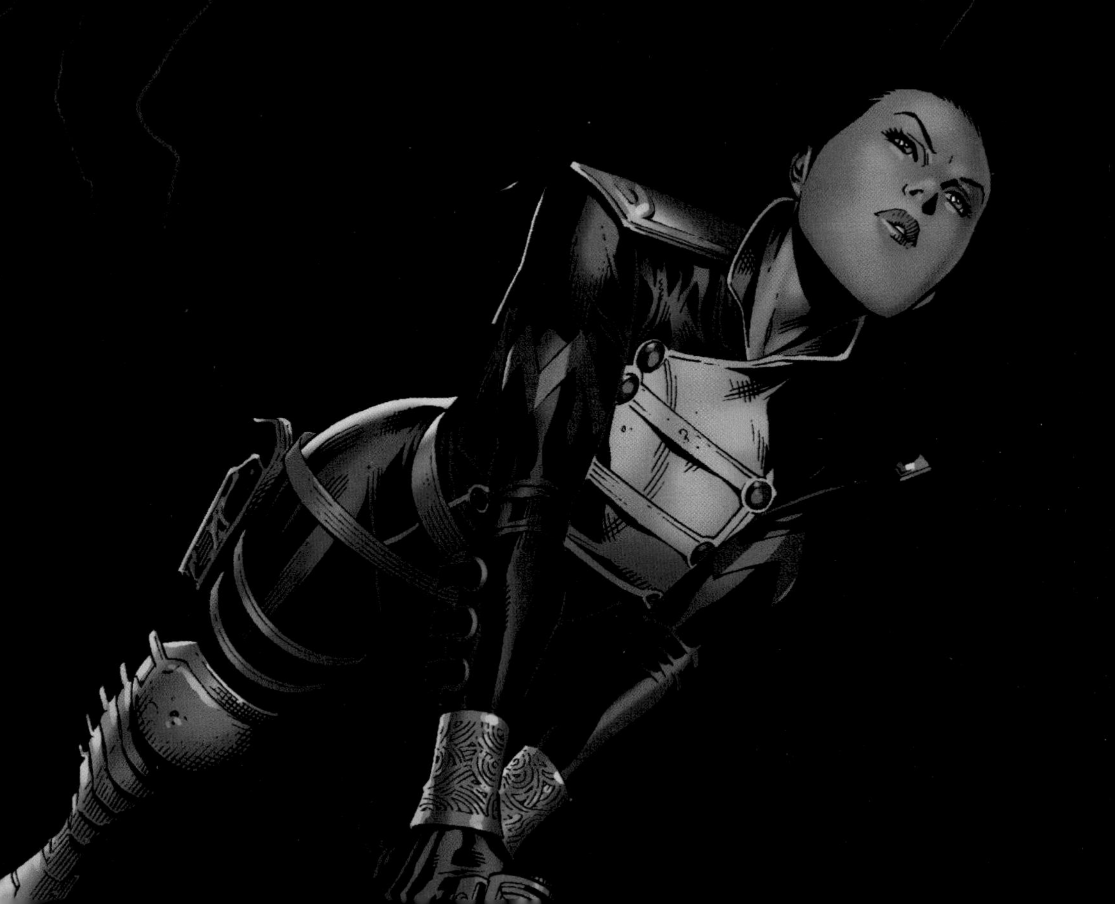

THE NEW AVENGERS

SECRET INVASION BOOK 2

WRITER: **Brian Michael Bendis**
PENCILS: **Billy Tan,**
Jim Cheung (Issue #45)
& Michael Gaydos (Issue #47)
INKS: **Danny Miki, Matt Banning,**
John Dell, Jay Leisten
& Michael Gaydos
COLORS: **Jason Keith & Justin Ponsor**
LETTERER: **RS & Comicraft's Albert Deschesne**

ASSOCIATE EDITOR: **Jeanine Schaefer**
EDITOR: **Tom Brevoort**

COLLECTION EDITOR: **Jennifer Grünwald**
EDITORIAL ASSISTANT: **Alex Starbuck**
ASSISTANT EDITORS: **Cory Levine & John Denning**
EDITOR, SPECIAL PROJECTS: **Mark D. Beazley**
SENIOR EDITOR, SPECIAL PROJECTS: **Jeff Youngquist**
SENIOR VICE PRESIDENT OF SALES: **David Gabriel**

PREVIOUSLY:

The New Avengers and Tony Stark have known there is a shape-shifting alien Skrull infestation on Earth, but they couldn't detect the Skrulls and now can't trust anyone to be who they seem to be. Including themselves.

When a Skrull ship crash-lands in the prehistoric area of Antarctica called the Savage Land, Tony Stark leads his team of Avengers on a chase to stop them...following Luke Cage and the "underground" Avengers, those who did not join Tony's new Initiative.

When both teams of Avengers get there the ship opens, revealing a shocking gathering of Marvel Heroes, icons from a more innocent time. These heroes declare that they have been held captive by the Skrull Empire and have just returned to Earth.

But if these are the real heroes, then who are the Avengers that have been living here on Earth?

The standoff between the Avengers of yesterday and today bursts into violence and is only interrupted when Captain America appears from the Skrull ship. But Captain America was recently assassinated...or was he?

The invasion has begun.

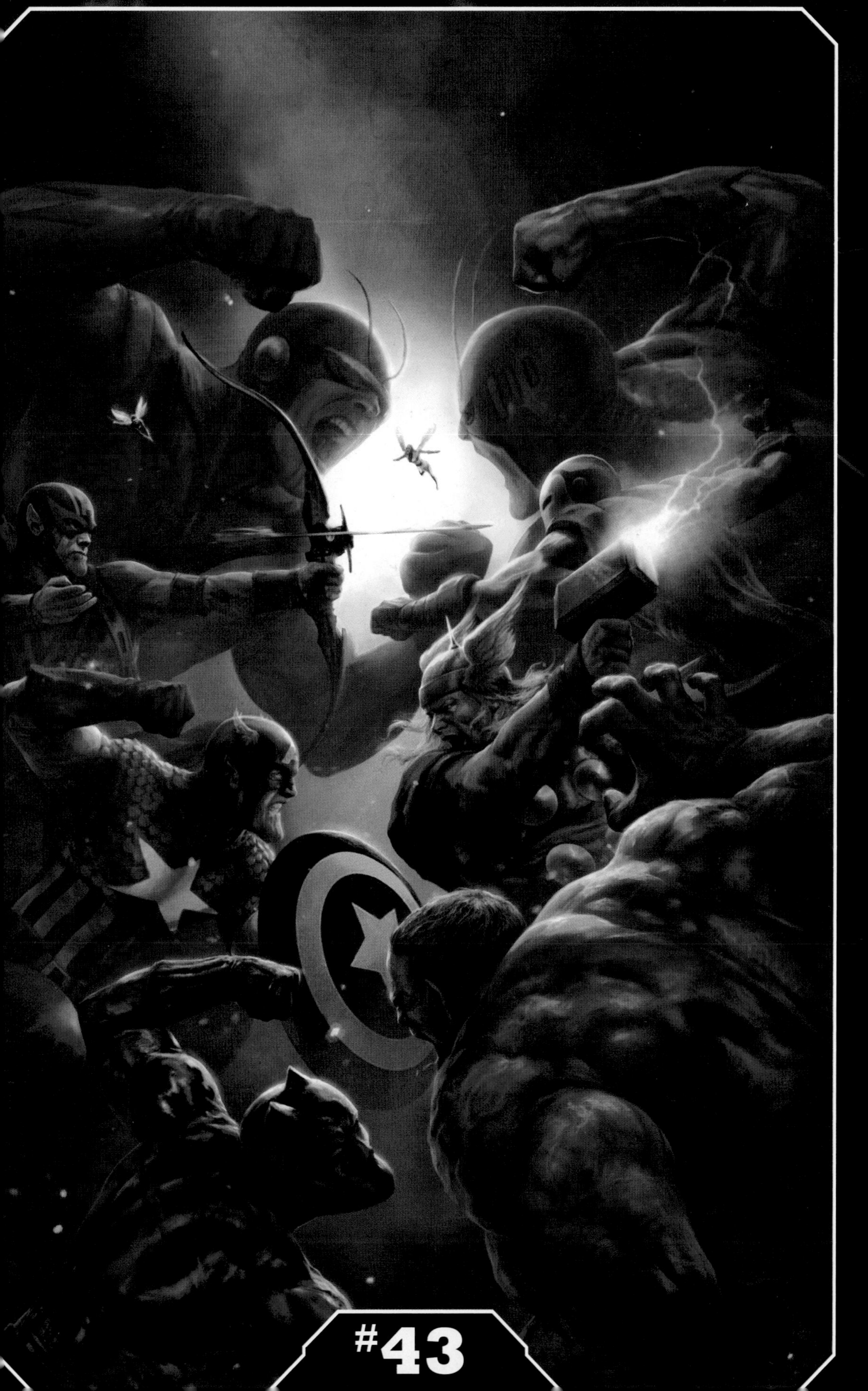
#43

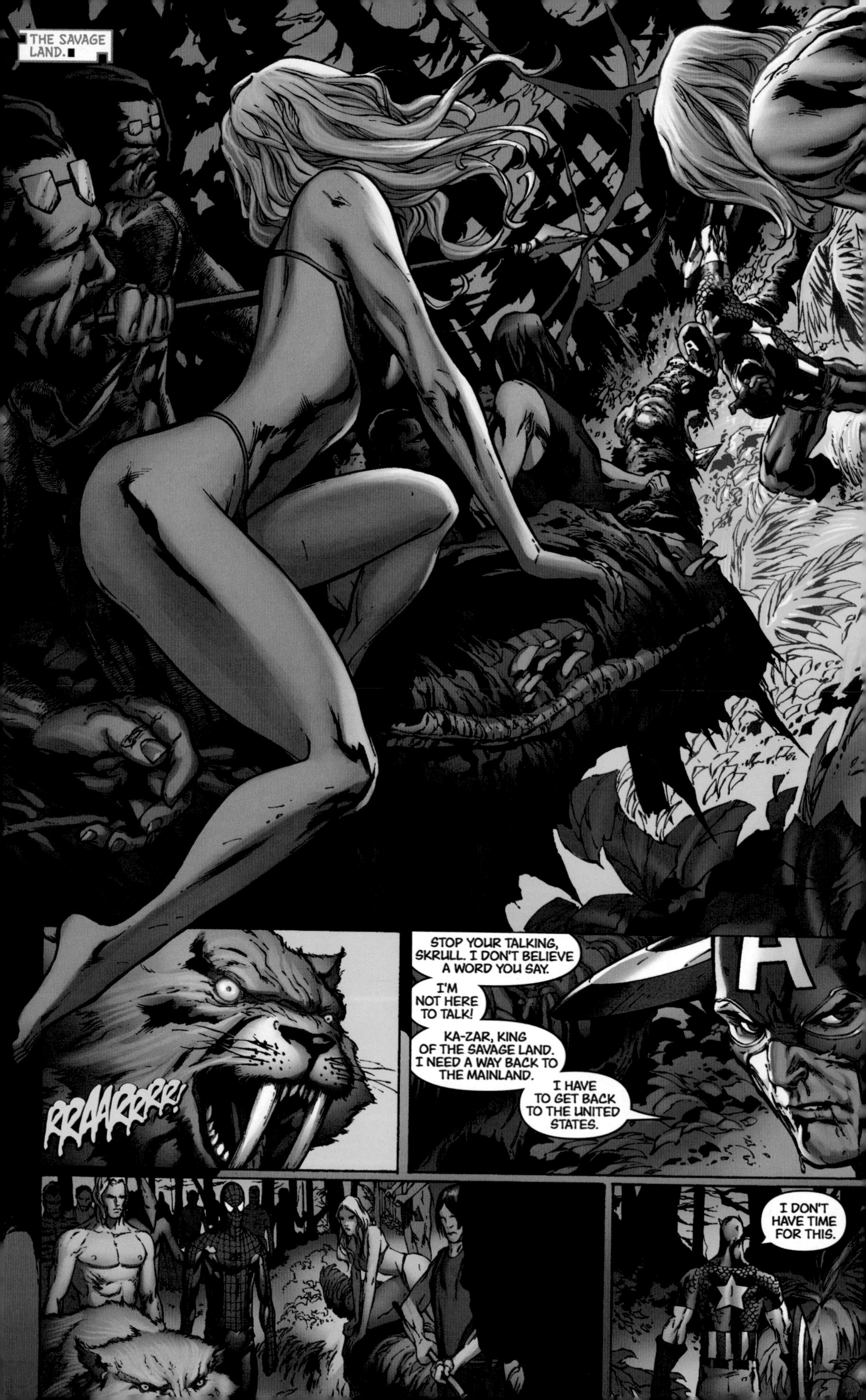
THE SAVAGE LAND.
RRAARRRR!
STOP YOUR TALKING, SKRULL. I DON'T BELIEVE A WORD YOU SAY.
I'M NOT HERE TO TALK!
KA-ZAR, KING OF THE SAVAGE LAND. I NEED A WAY BACK TO THE MAINLAND.
I HAVE TO GET BACK TO THE UNITED STATES.
I DON'T HAVE TIME FOR THIS.

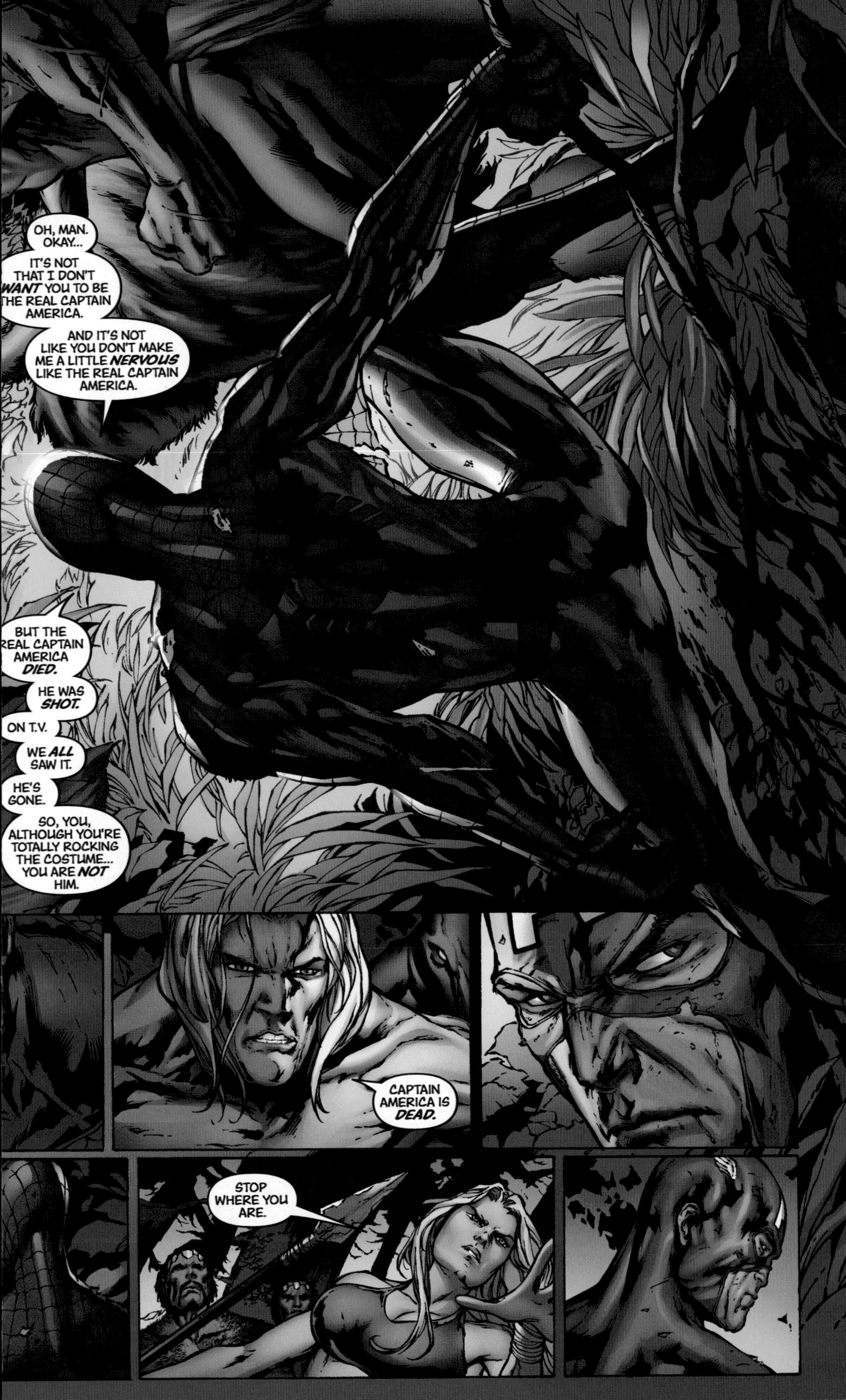
OH, MAN. OKAY...
IT'S NOT THAT I DON'T WANT YOU TO BE THE REAL CAPTAIN AMERICA.
AND IT'S NOT LIKE YOU DON'T MAKE ME A LITTLE NERVOUS LIKE THE REAL CAPTAIN AMERICA.
BUT THE REAL CAPTAIN AMERICA DIED.
HE WAS SHOT.
ON T.V.
WE ALL SAW IT.
HE'S GONE.
SO, YOU, ALTHOUGH YOU'RE TOTALLY ROCKING THE COSTUME... YOU ARE NOT HIM.
CAPTAIN AMERICA IS DEAD.
STOP WHERE YOU ARE.

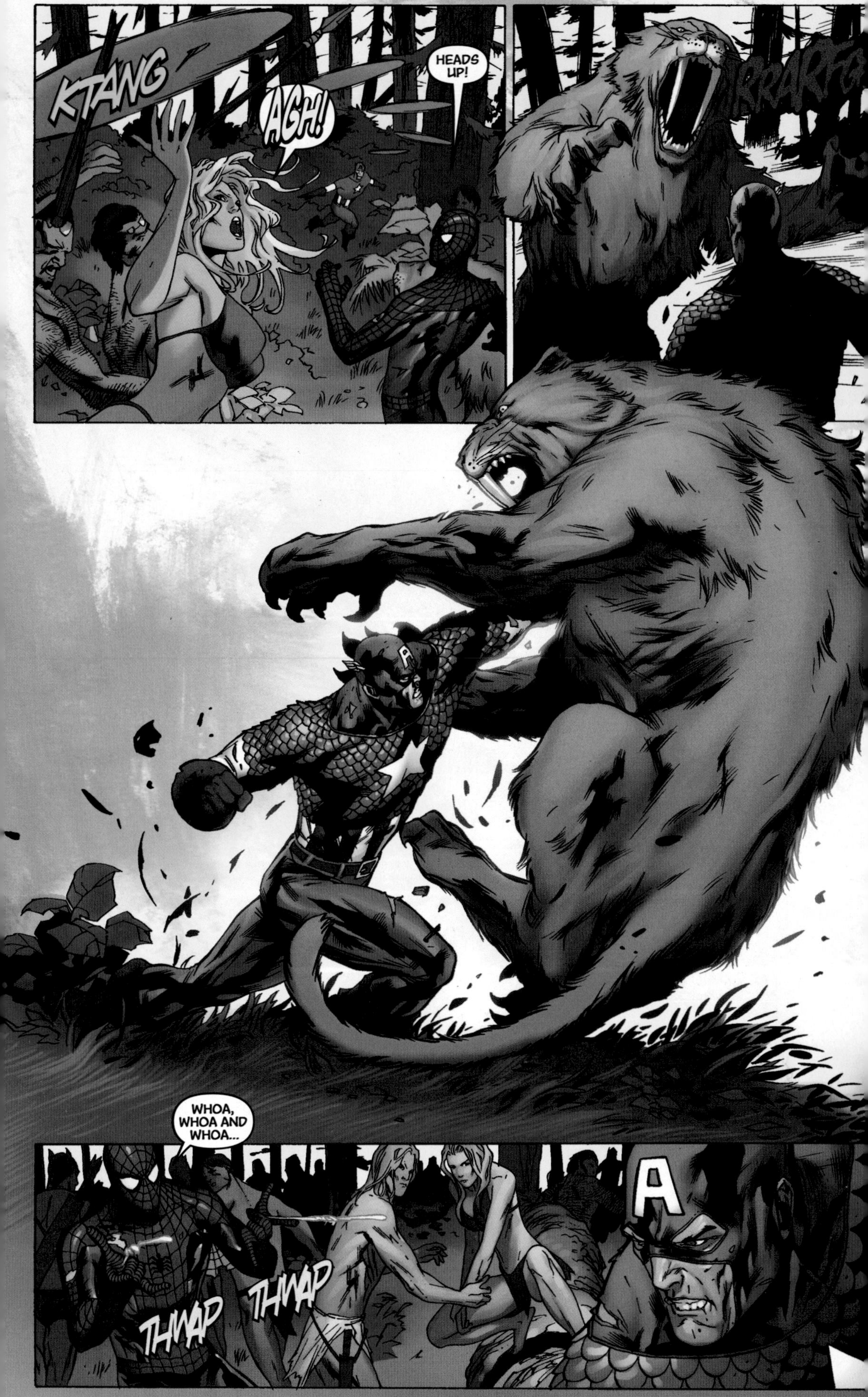
KTANG
AGH!
HEADS UP!
WHOA, WHOA AND WHOA...
THWAP
THWAP

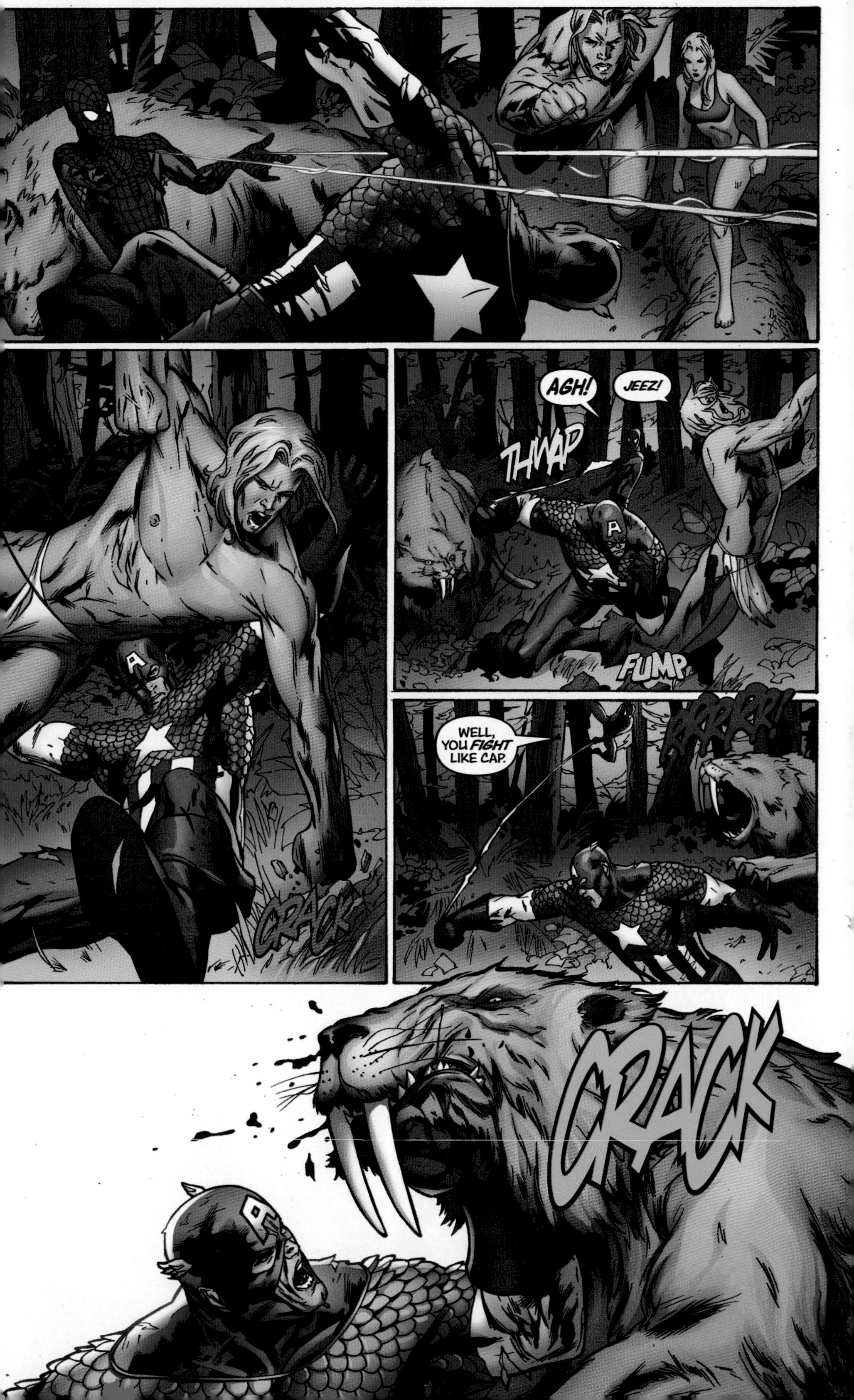
CRACK
AGH!
JEEZ!
THWAP
FUMP
WELL, YOU *FIGHT* LIKE CAP.
CRACK

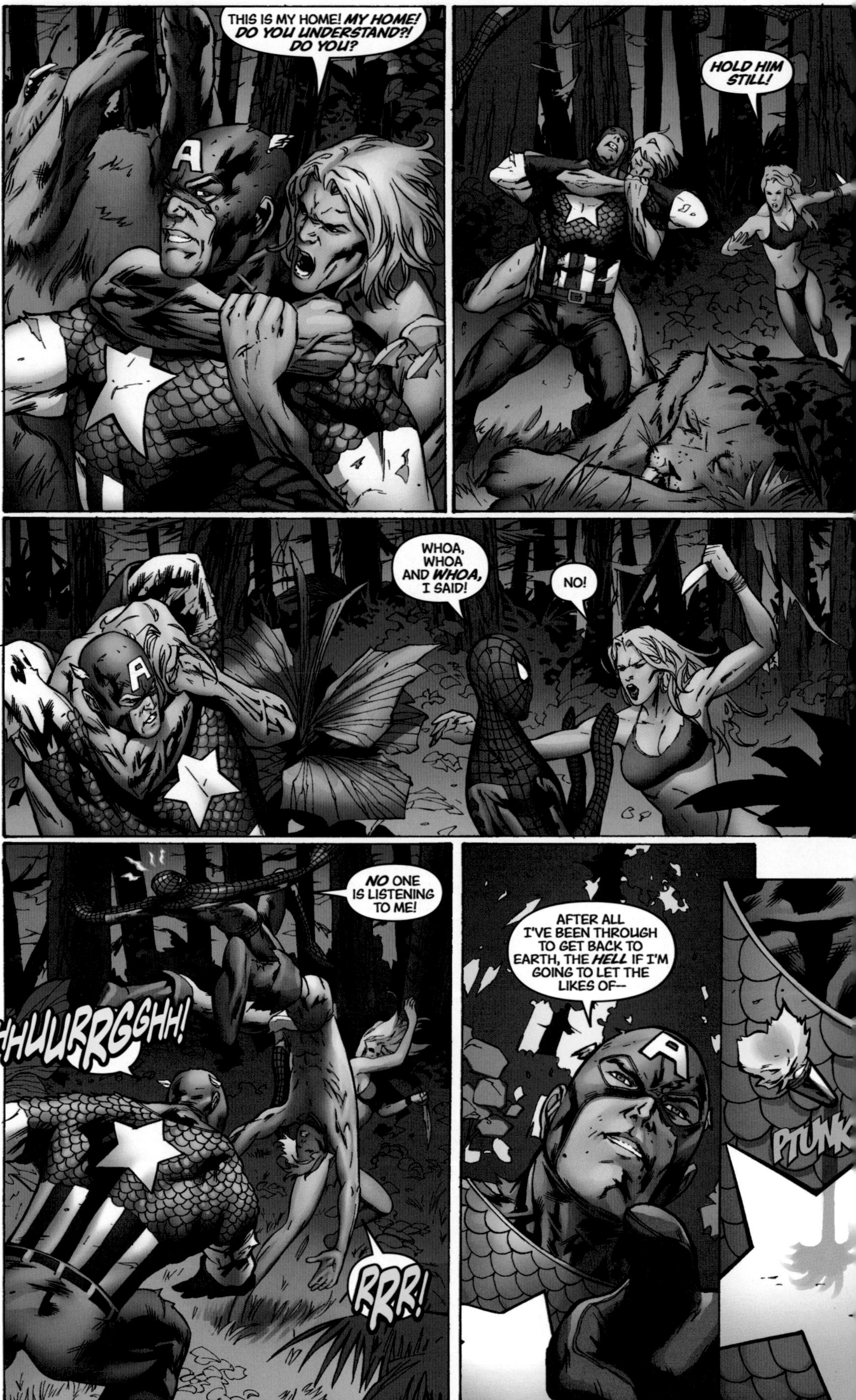
THIS IS MY HOME! MY HOME! DO YOU UNDERSTAND?! DO YOU?
HOLD HIM STILL!
WHOA, WHOA AND WHOA, I SAID!
NO!
NO ONE IS LISTENING TO ME!
HHUURRGGHH!
RRR!
AFTER ALL I'VE BEEN THROUGH TO GET BACK TO EARTH, THE HELL IF I'M GOING TO LET THE LIKES OF--
PTUNK

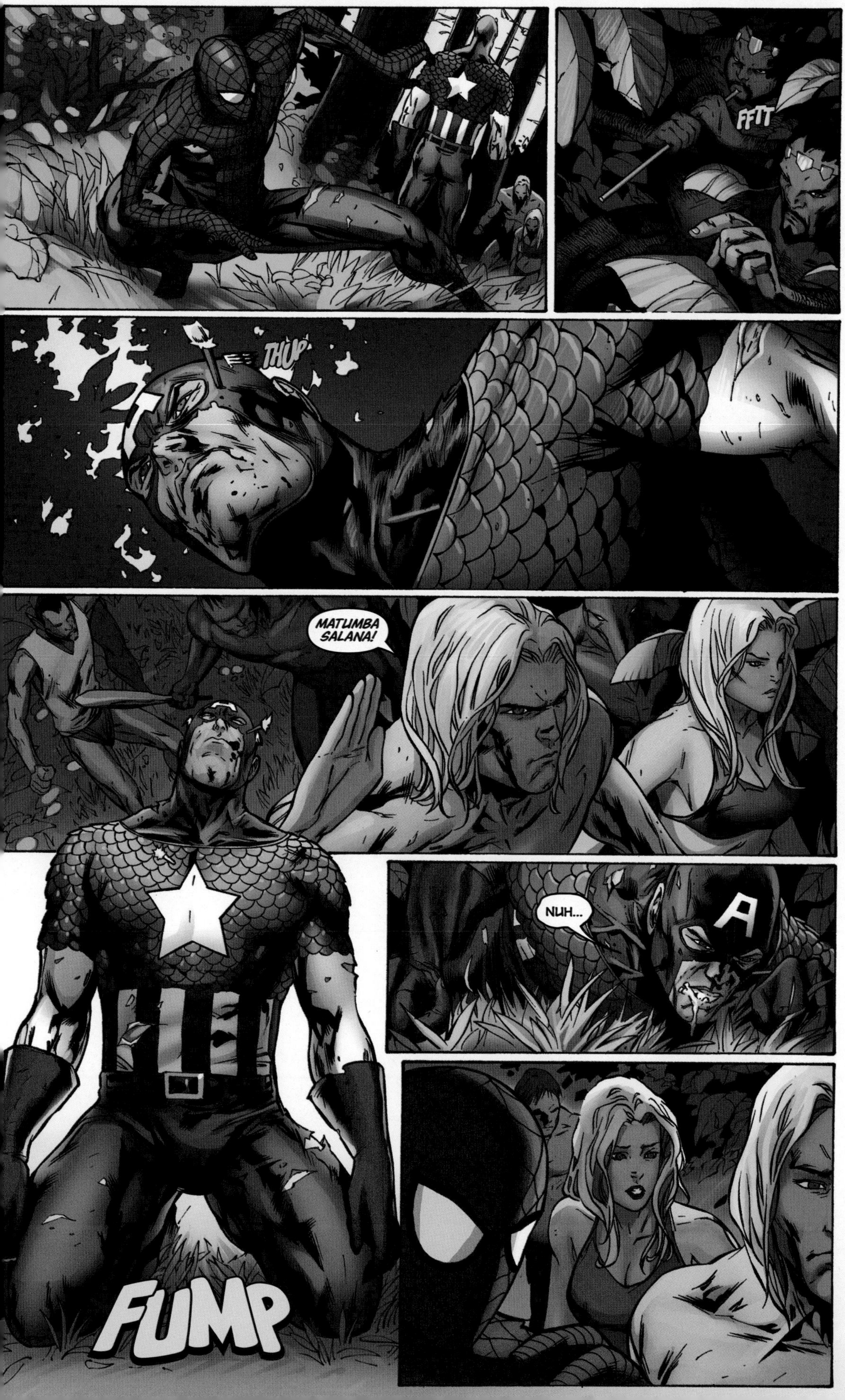
FFIT
THUP
MATUMBA SALANA!
NUH...
FUMP

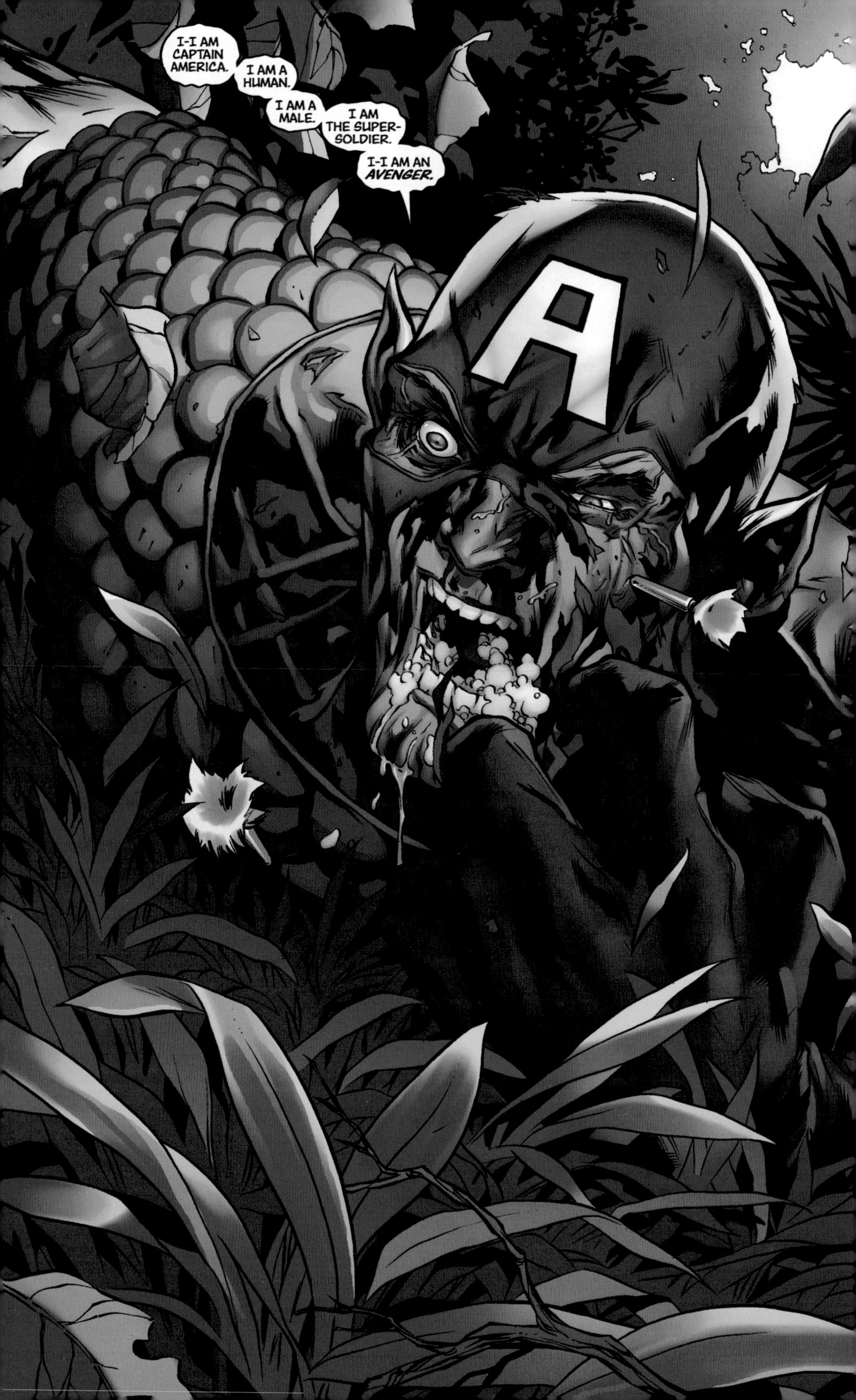
I-I AM CAPTAIN AMERICA.
I AM A HUMAN.
I AM A MALE.
I AM THE SUPER-SOLDIER.
I-I AM AN *AVENGER.*

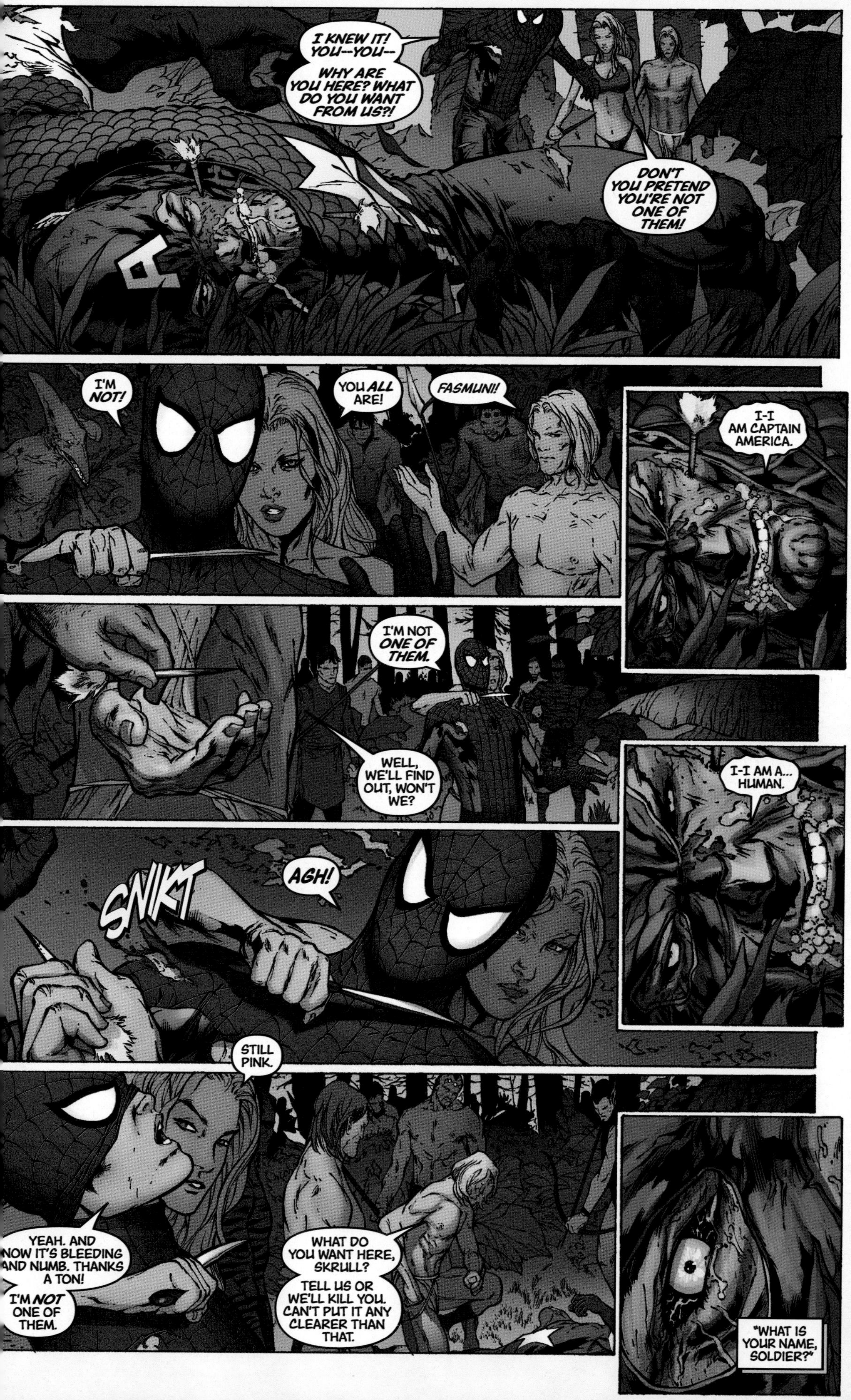
I KNEW IT! YOU--YOU--
WHY ARE YOU HERE? WHAT DO YOU WANT FROM US?!
DON'T YOU PRETEND YOU'RE NOT ONE OF THEM!
I'M NOT!
YOU ALL ARE!
FASMUNI!
I-I AM CAPTAIN AMERICA.
I'M NOT ONE OF THEM.
WELL, WE'LL FIND OUT, WON'T WE?
I-I AM A... HUMAN.
SNIKT
AGH!
STILL PINK.
YEAH. AND NOW IT'S BLEEDING AND NUMB. THANKS A TON!
I'M NOT ONE OF THEM.
WHAT DO YOU WANT HERE, SKRULL?
TELL US OR WE'LL KILL YOU. CAN'T PUT IT ANY CLEARER THAN THAT.
"WHAT IS YOUR NAME, SOLDIER?"

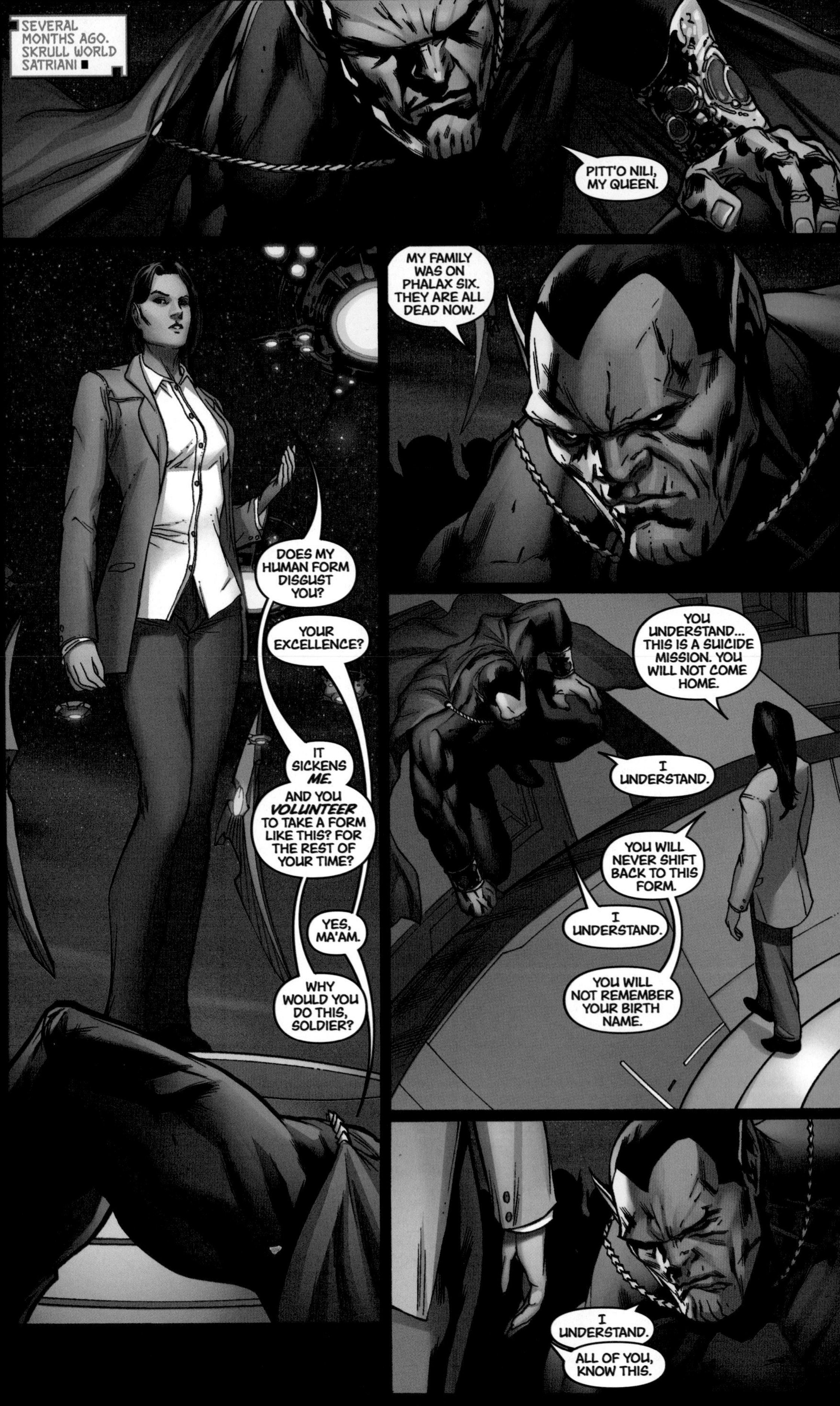

SEVERAL MONTHS AGO. SKRULL WORLD SATRIANI
PITT'O NILI, MY QUEEN.
DOES MY HUMAN FORM DISGUST YOU?
YOUR EXCELLENCE?
IT SICKENS *ME.*
AND YOU *VOLUNTEER* TO TAKE A FORM LIKE THIS? FOR THE REST OF YOUR TIME?
YES, MA'AM.
WHY WOULD YOU DO THIS, SOLDIER?
MY FAMILY WAS ON PHALAX SIX. THEY ARE ALL DEAD NOW.
YOU UNDERSTAND... THIS IS A SUICIDE MISSION. YOU WILL NOT COME HOME.
I UNDERSTAND.
YOU WILL NEVER SHIFT BACK TO THIS FORM.
I UNDERSTAND.
YOU WILL NOT REMEMBER YOUR BIRTH NAME.
I UNDERSTAND.
ALL OF YOU, KNOW THIS.

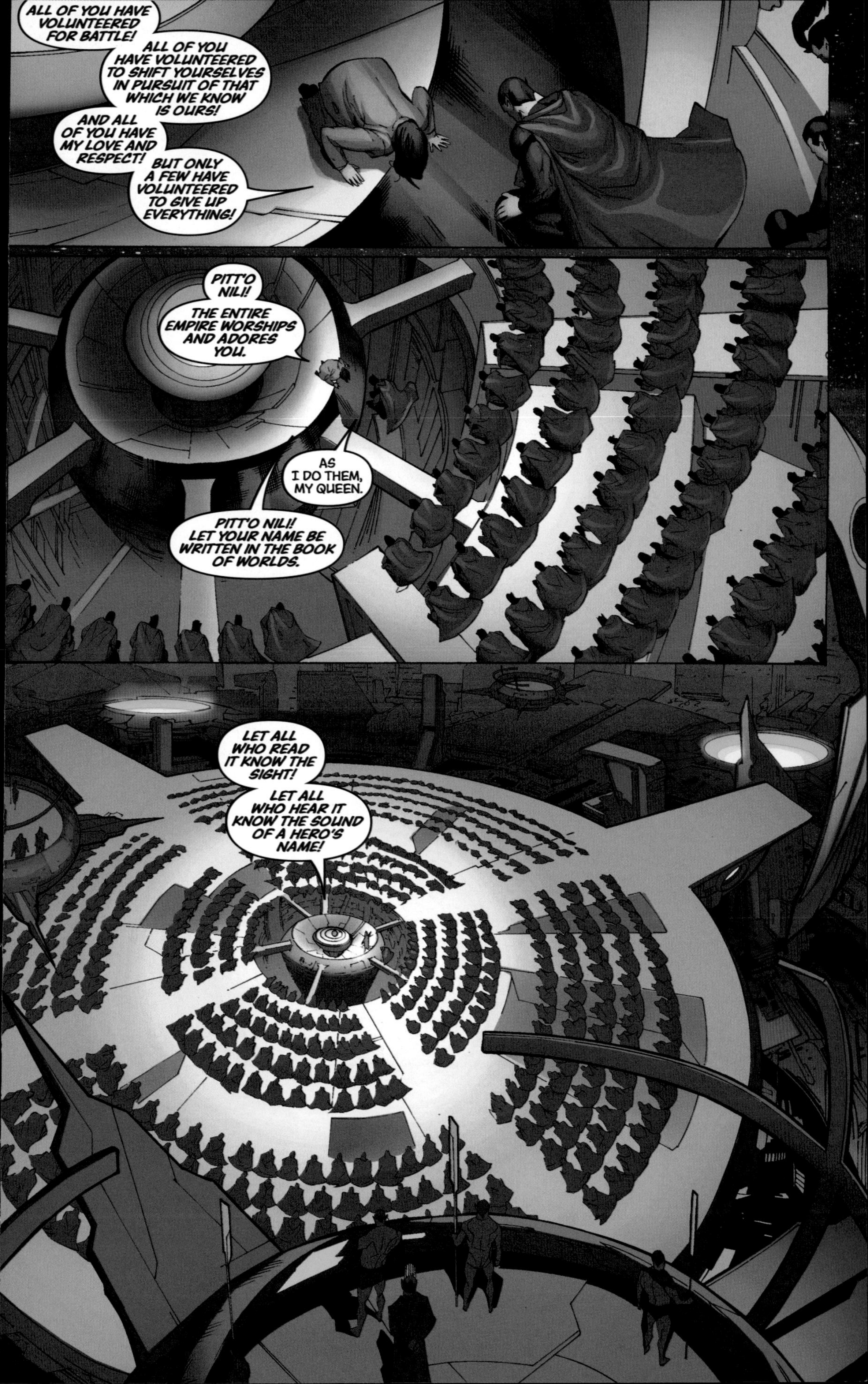
ALL OF YOU HAVE VOLUNTEERED FOR BATTLE!
ALL OF YOU HAVE VOLUNTEERED TO SHIFT YOURSELVES IN PURSUIT OF THAT WHICH WE KNOW IS OURS!
AND ALL OF YOU HAVE MY LOVE AND RESPECT!
BUT ONLY A FEW HAVE VOLUNTEERED TO GIVE UP EVERYTHING!
PITT'O NILI! THE ENTIRE EMPIRE WORSHIPS AND ADORES YOU.
AS I DO THEM, MY QUEEN.
PITT'O NILI! LET YOUR NAME BE WRITTEN IN THE BOOK OF WORLDS.
LET ALL WHO READ IT KNOW THE SIGHT!
LET ALL WHO HEAR IT KNOW THE SOUND OF A HERO'S NAME!

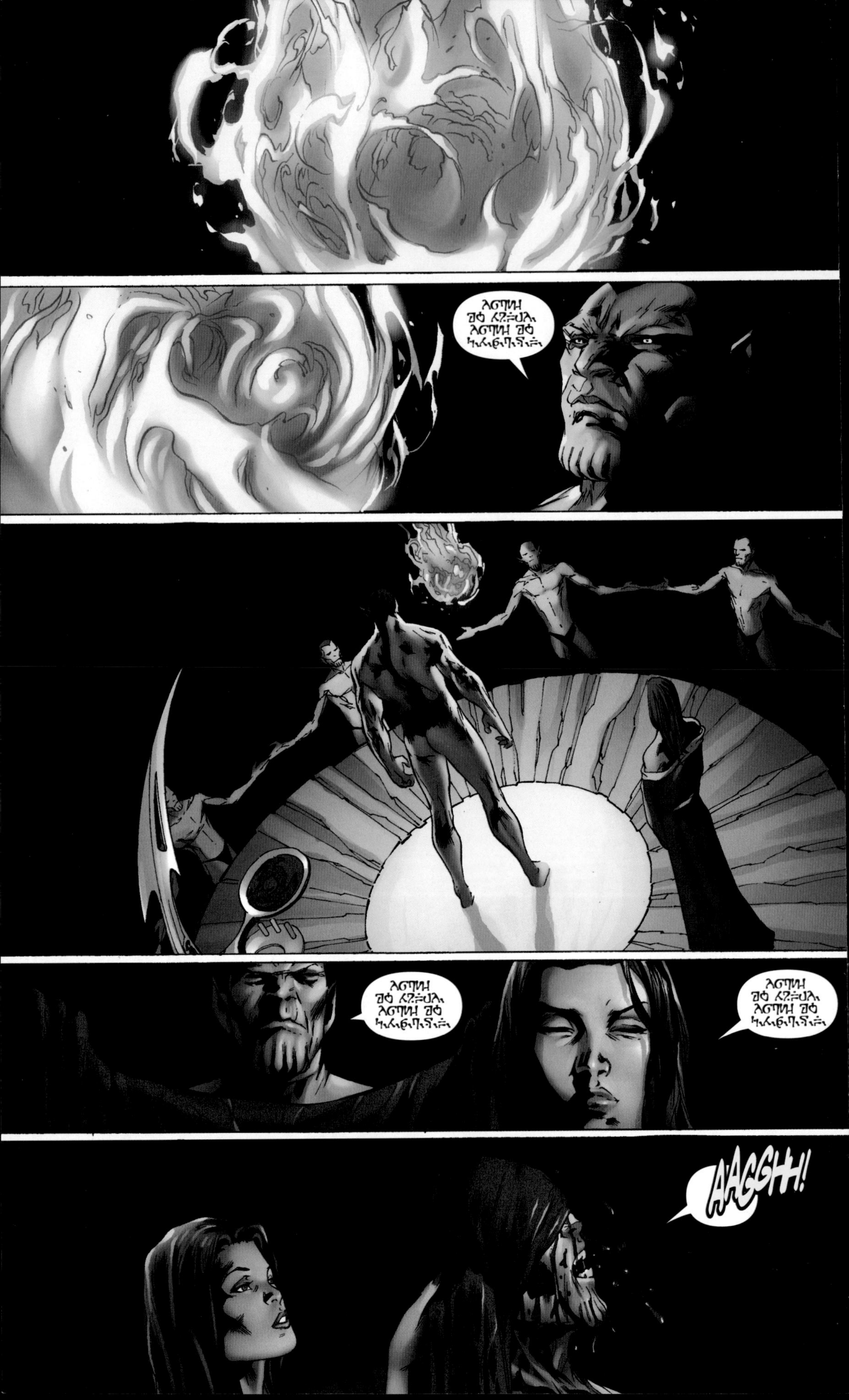
AAGGHH!

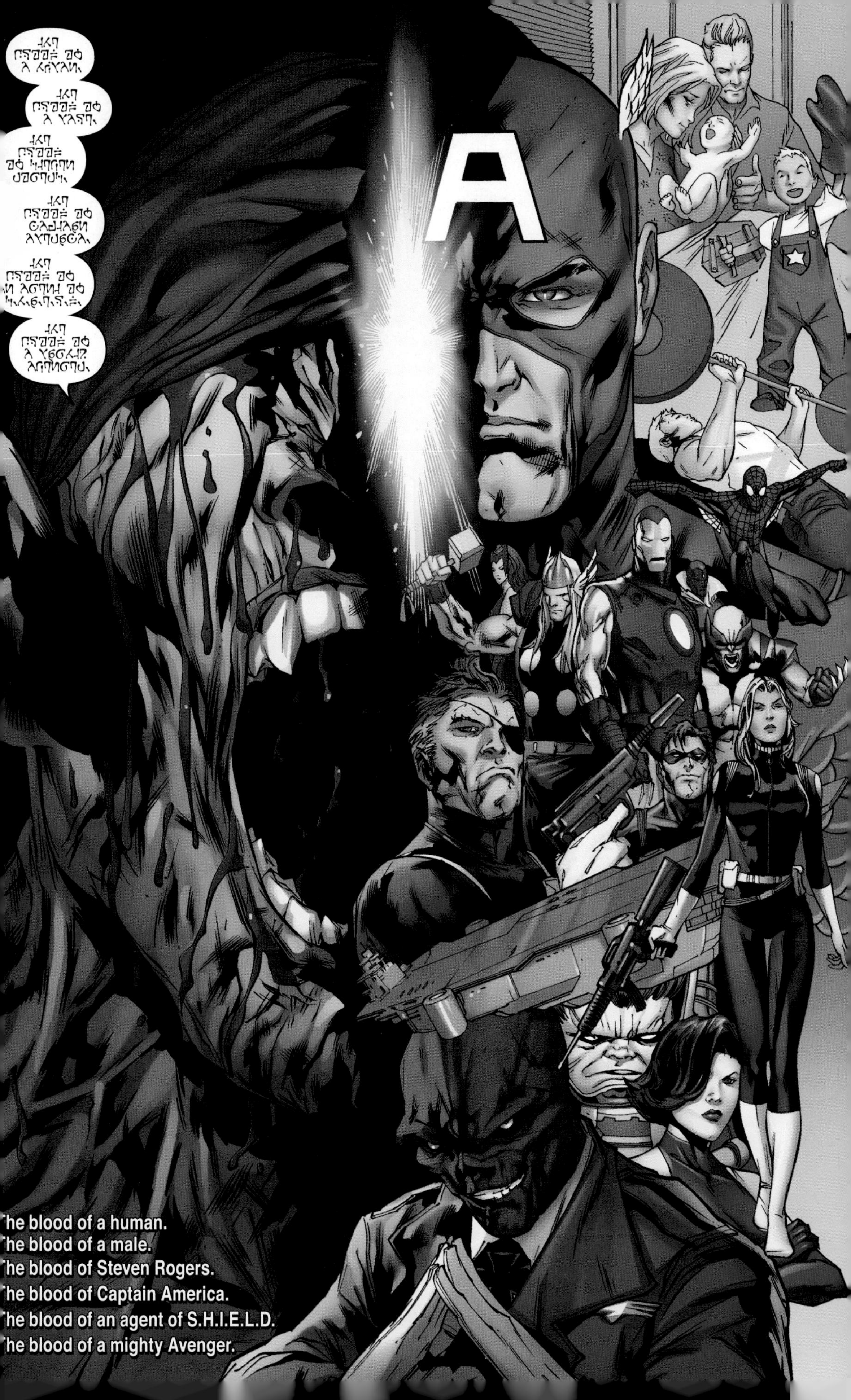
he blood of a human.
he blood of a male.
he blood of Steven Rogers.
he blood of Captain America.
he blood of an agent of S.H.I.E.L.D.
he blood of a mighty Avenger.

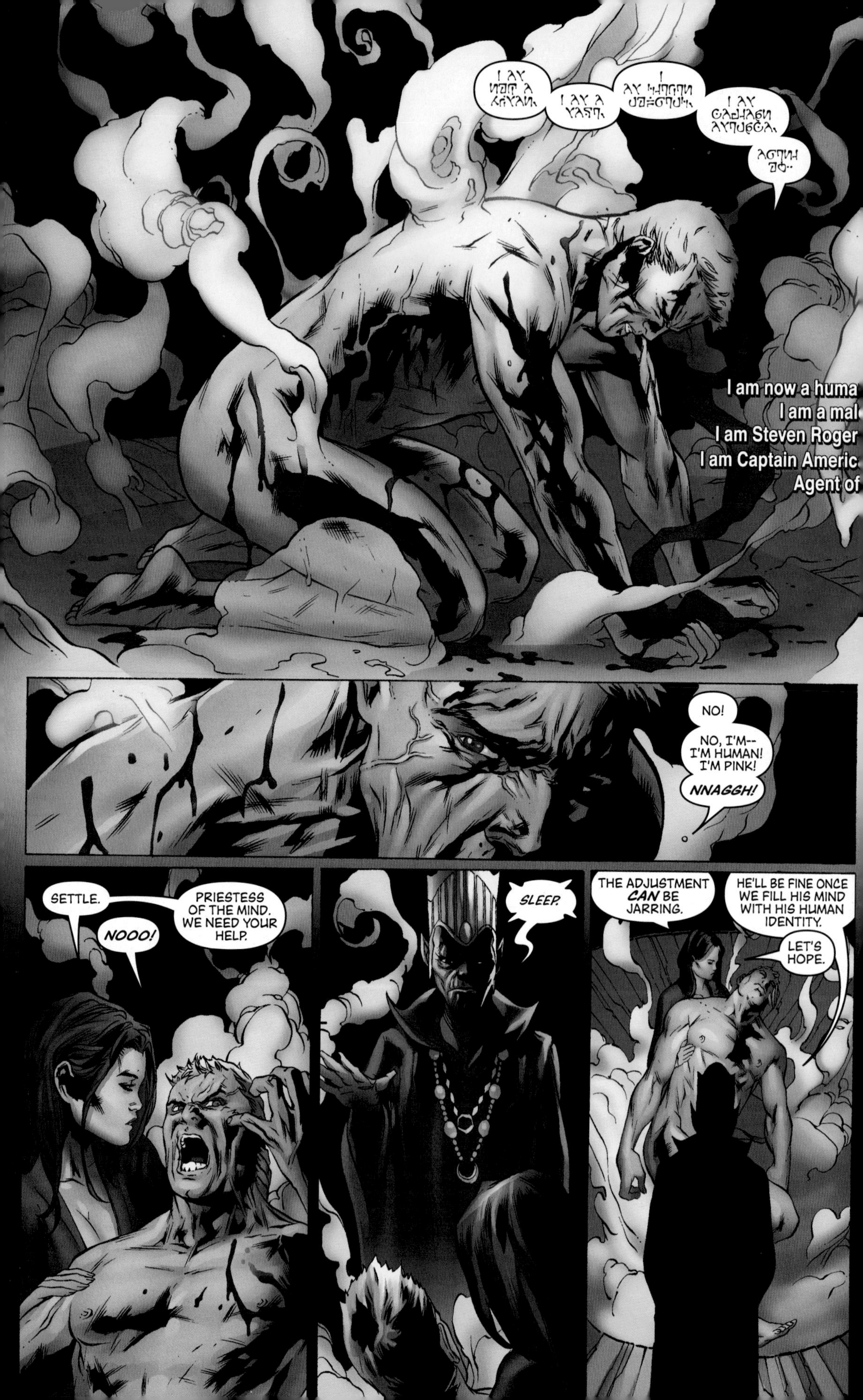
I am now a huma
I am a mal
I am Steven Roger
I am Captain Americ
Agent of
NO!
NO, I'M-- I'M HUMAN! I'M PINK!
NNAGGH!
SETTLE.
PRIESTESS OF THE MIND. WE NEED YOUR HELP.
NOOO!
SLEEP.
THE ADJUSTMENT CAN BE JARRING.
HE'LL BE FINE ONCE WE FILL HIS MIND WITH HIS HUMAN IDENTITY.
LET'S HOPE.

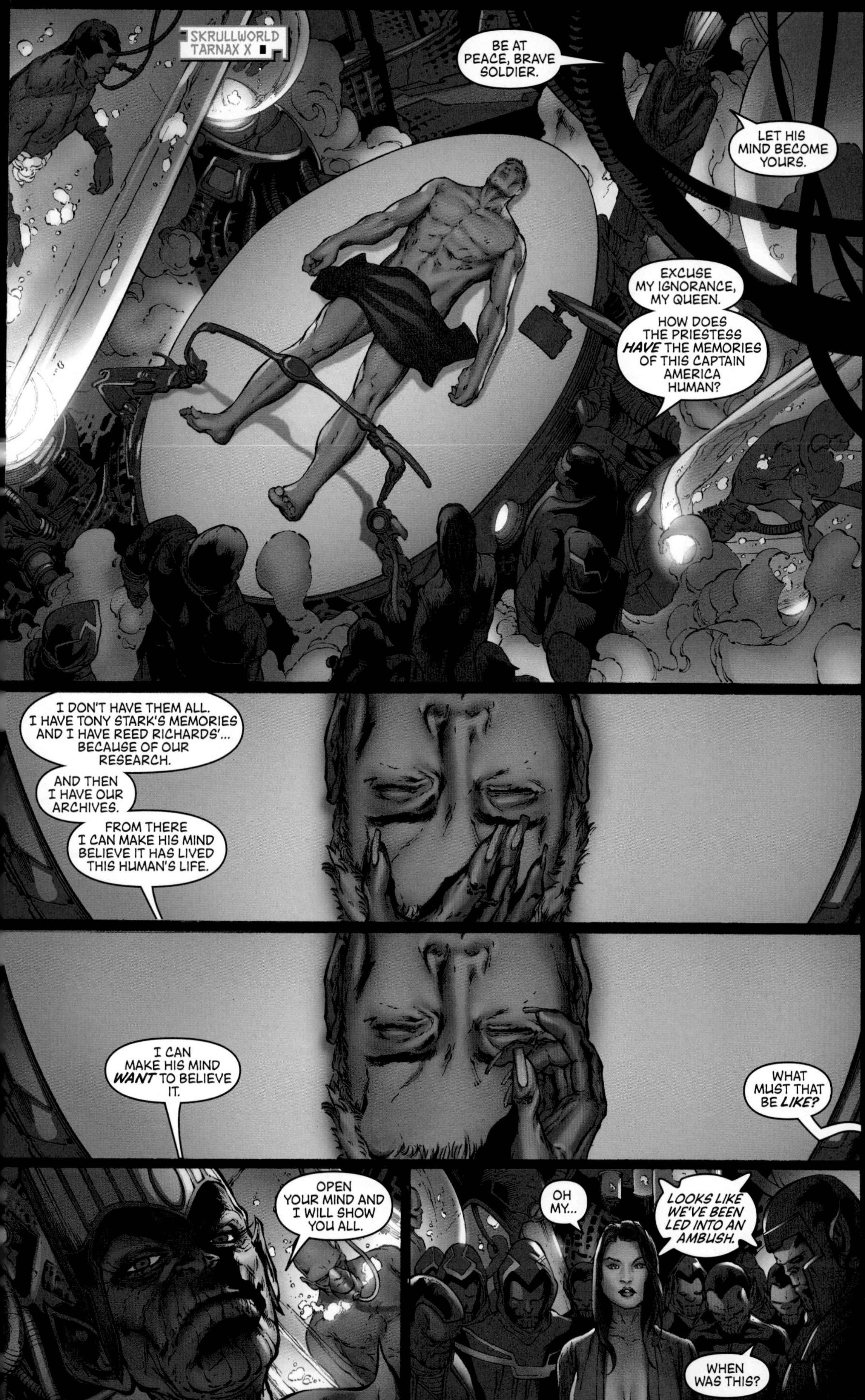
SKRULLWORLD TARNAX X
BE AT PEACE, BRAVE SOLDIER.
LET HIS MIND BECOME YOURS.
EXCUSE MY IGNORANCE, MY QUEEN.
HOW DOES THE PRIESTESS HAVE THE MEMORIES OF THIS CAPTAIN AMERICA HUMAN?
I DON'T HAVE THEM ALL. I HAVE TONY STARK'S MEMORIES AND I HAVE REED RICHARDS'... BECAUSE OF OUR RESEARCH.
AND THEN I HAVE OUR ARCHIVES.
FROM THERE I CAN MAKE HIS MIND BELIEVE IT HAS LIVED THIS HUMAN'S LIFE.
I CAN MAKE HIS MIND WANT TO BELIEVE IT.
WHAT MUST THAT BE LIKE?
OPEN YOUR MIND AND I WILL SHOW YOU ALL.
OH MY...
LOOKS LIKE WE'VE BEEN LED INTO AN AMBUSH.
WHEN WAS THIS?

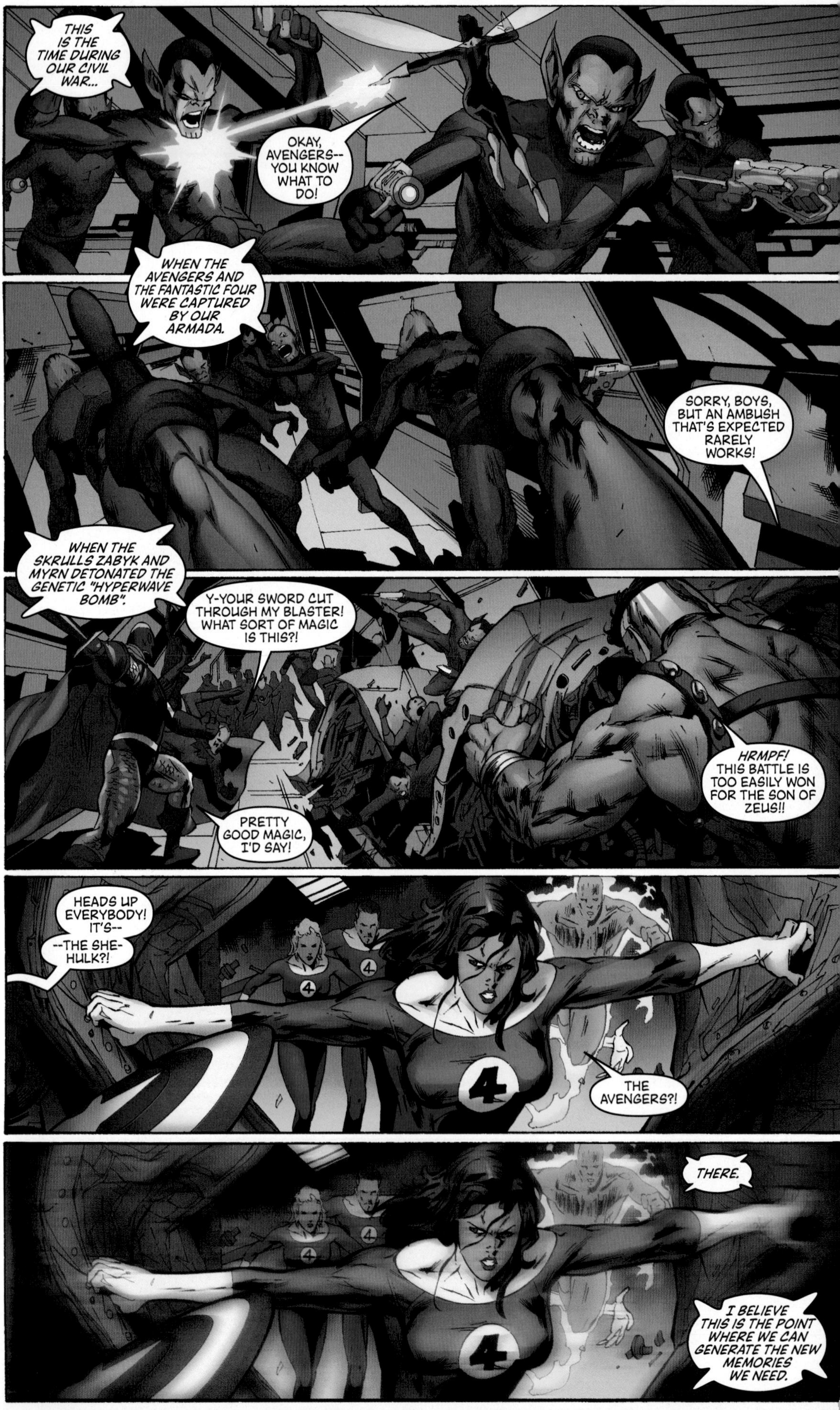
THIS IS THE TIME DURING OUR CIVIL WAR...
OKAY, AVENGERS-- YOU KNOW WHAT TO DO!
WHEN THE AVENGERS AND THE FANTASTIC FOUR WERE CAPTURED BY OUR ARMADA.
SORRY, BOYS, BUT AN AMBUSH THAT'S EXPECTED RARELY WORKS!
WHEN THE SKRULLS ZABYK AND MYRN DETONATED THE GENETIC "HYPERWAVE BOMB".
Y-YOUR SWORD CUT THROUGH MY BLASTER! WHAT SORT OF MAGIC IS THIS?!
PRETTY GOOD MAGIC, I'D SAY!
HRMPF! THIS BATTLE IS TOO EASILY WON FOR THE SON OF ZEUS!!
HEADS UP EVERYBODY! IT'S--
--THE SHE-HULK?!
THE AVENGERS?!
THERE.
I BELIEVE THIS IS THE POINT WHERE WE CAN GENERATE THE NEW MEMORIES WE NEED.

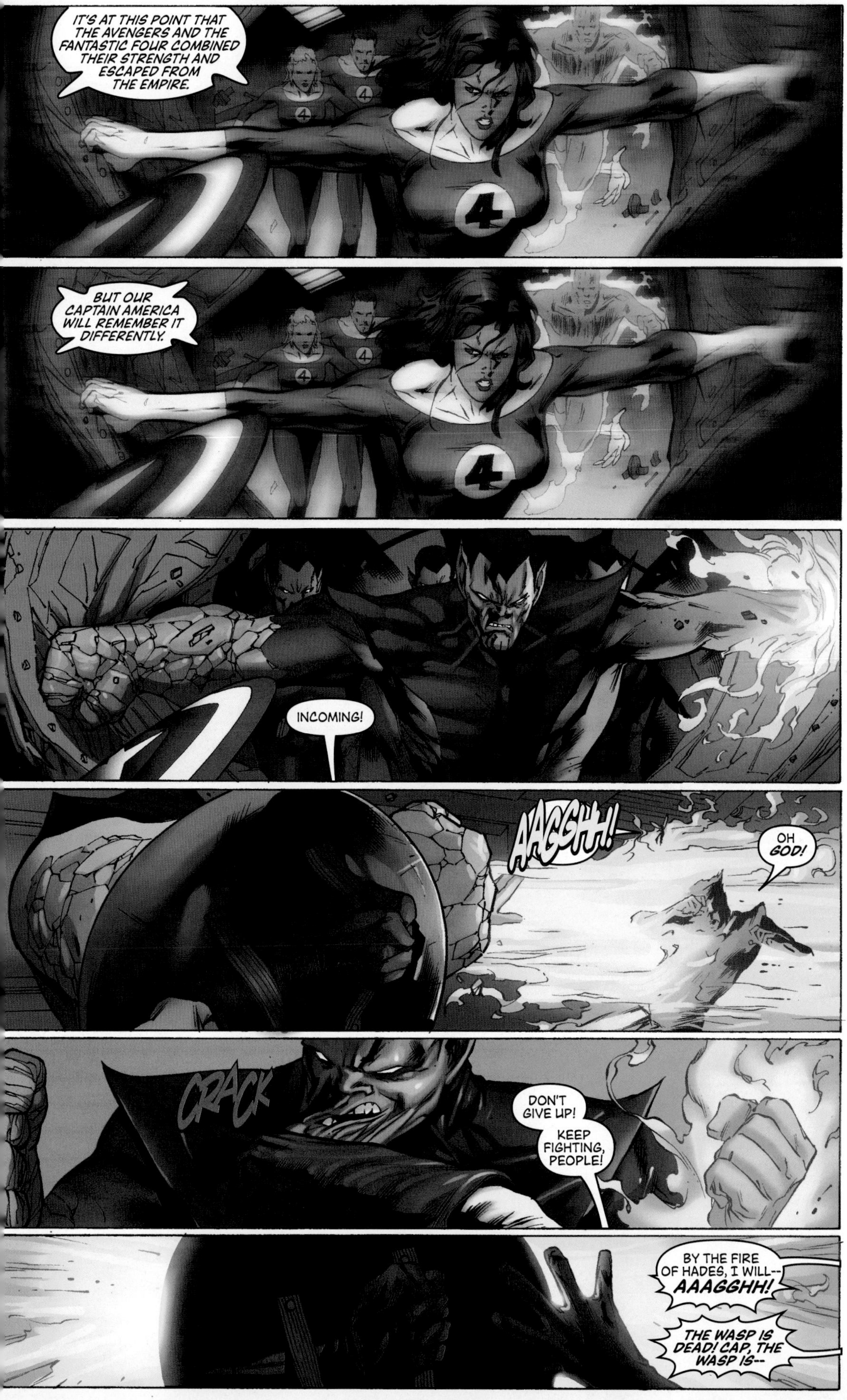
IT'S AT THIS POINT THAT THE AVENGERS AND THE FANTASTIC FOUR COMBINED THEIR STRENGTH AND ESCAPED FROM THE EMPIRE.
BUT OUR CAPTAIN AMERICA WILL REMEMBER IT DIFFERENTLY.
INCOMING!
AAGGHH!
OH GOD!
CRACK
DON'T GIVE UP!
KEEP FIGHTING, PEOPLE!
BY THE FIRE OF HADES, I WILL-- AAAGGHH!
THE WASP IS DEAD! CAP, THE WASP IS--

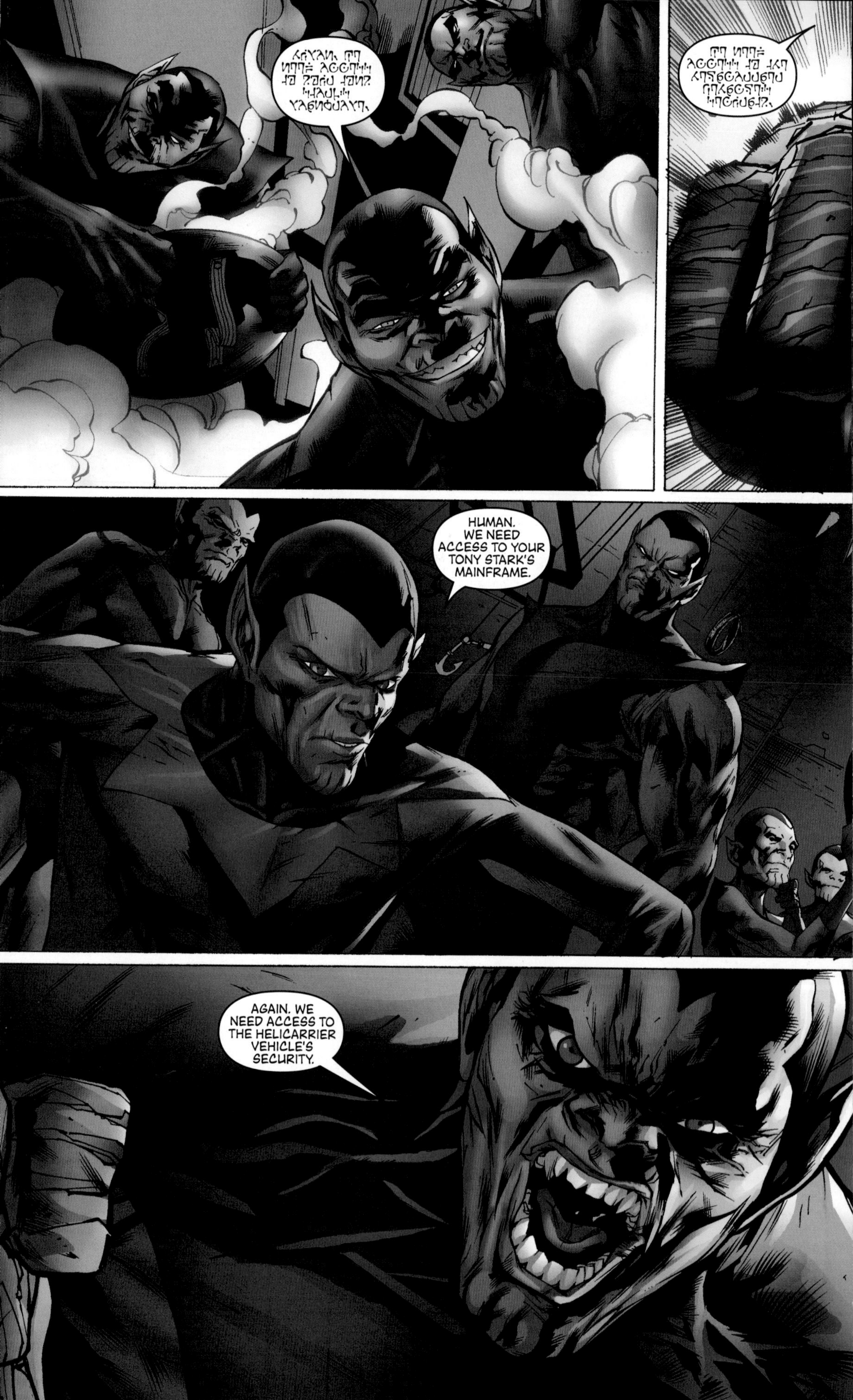
HUMAN. WE NEED ACCESS TO YOUR TONY STARK'S MAINFRAME.
AGAIN. WE NEED ACCESS TO THE HELICARRIER VEHICLE'S SECURITY.

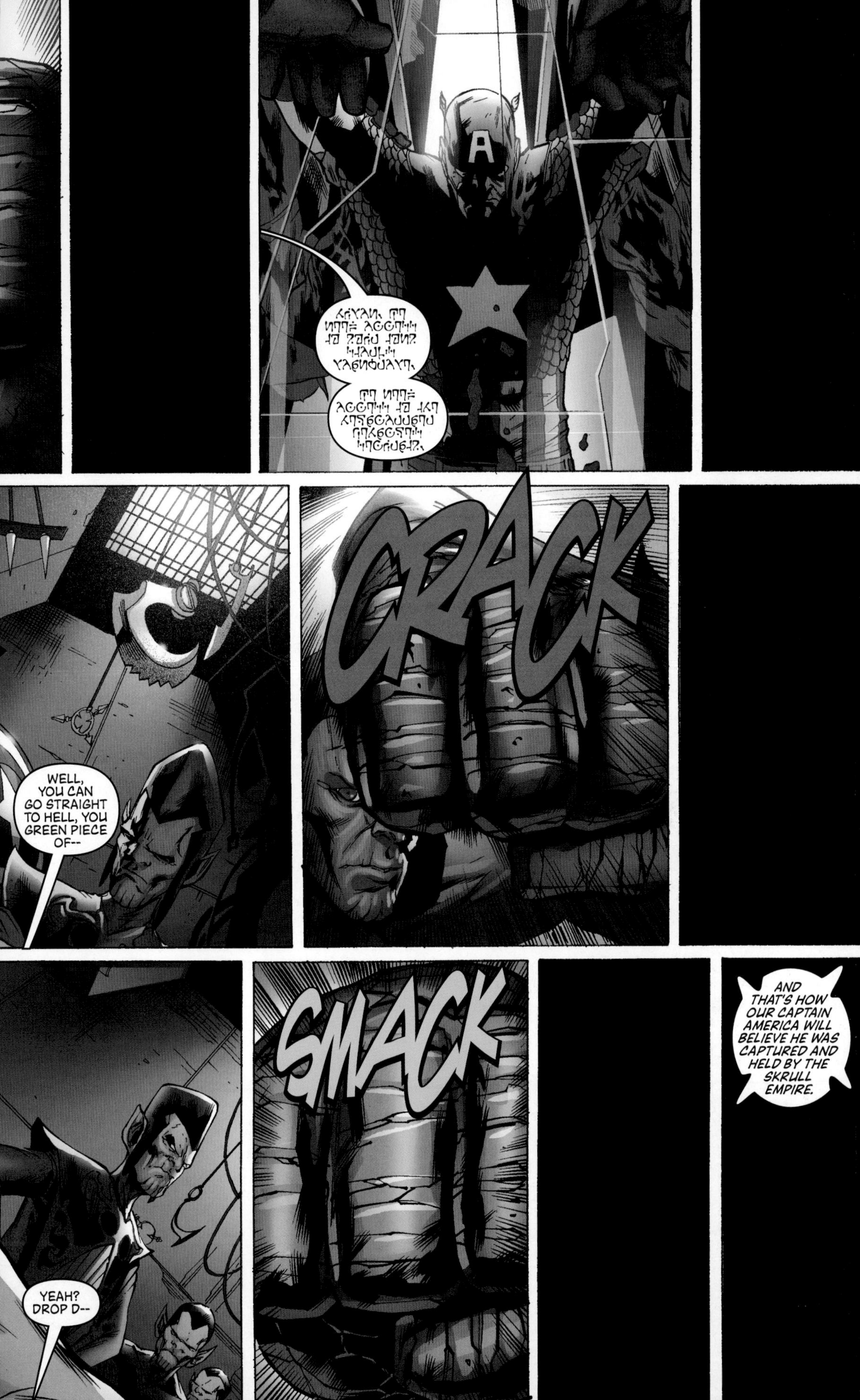
WELL, YOU CAN GO STRAIGHT TO HELL, YOU GREEN PIECE OF--
CRACK
YEAH? DROP D--
SMACK
AND THAT'S HOW OUR CAPTAIN AMERICA WILL BELIEVE HE WAS CAPTURED AND HELD BY THE SKRULL EMPIRE.

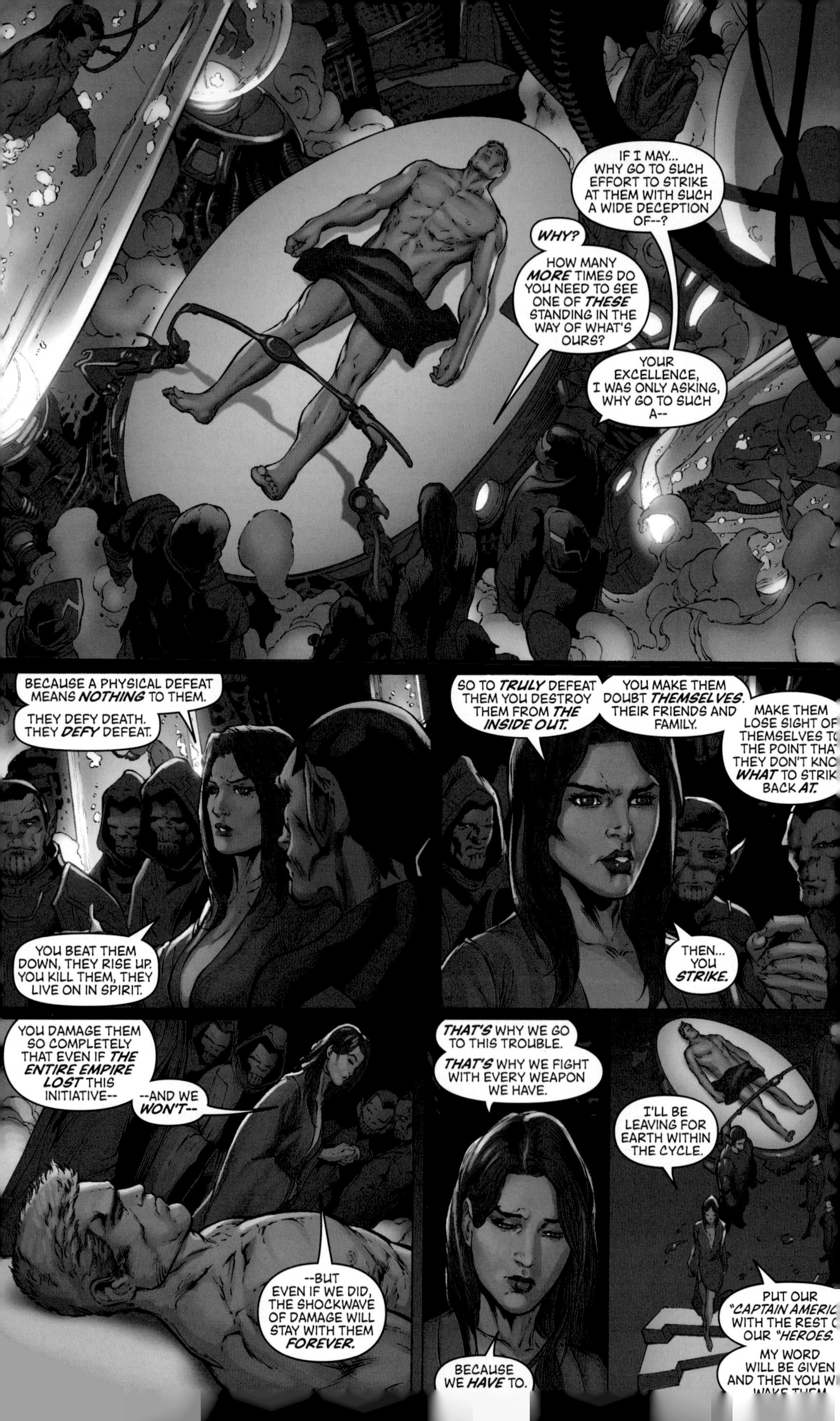
IF I MAY... WHY GO TO SUCH EFFORT TO STRIKE AT THEM WITH SUCH A WIDE DECEPTION OF--?
WHY?
HOW MANY MORE TIMES DO YOU NEED TO SEE ONE OF THESE STANDING IN THE WAY OF WHAT'S OURS?
YOUR EXCELLENCE, I WAS ONLY ASKING, WHY GO TO SUCH A--
BECAUSE A PHYSICAL DEFEAT MEANS NOTHING TO THEM.
THEY DEFY DEATH. THEY DEFY DEFEAT.
YOU BEAT THEM DOWN, THEY RISE UP. YOU KILL THEM, THEY LIVE ON IN SPIRIT.
SO TO TRULY DEFEAT THEM YOU DESTROY THEM FROM THE INSIDE OUT.
YOU MAKE THEM DOUBT THEMSELVES. THEIR FRIENDS AND FAMILY.
MAKE THEM LOSE SIGHT OF THEMSELVES TO THE POINT THA THEY DON'T KNO WHAT TO STRIK BACK AT.
THEN... YOU STRIKE.
YOU DAMAGE THEM SO COMPLETELY THAT EVEN IF THE ENTIRE EMPIRE LOST THIS INITIATIVE--
--AND WE WON'T--
--BUT EVEN IF WE DID, THE SHOCKWAVE OF DAMAGE WILL STAY WITH THEM FOREVER.
THAT'S WHY WE GO TO THIS TROUBLE.
THAT'S WHY WE FIGHT WITH EVERY WEAPON WE HAVE.
BECAUSE WE HAVE TO.
I'LL BE LEAVING FOR EARTH WITHIN THE CYCLE.
PUT OUR "CAPTAIN AMERIC WITH THE REST O OUR "HEROES."
MY WORD WILL BE GIVEN AND THEN YOU W

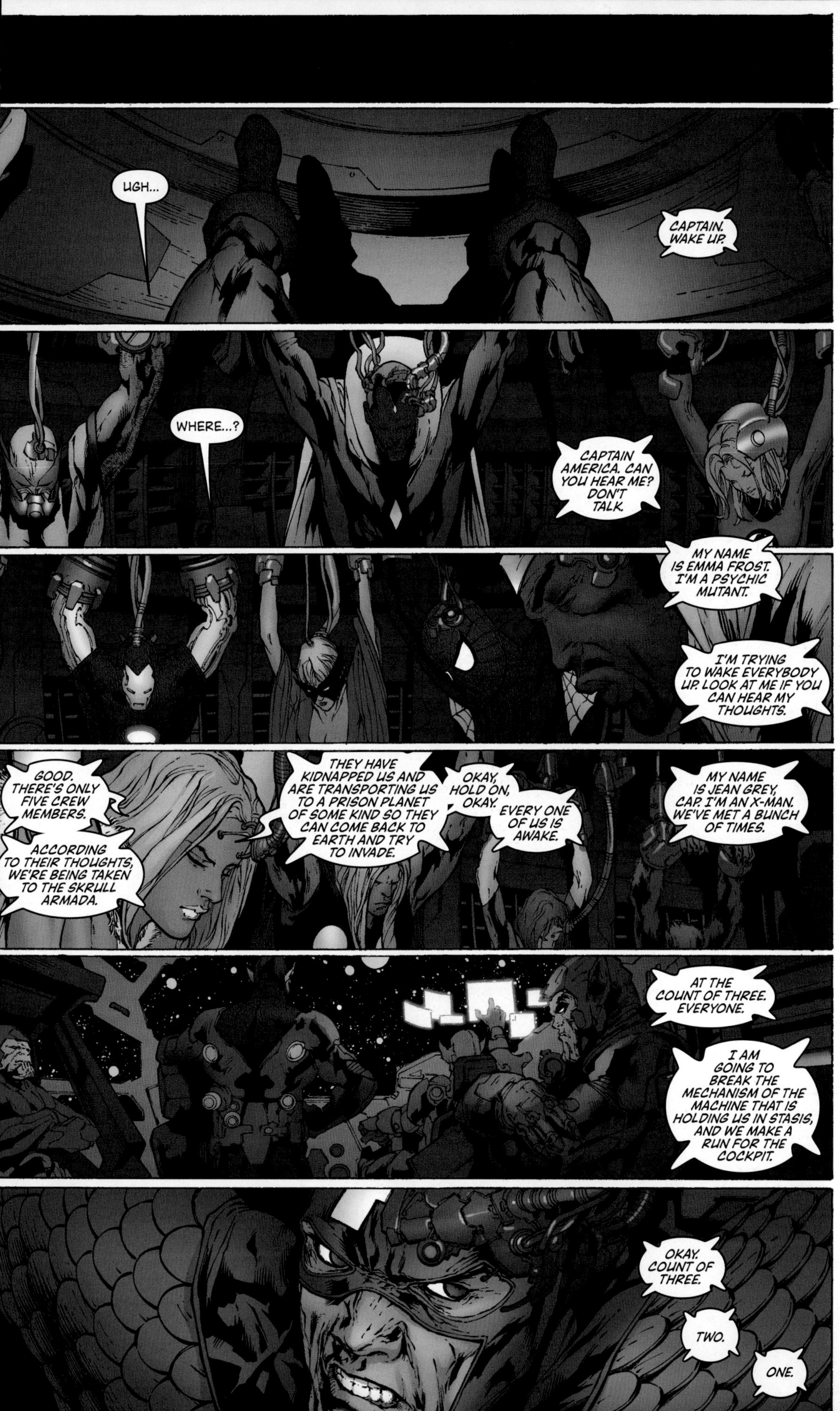
UGH...
CAPTAIN. WAKE UP.
WHERE...?
CAPTAIN AMERICA. CAN YOU HEAR ME? DON'T TALK.
MY NAME IS EMMA FROST. I'M A PSYCHIC MUTANT.
I'M TRYING TO WAKE EVERYBODY UP. LOOK AT ME IF YOU CAN HEAR MY THOUGHTS.
GOOD. THERE'S ONLY FIVE CREW MEMBERS.
ACCORDING TO THEIR THOUGHTS, WE'RE BEING TAKEN TO THE SKRULL ARMADA.
THEY HAVE KIDNAPPED US AND ARE TRANSPORTING US TO A PRISON PLANET OF SOME KIND SO THEY CAN COME BACK TO EARTH AND TRY TO INVADE.
OKAY, HOLD ON, OKAY.
EVERY ONE OF US IS AWAKE.
MY NAME IS JEAN GREY, CAP. I'M AN X-MAN. WE'VE MET A BUNCH OF TIMES.
AT THE COUNT OF THREE. EVERYONE.
I AM GOING TO BREAK THE MECHANISM OF THE MACHINE THAT IS HOLDING US IN STASIS, AND WE MAKE A RUN FOR THE COCKPIT.
OKAY. COUNT OF THREE.
TWO.
ONE.

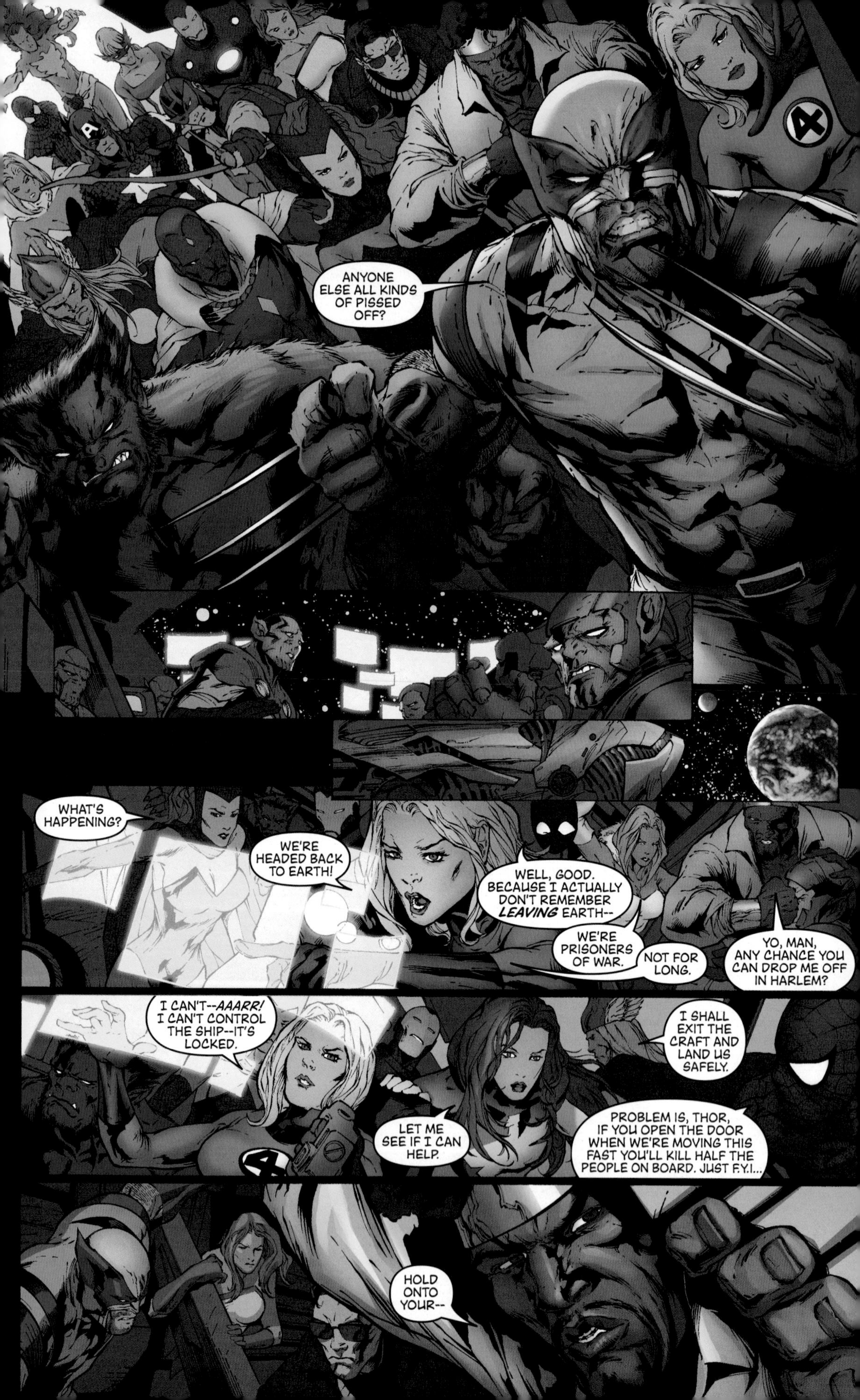
ANYONE ELSE ALL KINDS OF PISSED OFF?
WHAT'S HAPPENING?
WE'RE HEADED BACK TO EARTH!
WELL, GOOD. BECAUSE I ACTUALLY DON'T REMEMBER *LEAVING* EARTH--
WE'RE PRISONERS OF WAR.
NOT FOR LONG.
YO, MAN, ANY CHANCE YOU CAN DROP ME OFF IN HARLEM?
I CAN'T--*AAARR!* I CAN'T CONTROL THE SHIP--IT'S LOCKED.
I SHALL EXIT THE CRAFT AND LAND US SAFELY.
LET ME SEE IF I CAN HELP.
PROBLEM IS, THOR, IF YOU OPEN THE DOOR WHEN WE'RE MOVING THIS FAST YOU'LL KILL HALF THE PEOPLE ON BOARD. JUST F.Y.I...
HOLD ONTO YOUR--

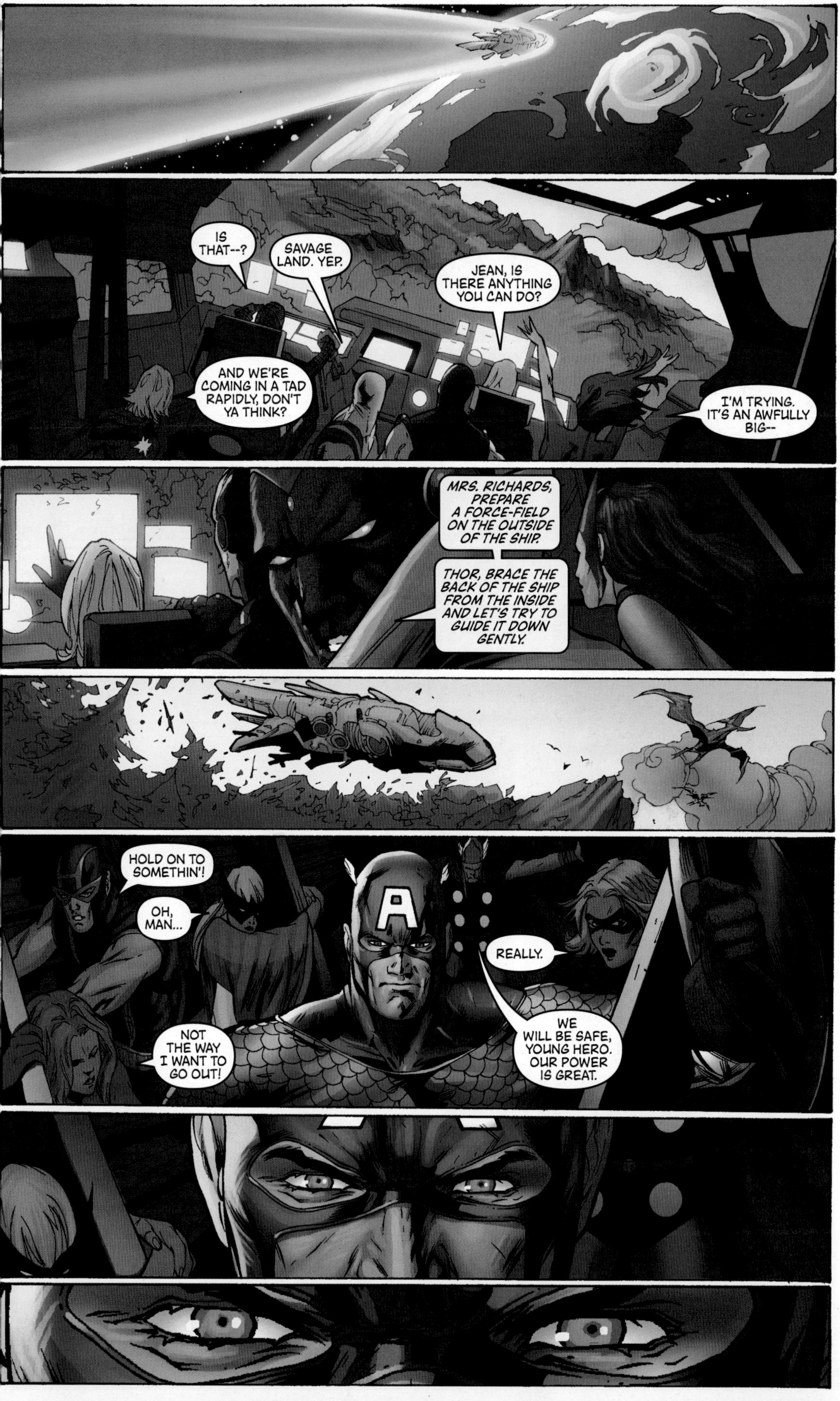

IS THAT--?
SAVAGE LAND. YEP.
AND WE'RE COMING IN A TAD RAPIDLY, DON'T YA THINK?
JEAN, IS THERE ANYTHING YOU CAN DO?
I'M TRYING. IT'S AN AWFULLY BIG--
MRS. RICHARDS, PREPARE A FORCE-FIELD ON THE OUTSIDE OF THE SHIP.
THOR, BRACE THE BACK OF THE SHIP FROM THE INSIDE AND LET'S TRY TO GUIDE IT DOWN GENTLY.
HOLD ON TO SOMETHIN'!
OH, MAN...
REALLY.
NOT THE WAY I WANT TO GO OUT!
WE WILL BE SAFE, YOUNG HERO. OUR POWER IS GREAT.

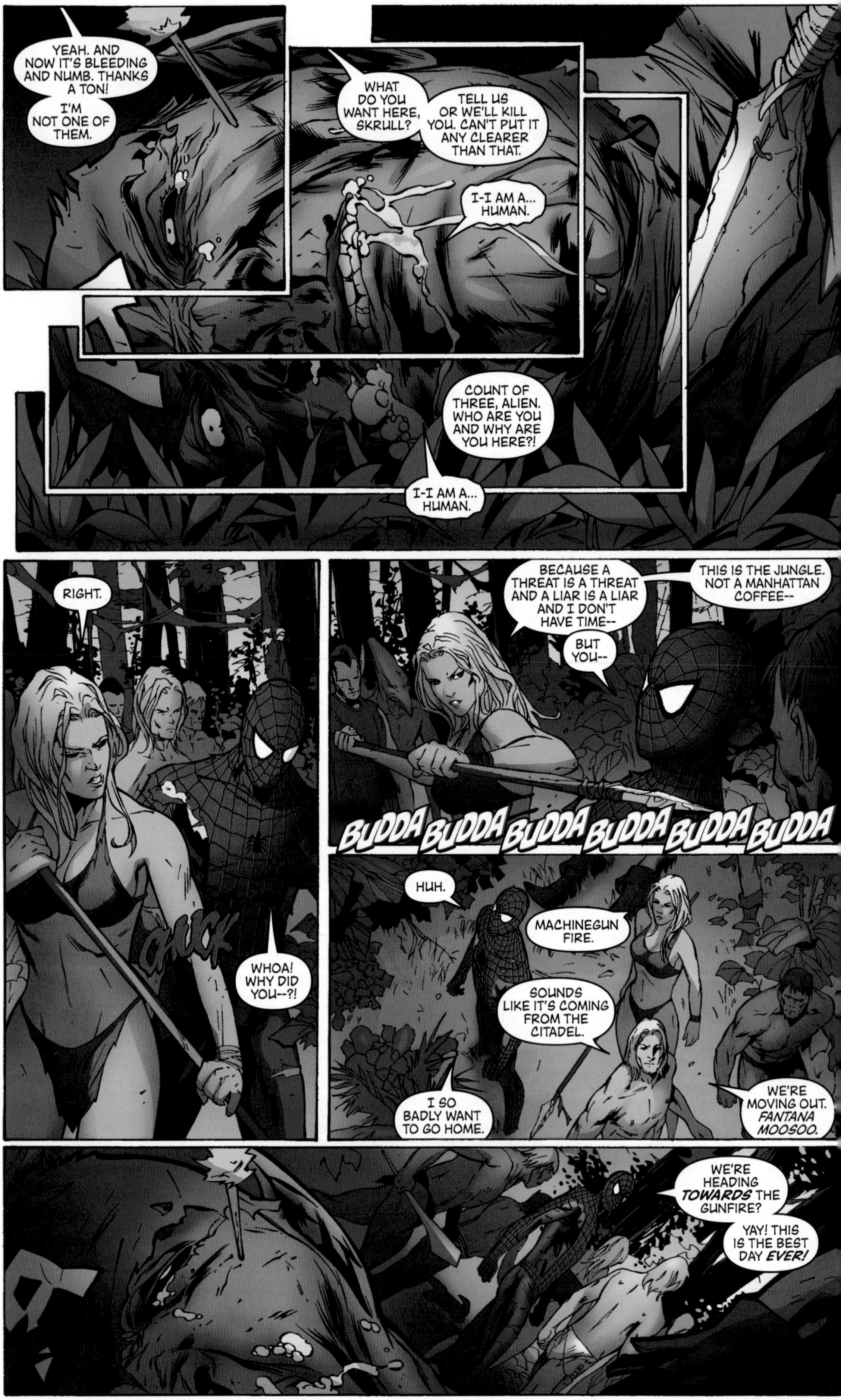

YEAH. AND NOW IT'S BLEEDING AND NUMB. THANKS A TON!
I'M NOT ONE OF THEM.
WHAT DO YOU WANT HERE, SKRULL?
TELL US OR WE'LL KILL YOU. CAN'T PUT IT ANY CLEARER THAN THAT.
I-I AM A... HUMAN.
COUNT OF THREE, ALIEN. WHO ARE YOU AND WHY ARE YOU HERE?!
I-I AM A... HUMAN.
RIGHT.
CHUCK
WHOA! WHY DID YOU--?!
BECAUSE A THREAT IS A THREAT AND A LIAR IS A LIAR AND I DON'T HAVE TIME--
BUT YOU--
THIS IS THE JUNGLE. NOT A MANHATTAN COFFEE--
BUDDA BUDDA BUDDA BUDDA BUDDA BUDDA
HUH.
MACHINEGUN FIRE.
SOUNDS LIKE IT'S COMING FROM THE CITADEL.
I SO BADLY WANT TO GO HOME.
WE'RE MOVING OUT. *FANTANA MOOSOO.*
WE'RE HEADING *TOWARDS* THE GUNFIRE?
YAY! THIS IS THE BEST DAY *EVER!*

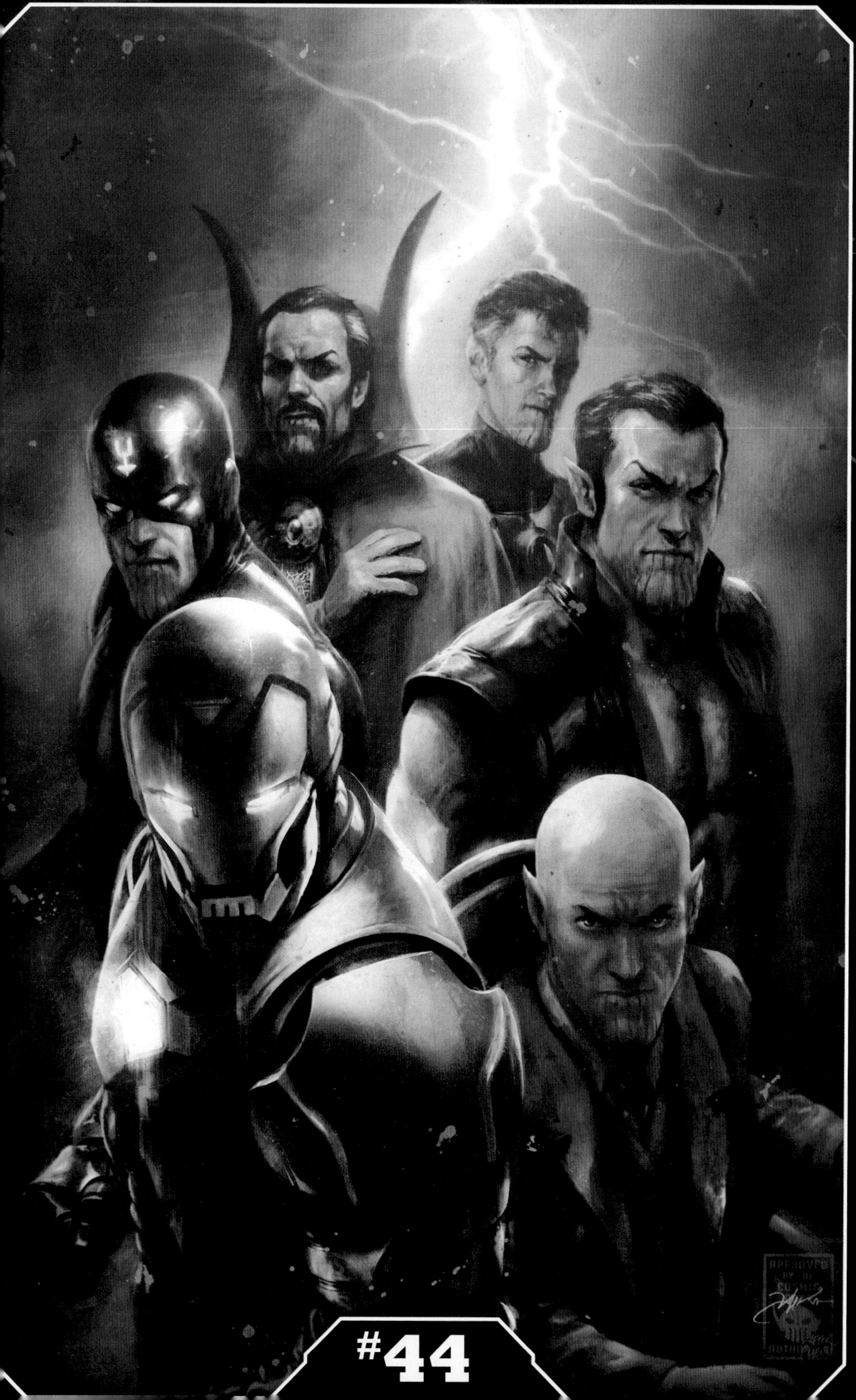
#44

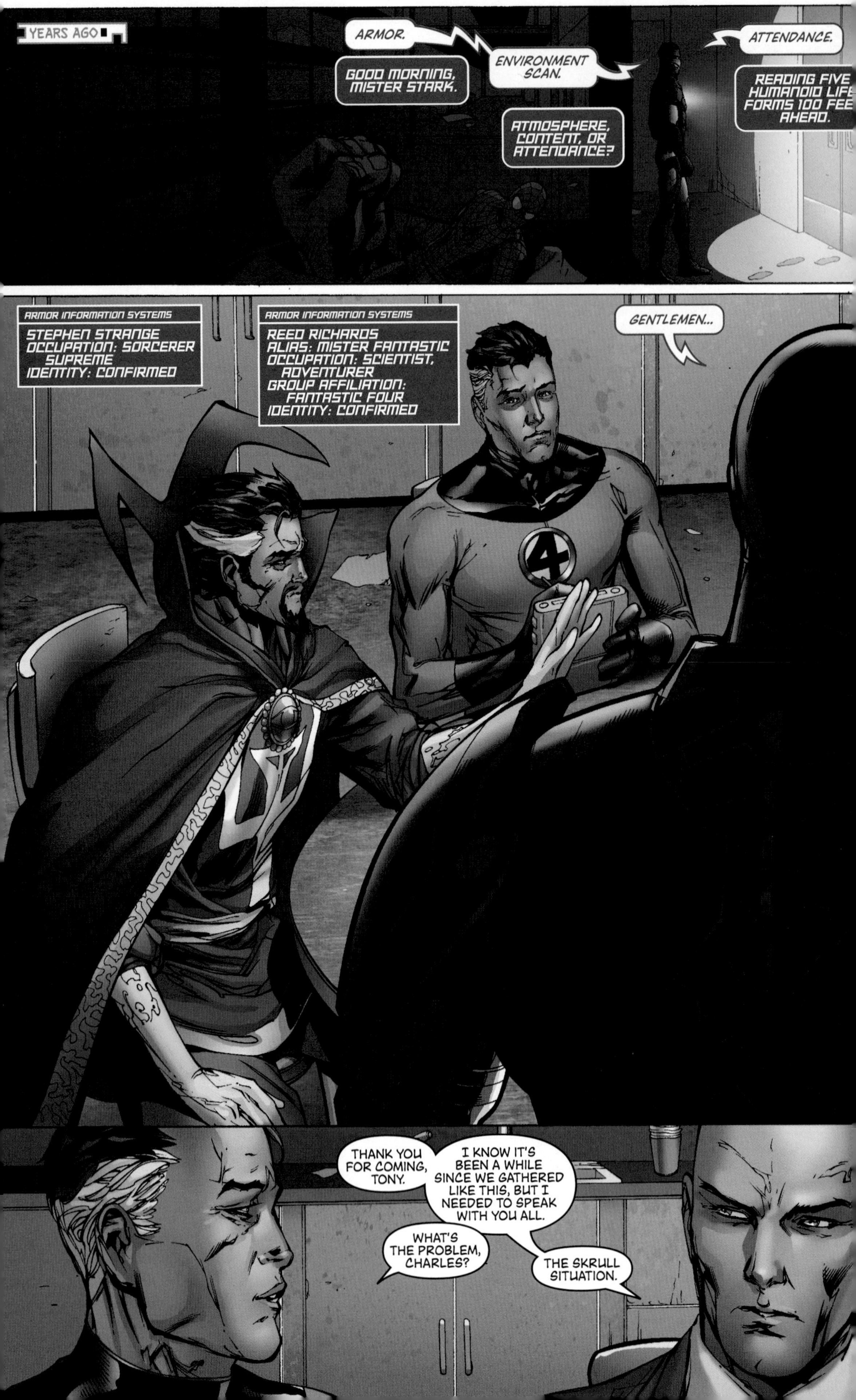

YEARS AGO
ARMOR.
GOOD MORNING, MISTER STARK.
ENVIRONMENT SCAN.
ATMOSPHERE, CONTENT, OR ATTENDANCE?
ATTENDANCE.
READING FIVE HUMANOID LIFE FORMS 100 FEE AHEAD.
ARMOR INFORMATION SYSTEMS
STEPHEN STRANGE
OCCUPATION: SORCERER SUPREME
IDENTITY: CONFIRMED
ARMOR INFORMATION SYSTEMS
REED RICHARDS
ALIAS: MISTER FANTASTIC
OCCUPATION: SCIENTIST, ADVENTURER
GROUP AFFILIATION: FANTASTIC FOUR
IDENTITY: CONFIRMED
GENTLEMEN...
THANK YOU FOR COMING, TONY.
I KNOW IT'S BEEN A WHILE SINCE WE GATHERED LIKE THIS, BUT I NEEDED TO SPEAK WITH YOU ALL.
WHAT'S THE PROBLEM, CHARLES?
THE SKRULL SITUATION.

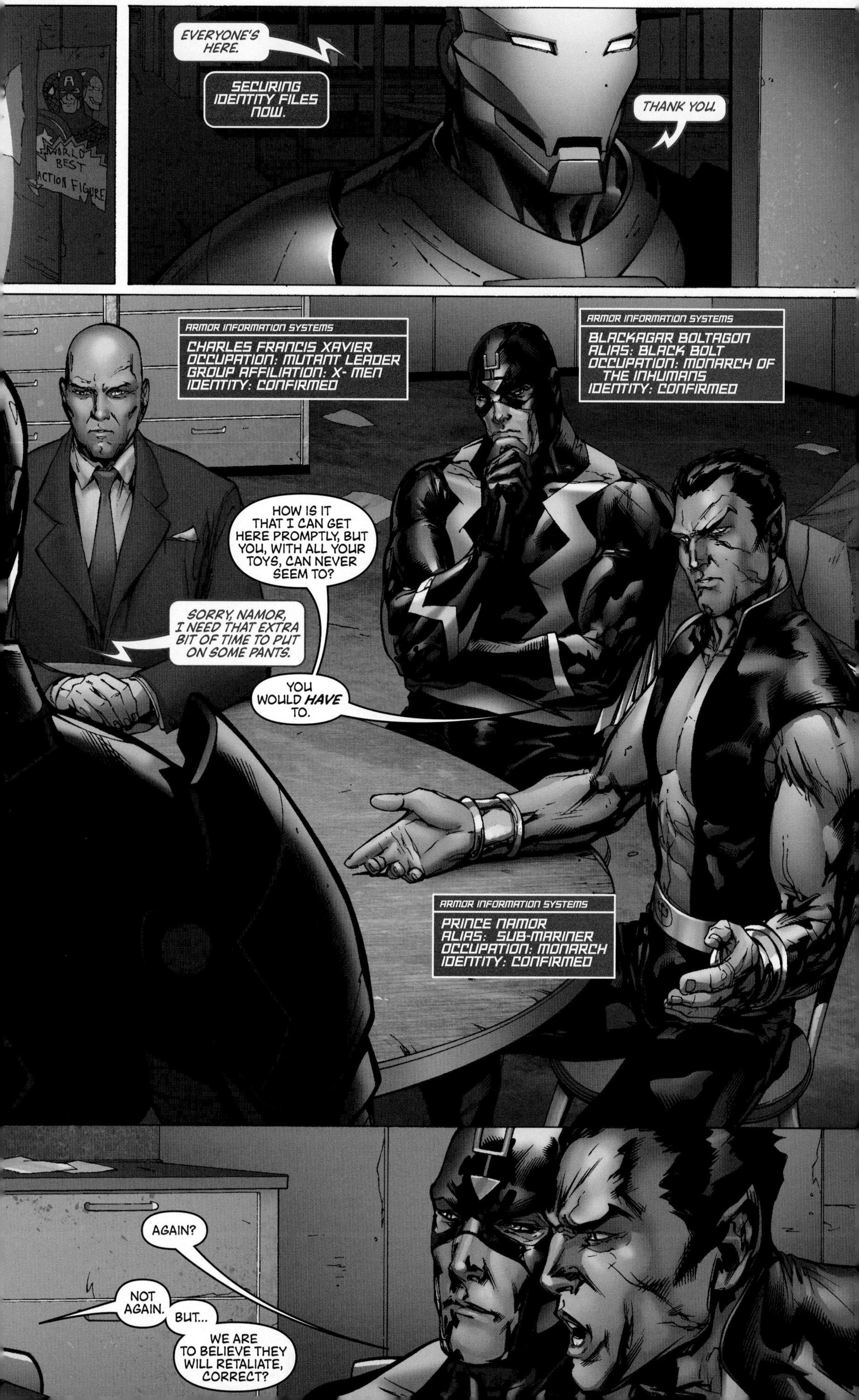

WORLD BEST ACTION FIGURE
EVERYONE'S HERE.
SECURING IDENTITY FILES NOW.
THANK YOU.
ARMOR INFORMATION SYSTEMS
CHARLES FRANCIS XAVIER
OCCUPATION: MUTANT LEADER
GROUP AFFILIATION: X- MEN
IDENTITY: CONFIRMED
ARMOR INFORMATION SYSTEMS
BLACKAGAR BOLTAGON
ALIAS: BLACK BOLT
OCCUPATION: MONARCH OF THE INHUMANS
IDENTITY: CONFIRMED
HOW IS IT THAT I CAN GET HERE PROMPTLY, BUT YOU, WITH ALL YOUR TOYS, CAN NEVER SEEM TO?
SORRY, NAMOR, I NEED THAT EXTRA BIT OF TIME TO PUT ON SOME PANTS.
YOU WOULD *HAVE* TO.
ARMOR INFORMATION SYSTEMS
PRINCE NAMOR
ALIAS: SUB-MARINER
OCCUPATION: MONARCH
IDENTITY: CONFIRMED
AGAIN?
NOT AGAIN.
BUT...
WE ARE TO BELIEVE THEY WILL RETALIATE, CORRECT?

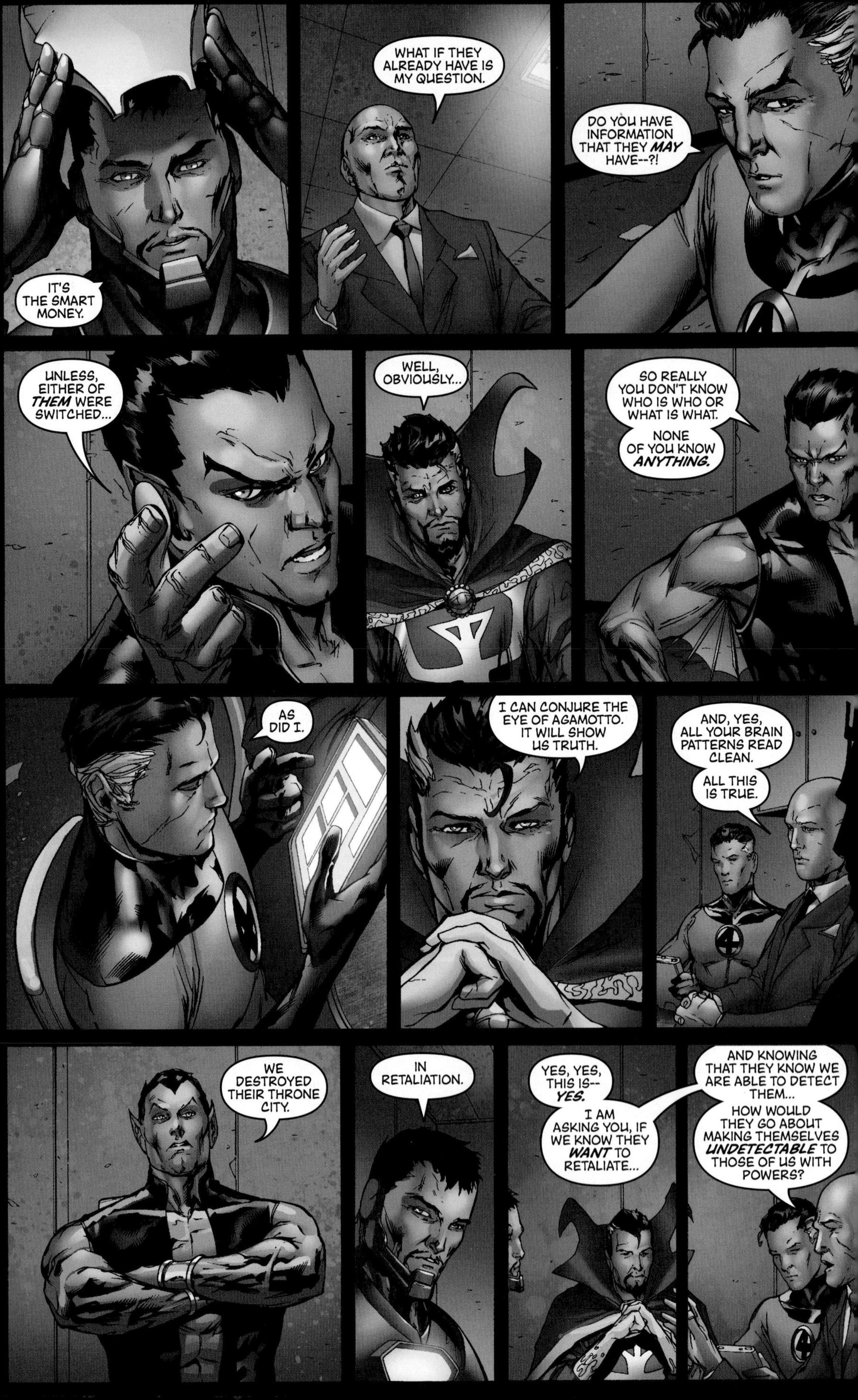
IT'S THE SMART MONEY.
WHAT IF THEY ALREADY HAVE IS MY QUESTION.
DO YOU HAVE INFORMATION THAT THEY MAY HAVE--?!
UNLESS, EITHER OF THEM WERE SWITCHED...
WELL, OBVIOUSLY...
SO REALLY YOU DON'T KNOW WHO IS WHO OR WHAT IS WHAT.
NONE OF YOU KNOW ANYTHING.
AS DID I.
I CAN CONJURE THE EYE OF AGAMOTTO. IT WILL SHOW US TRUTH.
AND, YES, ALL YOUR BRAIN PATTERNS READ CLEAN.
ALL THIS IS TRUE.
WE DESTROYED THEIR THRONE CITY.
IN RETALIATION.
YES, YES, THIS IS-- YES.
I AM ASKING YOU, IF WE KNOW THEY WANT TO RETALIATE...
AND KNOWING THAT THEY KNOW WE ARE ABLE TO DETECT THEM...
HOW WOULD THEY GO ABOUT MAKING THEMSELVES UNDETECTABLE TO THOSE OF US WITH POWERS?

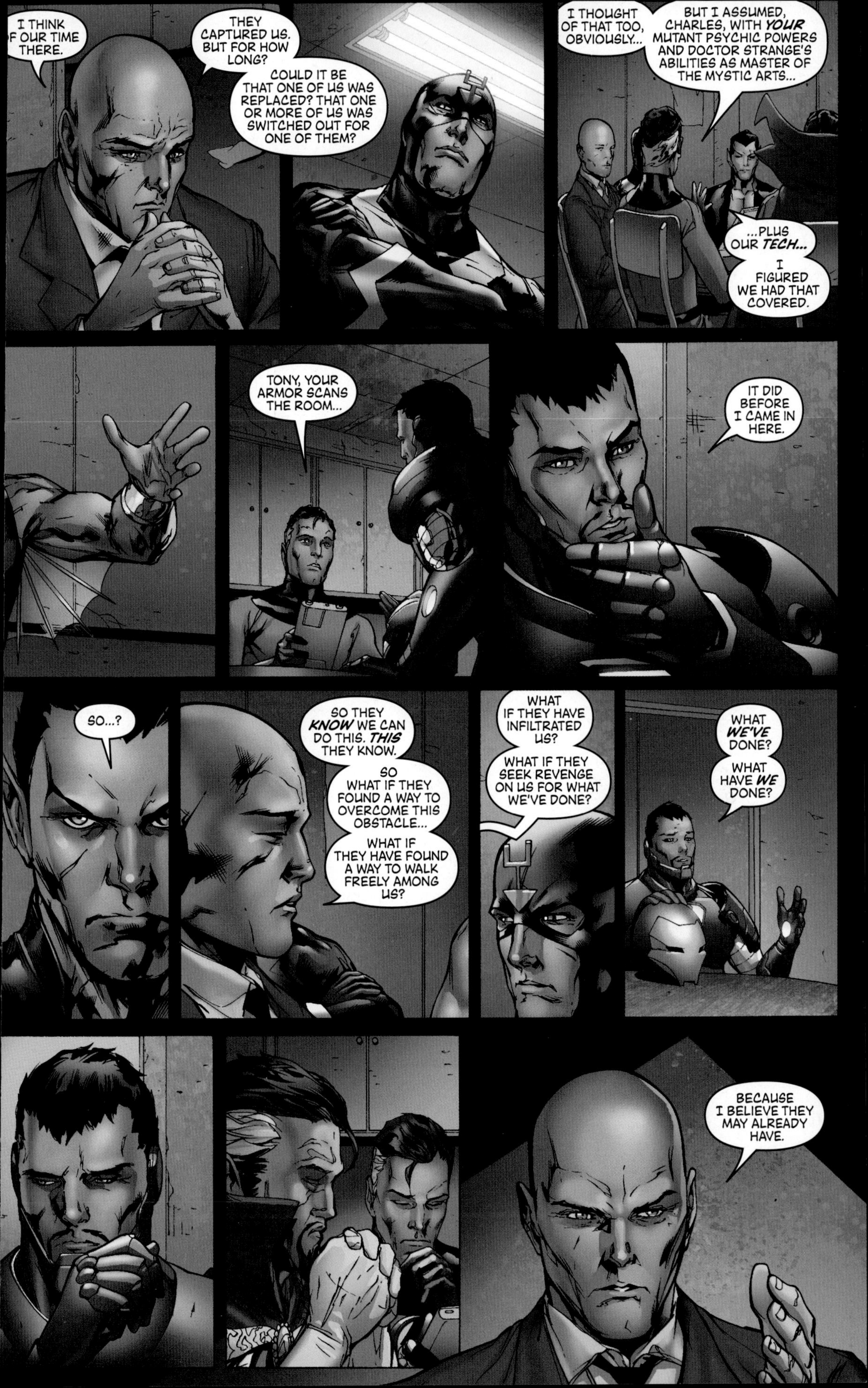
I THINK OF OUR TIME THERE.
THEY CAPTURED US. BUT FOR HOW LONG?
COULD IT BE THAT ONE OF US WAS REPLACED? THAT ONE OR MORE OF US WAS SWITCHED OUT FOR ONE OF THEM?
I THOUGHT OF THAT TOO, OBVIOUSLY...
BUT I ASSUMED, CHARLES, WITH YOUR MUTANT PSYCHIC POWERS AND DOCTOR STRANGE'S ABILITIES AS MASTER OF THE MYSTIC ARTS...
...PLUS OUR TECH...
I FIGURED WE HAD THAT COVERED.
TONY, YOUR ARMOR SCANS THE ROOM...
IT DID BEFORE I CAME IN HERE.
SO...?
SO THEY KNOW WE CAN DO THIS. THIS THEY KNOW.
SO WHAT IF THEY FOUND A WAY TO OVERCOME THIS OBSTACLE...
WHAT IF THEY HAVE FOUND A WAY TO WALK FREELY AMONG US?
WHAT IF THEY HAVE INFILTRATED US?
WHAT IF THEY SEEK REVENGE ON US FOR WHAT WE'VE DONE?
WHAT WE'VE DONE?
WHAT HAVE WE DONE?
BECAUSE I BELIEVE THEY MAY ALREADY HAVE.

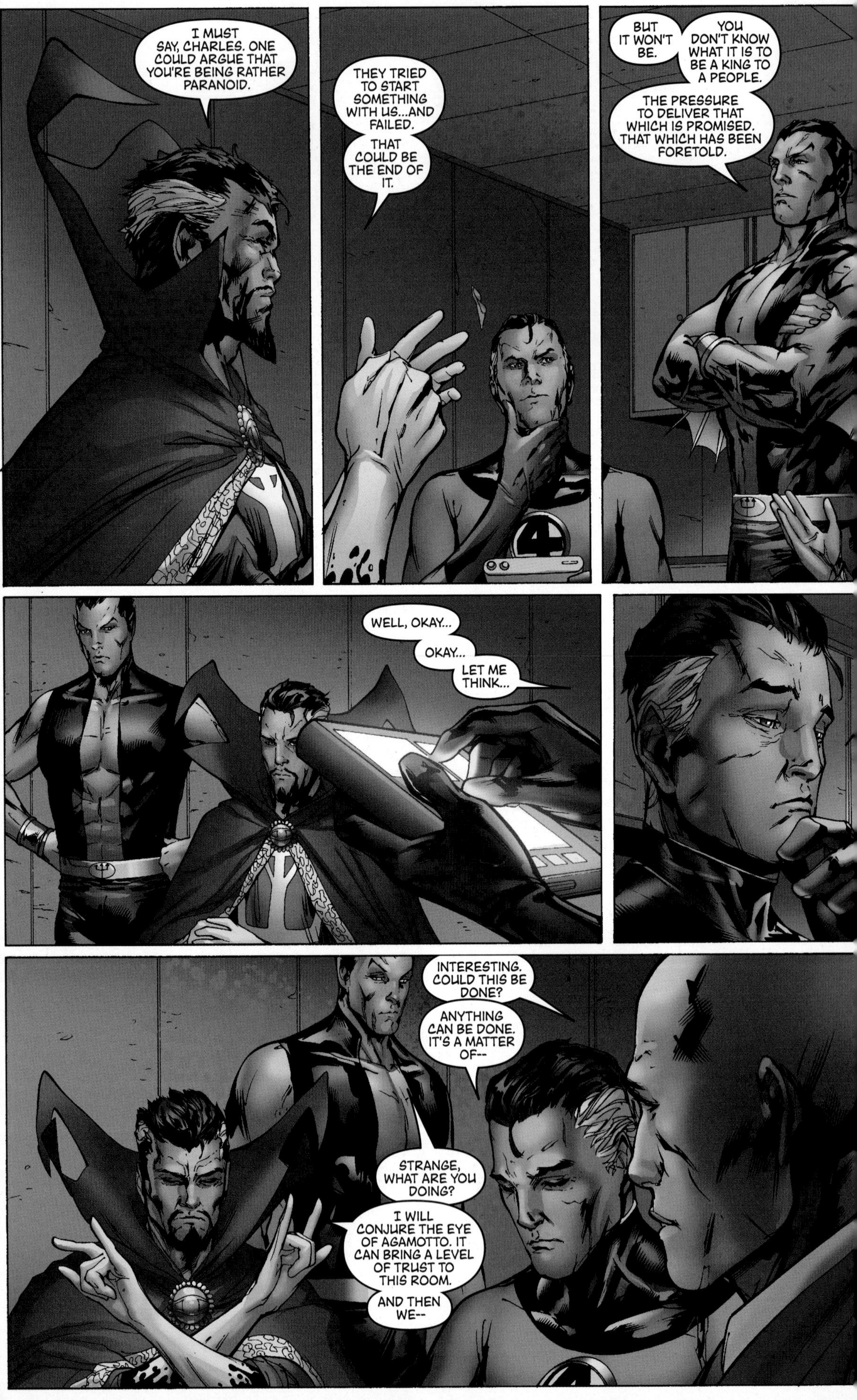

I MUST SAY, CHARLES. ONE COULD ARGUE THAT YOU'RE BEING RATHER PARANOID.
THEY TRIED TO START SOMETHING WITH US...AND FAILED.
THAT COULD BE THE END OF IT.
BUT IT WON'T BE.
YOU DON'T KNOW WHAT IT IS TO BE A KING TO A PEOPLE.
THE PRESSURE TO DELIVER THAT WHICH IS PROMISED. THAT WHICH HAS BEEN FORETOLD.
WELL, OKAY...
OKAY...
LET ME THINK...
INTERESTING. COULD THIS BE DONE?
ANYTHING CAN BE DONE. IT'S A MATTER OF--
STRANGE, WHAT ARE YOU DOING?
I WILL CONJURE THE EYE OF AGAMOTTO. IT CAN BRING A LEVEL OF TRUST TO THIS ROOM.
AND THEN WE--

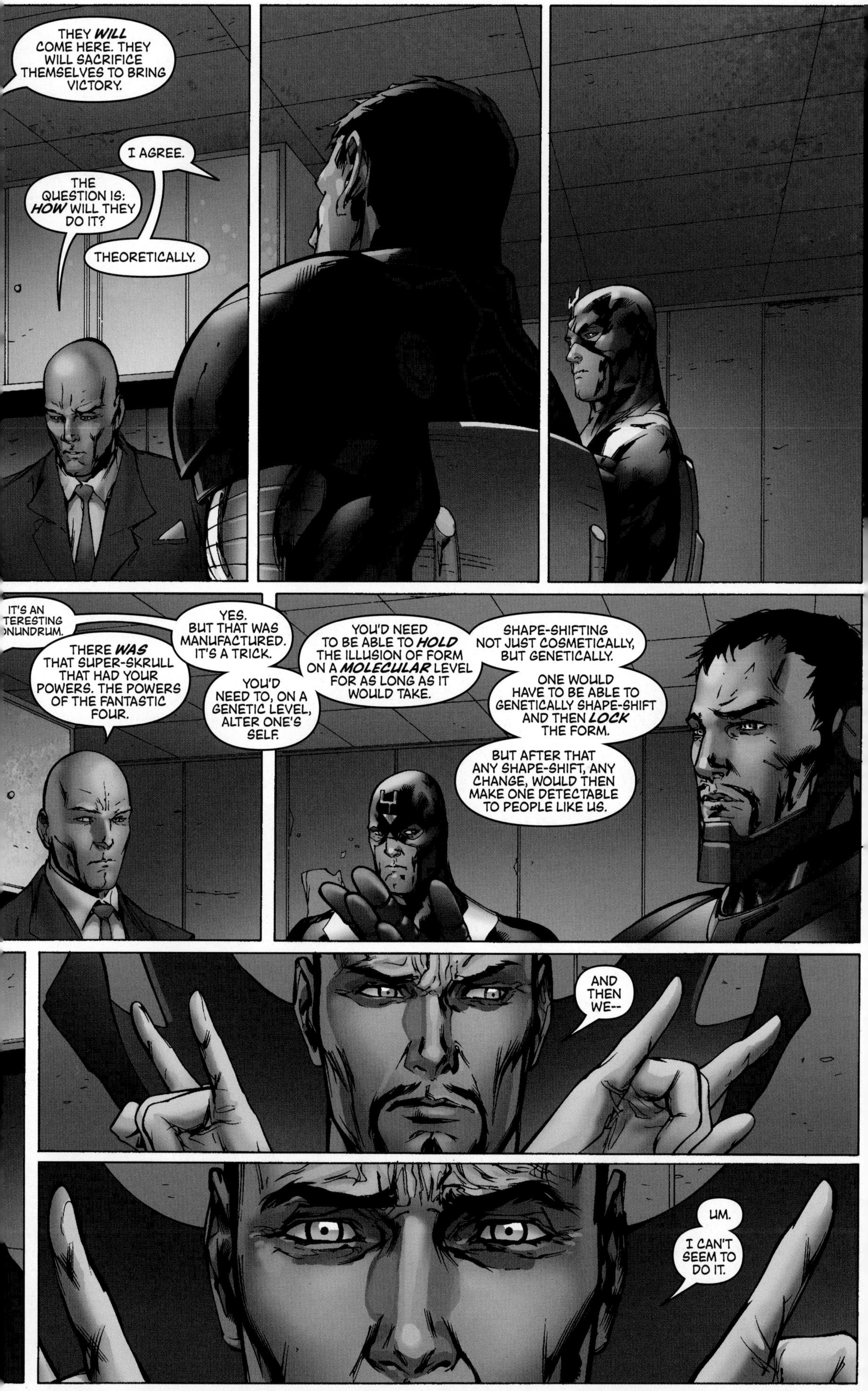
THEY WILL COME HERE. THEY WILL SACRIFICE THEMSELVES TO BRING VICTORY.
I AGREE.
THE QUESTION IS: HOW WILL THEY DO IT?
THEORETICALLY.
IT'S AN TERESTING ONUNDRUM.
THERE WAS THAT SUPER-SKRULL THAT HAD YOUR POWERS. THE POWERS OF THE FANTASTIC FOUR.
YES. BUT THAT WAS MANUFACTURED. IT'S A TRICK.
YOU'D NEED TO, ON A GENETIC LEVEL, ALTER ONE'S SELF.
YOU'D NEED TO BE ABLE TO HOLD THE ILLUSION OF FORM ON A MOLECULAR LEVEL FOR AS LONG AS IT WOULD TAKE.
SHAPE-SHIFTING NOT JUST COSMETICALLY, BUT GENETICALLY.
ONE WOULD HAVE TO BE ABLE TO GENETICALLY SHAPE-SHIFT AND THEN LOCK THE FORM.
BUT AFTER THAT ANY SHAPE-SHIFT, ANY CHANGE, WOULD THEN MAKE ONE DETECTABLE TO PEOPLE LIKE US.
AND THEN WE--
UM.
I CAN'T SEEM TO DO IT.

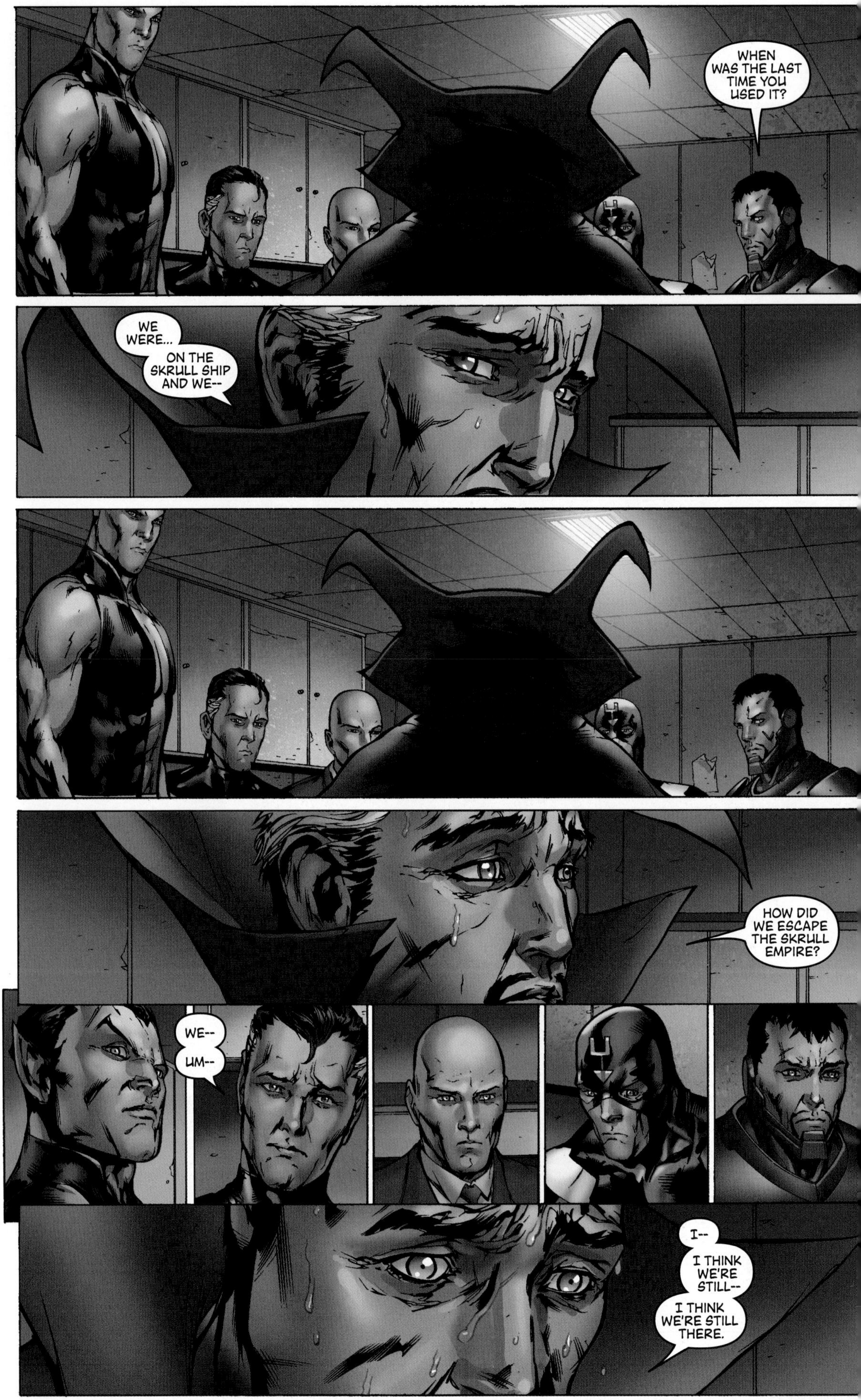
WHEN WAS THE LAST TIME YOU USED IT?
WE WERE...
ON THE SKRULL SHIP AND WE--
HOW DID WE ESCAPE THE SKRULL EMPIRE?
WE--
UM--
I--
I THINK WE'RE STILL--
I THINK WE'RE STILL THERE.

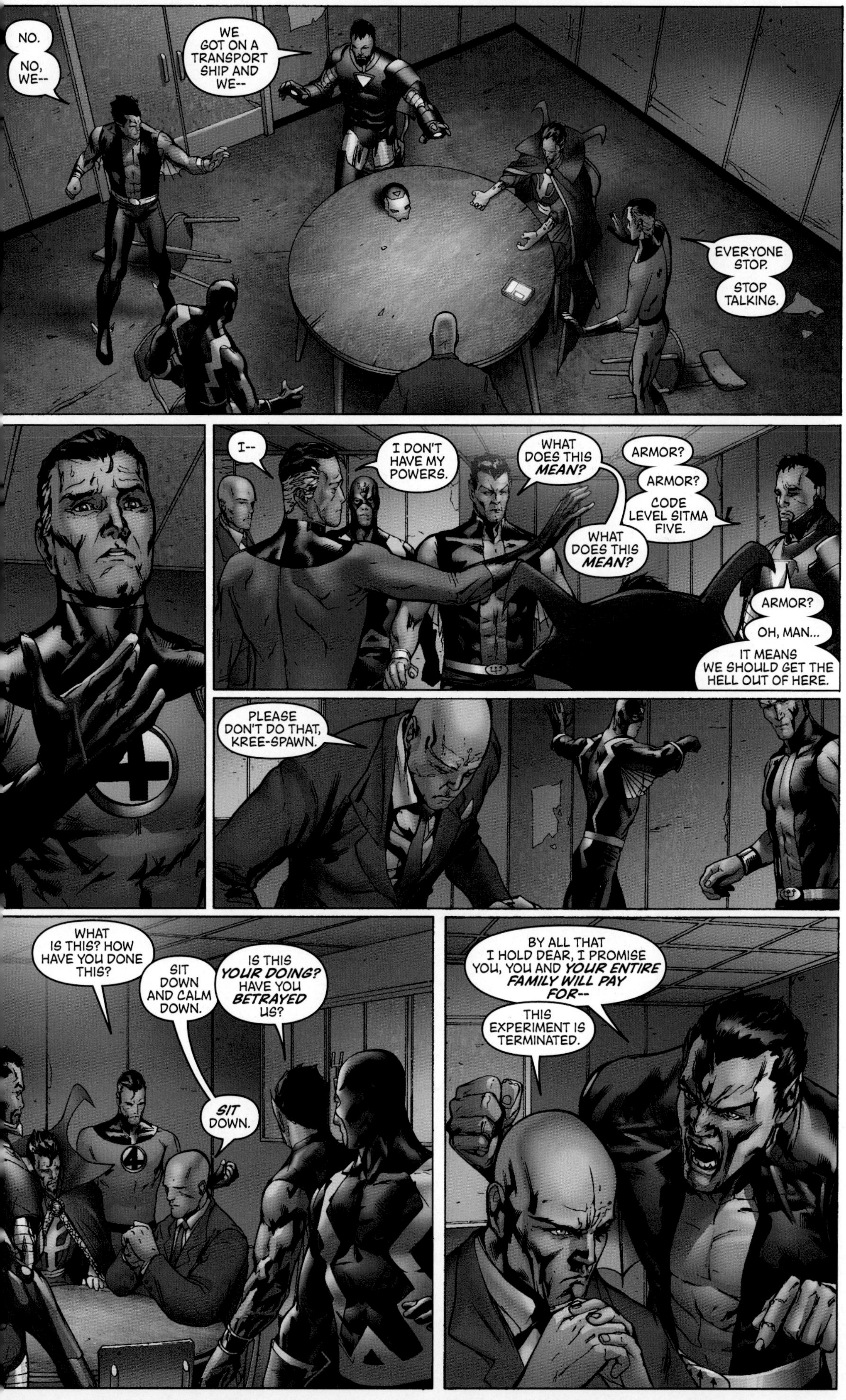
NO.
NO, WE--
WE GOT ON A TRANSPORT SHIP AND WE--
EVERYONE STOP.
STOP TALKING.
I--
I DON'T HAVE MY POWERS.
WHAT DOES THIS *MEAN?*
ARMOR?
ARMOR?
CODE LEVEL SITMA FIVE.
WHAT DOES THIS *MEAN?*
ARMOR?
OH, MAN...
IT MEANS WE SHOULD GET THE HELL OUT OF HERE.
PLEASE DON'T DO THAT, KREE-SPAWN.
WHAT IS THIS? HOW HAVE YOU DONE THIS?
SIT DOWN AND CALM DOWN.
IS THIS *YOUR DOING?* HAVE YOU *BETRAYED* US?
SIT DOWN.
BY ALL THAT I HOLD DEAR, I PROMISE YOU, YOU AND *YOUR ENTIRE FAMILY WILL PAY FOR--*
THIS EXPERIMENT IS TERMINATED.

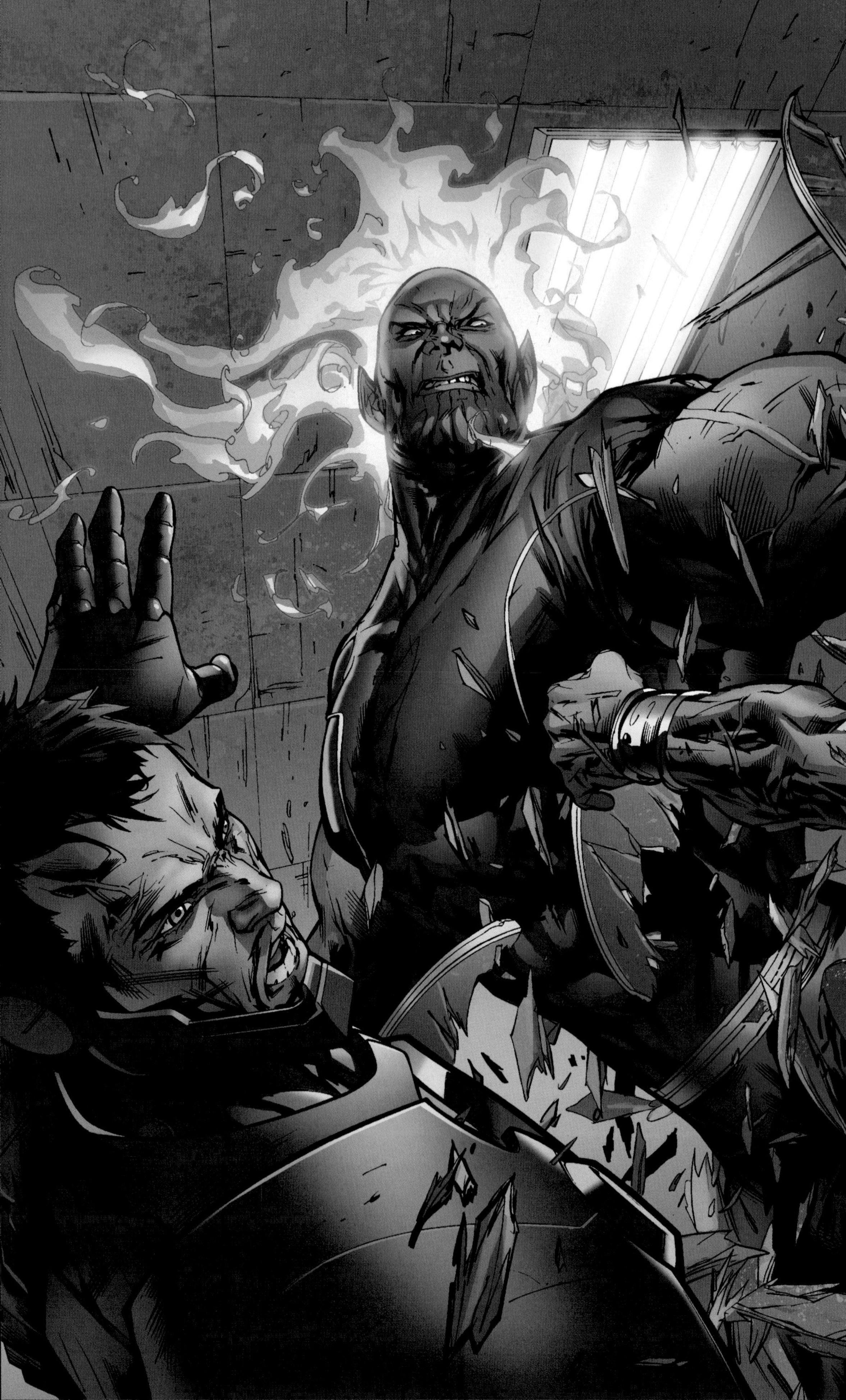

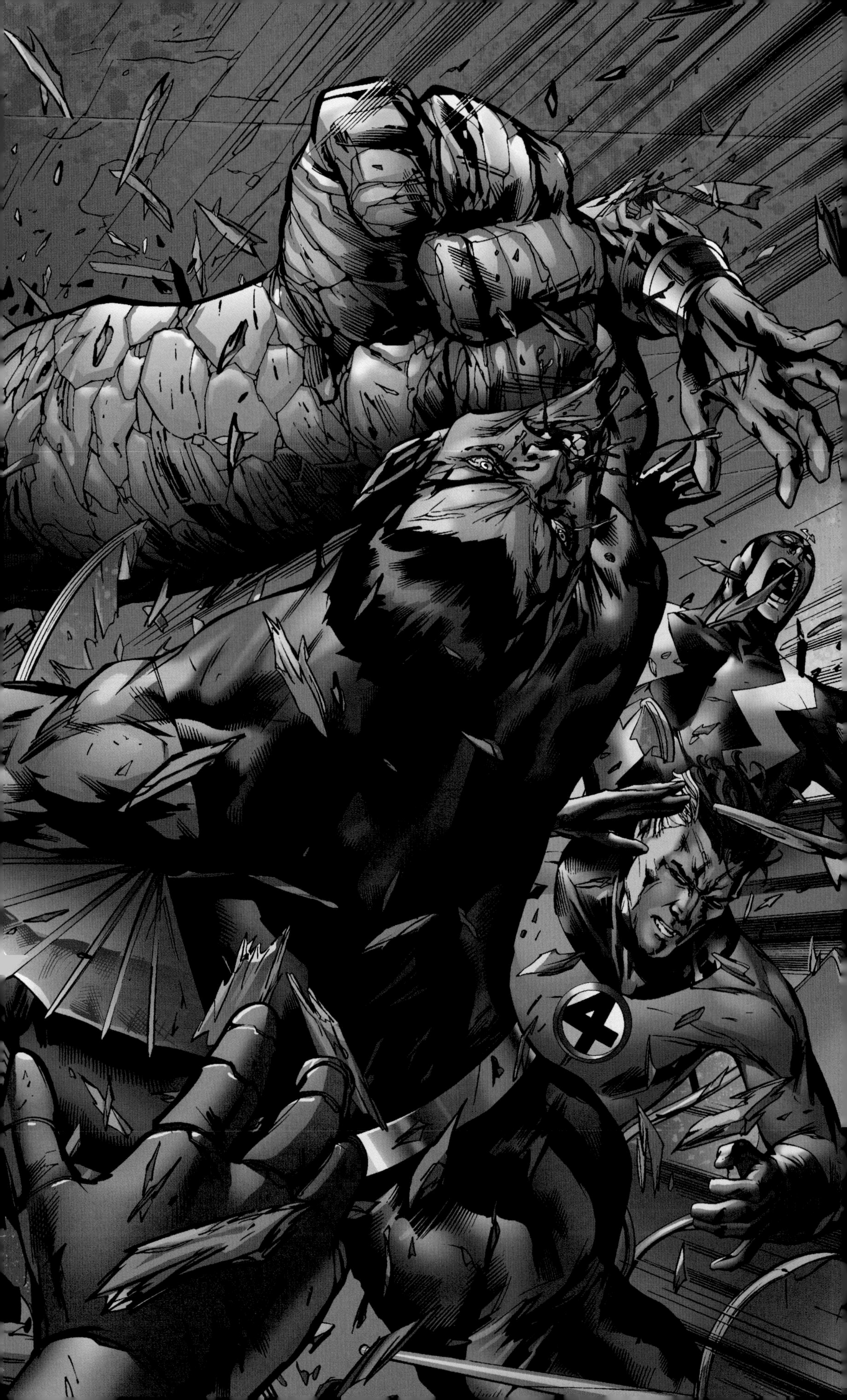

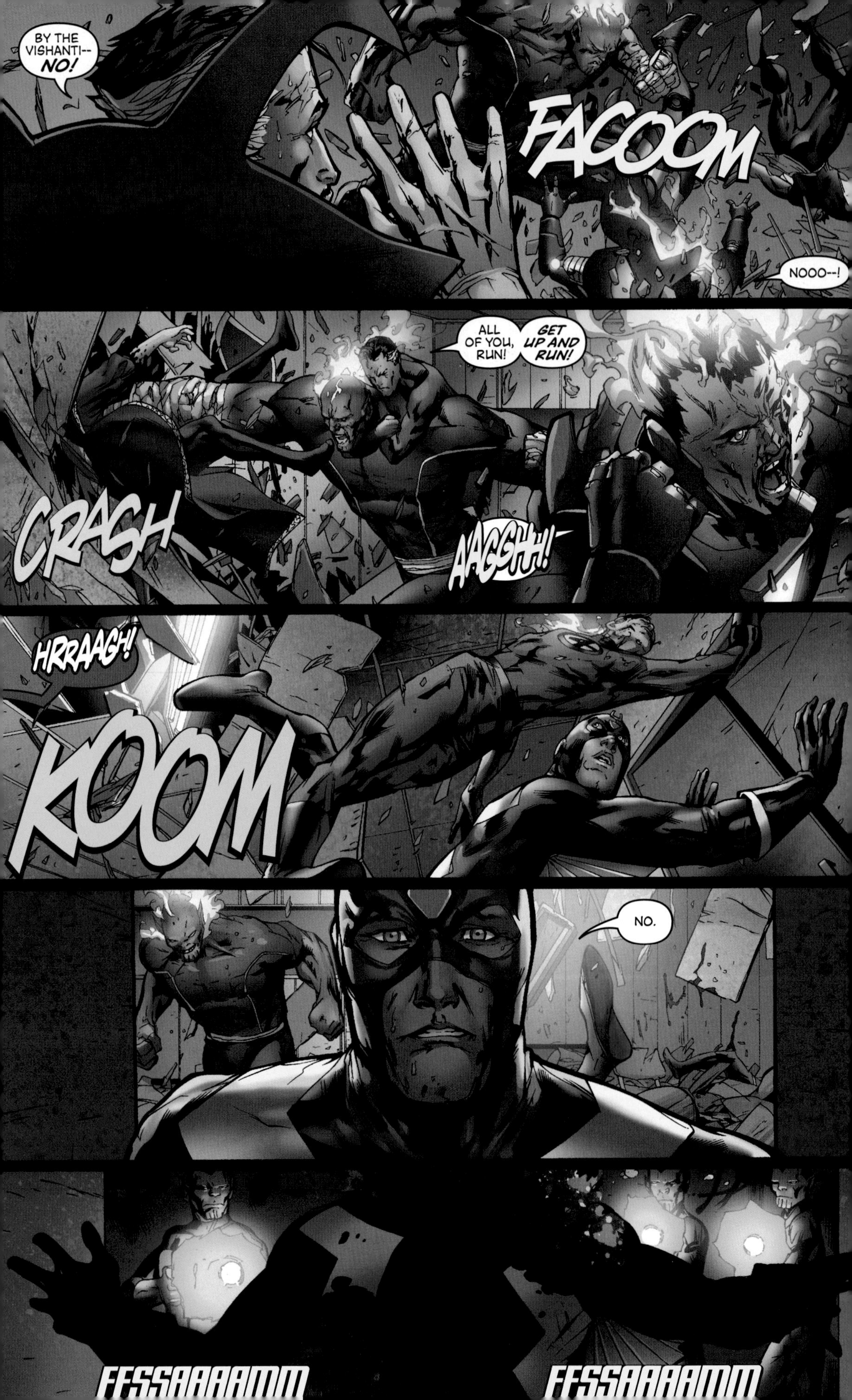
BY THE VISHANTI-- NO!
FACOOM
NOOO--!
ALL OF YOU, RUN!
GET UP AND RUN!
CRASH
AAGGHH!
HRRAAGH!
KOOM
NO.
FFSSAAAAAMM
FFSSAAAAAMM

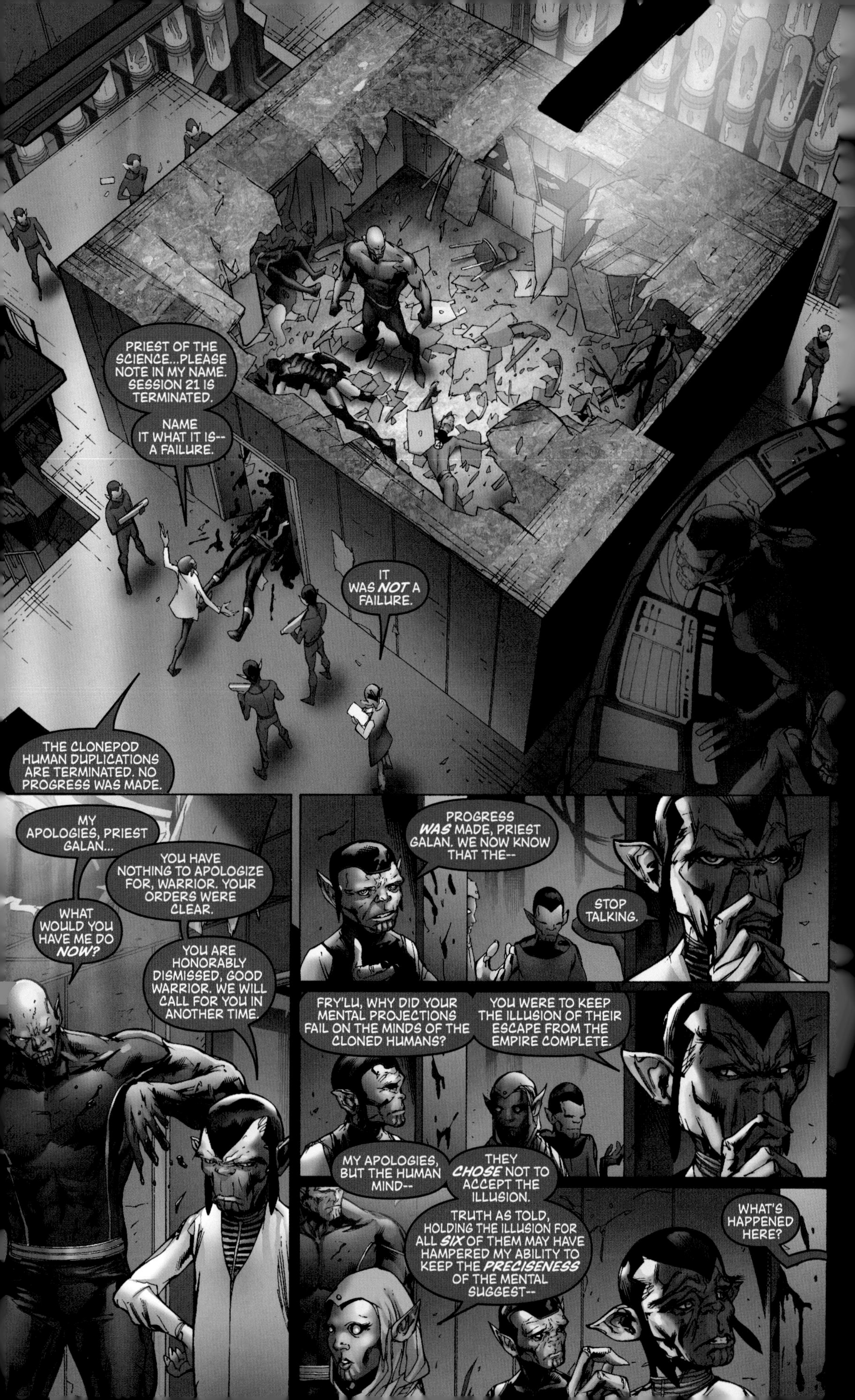
PRIEST OF THE SCIENCE...PLEASE NOTE IN MY NAME. SESSION 21 IS TERMINATED.
NAME IT WHAT IT IS-- A FAILURE.
IT WAS *NOT* A FAILURE.
THE CLONEPOD HUMAN DUPLICATIONS ARE TERMINATED. NO PROGRESS WAS MADE.
MY APOLOGIES, PRIEST GALAN...
YOU HAVE NOTHING TO APOLOGIZE FOR, WARRIOR. YOUR ORDERS WERE CLEAR.
WHAT WOULD YOU HAVE ME DO *NOW?*
YOU ARE HONORABLY DISMISSED, GOOD WARRIOR. WE WILL CALL FOR YOU IN ANOTHER TIME.
PROGRESS *WAS* MADE, PRIEST GALAN. WE NOW KNOW THAT THE--
STOP TALKING.
FRY'LU, WHY DID YOUR MENTAL PROJECTIONS FAIL ON THE MINDS OF THE CLONED HUMANS?
YOU WERE TO KEEP THE ILLUSION OF THEIR ESCAPE FROM THE EMPIRE COMPLETE.
MY APOLOGIES, BUT THE HUMAN MIND--
THEY *CHOSE* NOT TO ACCEPT THE ILLUSION.
TRUTH AS TOLD, HOLDING THE ILLUSION FOR ALL *SIX* OF THEM MAY HAVE HAMPERED MY ABILITY TO KEEP THE *PRECISENESS* OF THE MENTAL SUGGEST--
WHAT'S HAPPENED HERE?

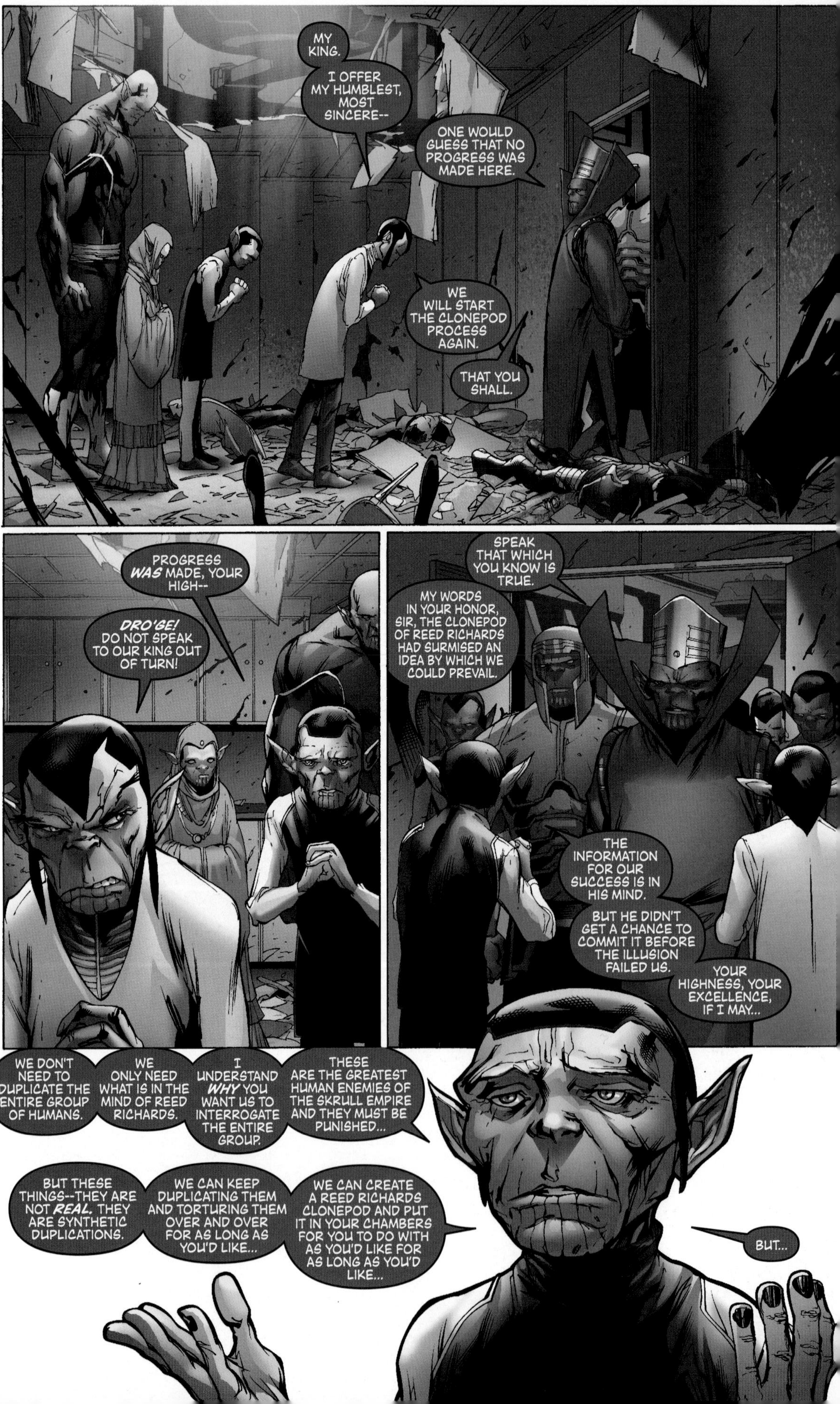

MY KING.
I OFFER MY HUMBLEST, MOST SINCERE--
ONE WOULD GUESS THAT NO PROGRESS WAS MADE HERE.
WE WILL START THE CLONEPOD PROCESS AGAIN.
THAT YOU SHALL.
PROGRESS *WAS* MADE, YOUR HIGH--
DRO'GE! DO NOT SPEAK TO OUR KING OUT OF TURN!
SPEAK THAT WHICH YOU KNOW IS TRUE.
MY WORDS IN YOUR HONOR, SIR, THE CLONEPOD OF REED RICHARDS HAD SURMISED AN IDEA BY WHICH WE COULD PREVAIL.
THE INFORMATION FOR OUR SUCCESS IS IN HIS MIND.
BUT HE DIDN'T GET A CHANCE TO COMMIT IT BEFORE THE ILLUSION FAILED US.
YOUR HIGHNESS, YOUR EXCELLENCE, IF I MAY...
WE DON'T NEED TO DUPLICATE THE ENTIRE GROUP OF HUMANS.
WE ONLY NEED WHAT IS IN THE MIND OF REED RICHARDS.
I UNDERSTAND *WHY* YOU WANT US TO INTERROGATE THE ENTIRE GROUP.
THESE ARE THE GREATEST HUMAN ENEMIES OF THE SKRULL EMPIRE AND THEY MUST BE PUNISHED...
BUT THESE THINGS--THEY ARE NOT *REAL.* THEY ARE SYNTHETIC DUPLICATIONS.
WE CAN KEEP DUPLICATING THEM AND TORTURING THEM OVER AND OVER FOR AS LONG AS YOU'D LIKE...
WE CAN CREATE A REED RICHARDS CLONEPOD AND PUT IT IN YOUR CHAMBERS FOR YOU TO DO WITH AS YOU'D LIKE FOR AS LONG AS YOU'D LIKE...
BUT...

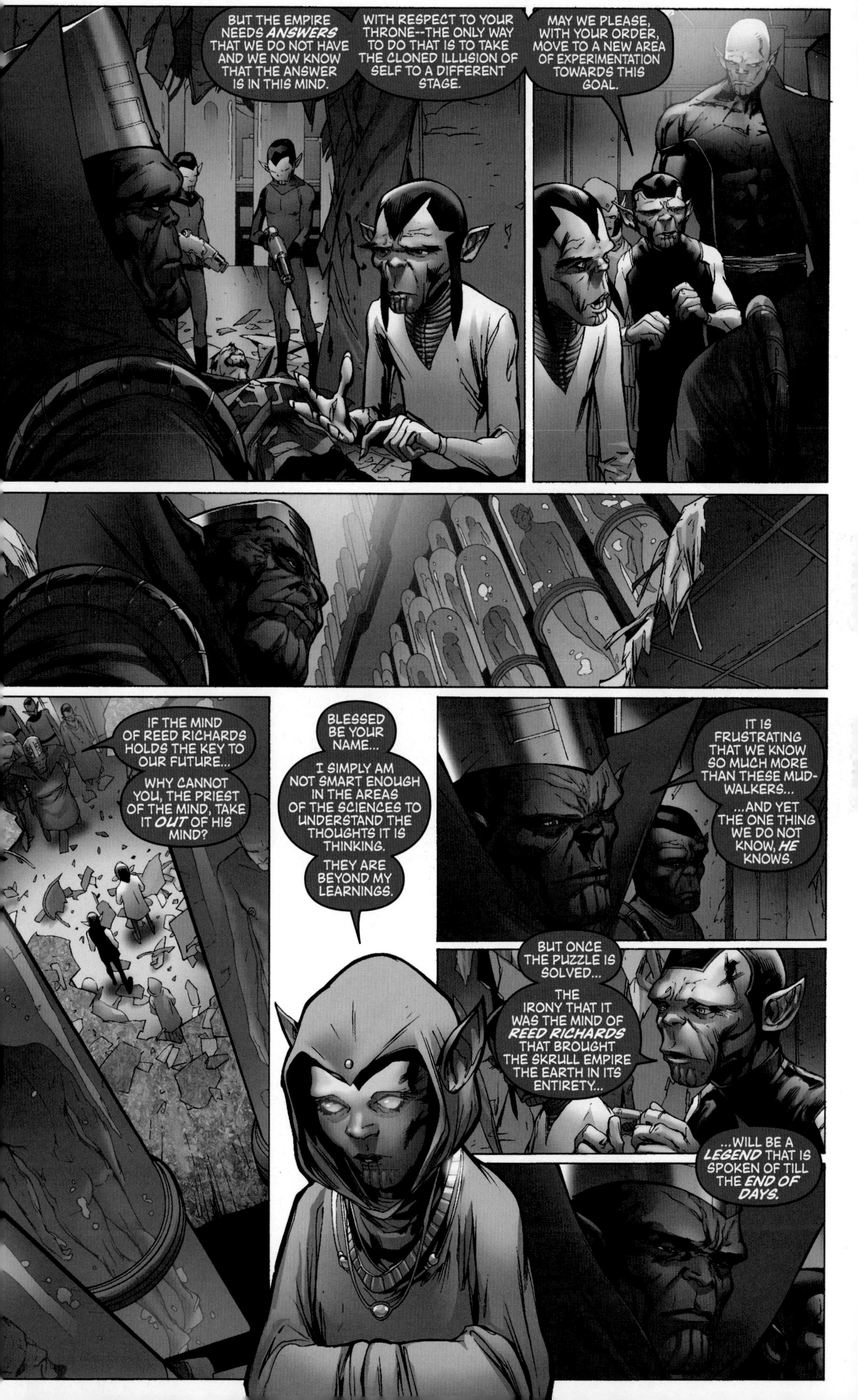

BUT THE EMPIRE NEEDS ANSWERS THAT WE DO NOT HAVE AND WE NOW KNOW THAT THE ANSWER IS IN THIS MIND.
WITH RESPECT TO YOUR THRONE--THE ONLY WAY TO DO THAT IS TO TAKE THE CLONED ILLUSION OF SELF TO A DIFFERENT STAGE.
MAY WE PLEASE, WITH YOUR ORDER, MOVE TO A NEW AREA OF EXPERIMENTATION TOWARDS THIS GOAL.
IF THE MIND OF REED RICHARDS HOLDS THE KEY TO OUR FUTURE...
WHY CANNOT YOU, THE PRIEST OF THE MIND, TAKE IT OUT OF HIS MIND?
BLESSED BE YOUR NAME...
I SIMPLY AM NOT SMART ENOUGH IN THE AREAS OF THE SCIENCES TO UNDERSTAND THE THOUGHTS IT IS THINKING.
THEY ARE BEYOND MY LEARNINGS.
IT IS FRUSTRATING THAT WE KNOW SO MUCH MORE THAN THESE MUD-WALKERS...
...AND YET THE ONE THING WE DO NOT KNOW, HE KNOWS.
BUT ONCE THE PUZZLE IS SOLVED...
THE IRONY THAT IT WAS THE MIND OF REED RICHARDS THAT BROUGHT THE SKRULL EMPIRE THE EARTH IN ITS ENTIRETY...
...WILL BE A LEGEND THAT IS SPOKEN OF TILL THE END OF DAYS.

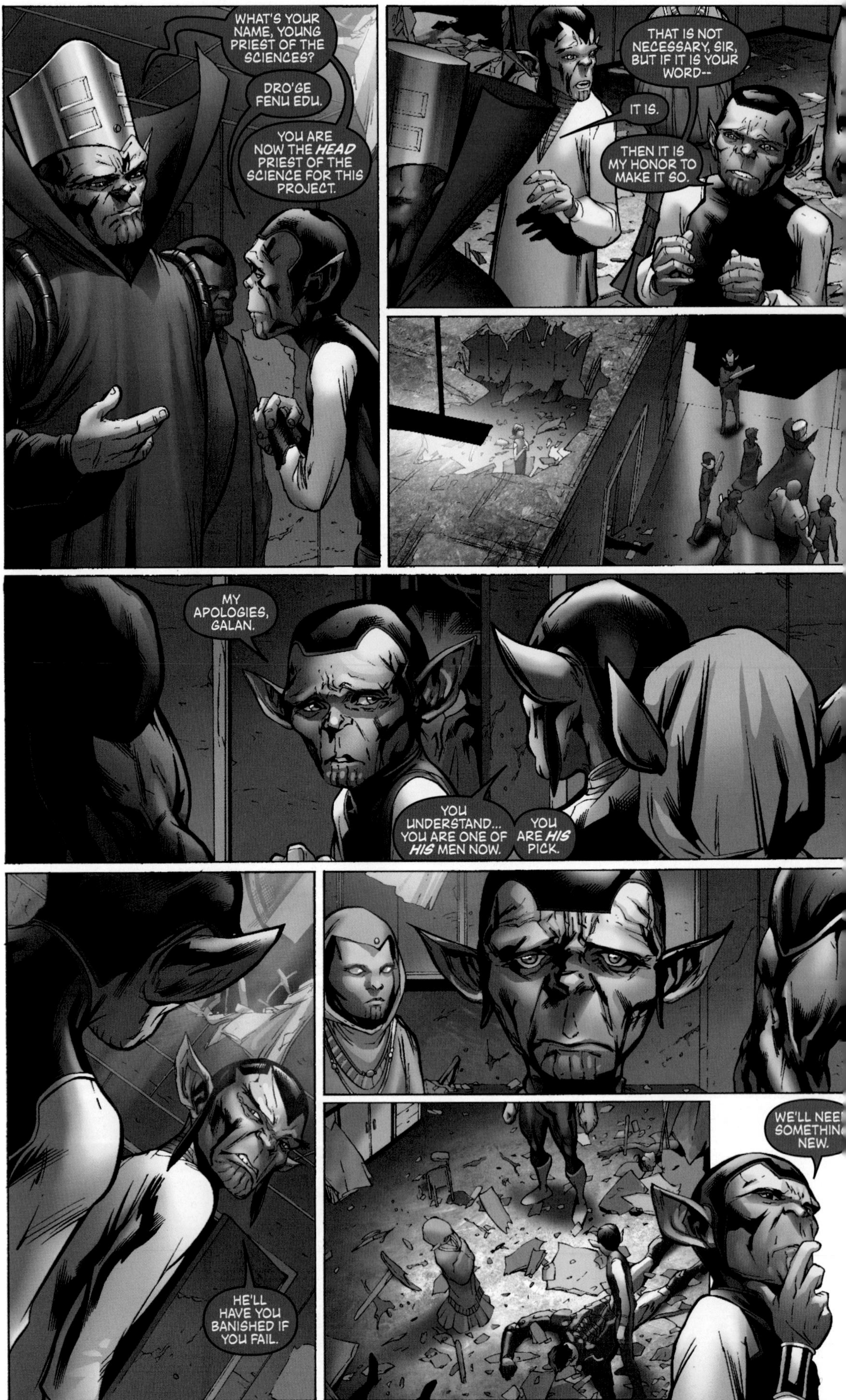

WHAT'S YOUR NAME, YOUNG PRIEST OF THE SCIENCES?
DRO'GE FENU EDU.
YOU ARE NOW THE *HEAD* PRIEST OF THE SCIENCE FOR THIS PROJECT.
THAT IS NOT NECESSARY, SIR, BUT IF IT IS YOUR WORD--
IT IS.
THEN IT IS MY HONOR TO MAKE IT SO.
MY APOLOGIES, GALAN.
YOU UNDERSTAND... YOU ARE ONE OF *HIS* MEN NOW.
YOU ARE *HIS* PICK.
HE'LL HAVE YOU BANISHED IF YOU FAIL.
WE'LL NEE SOMETHIN NEW.

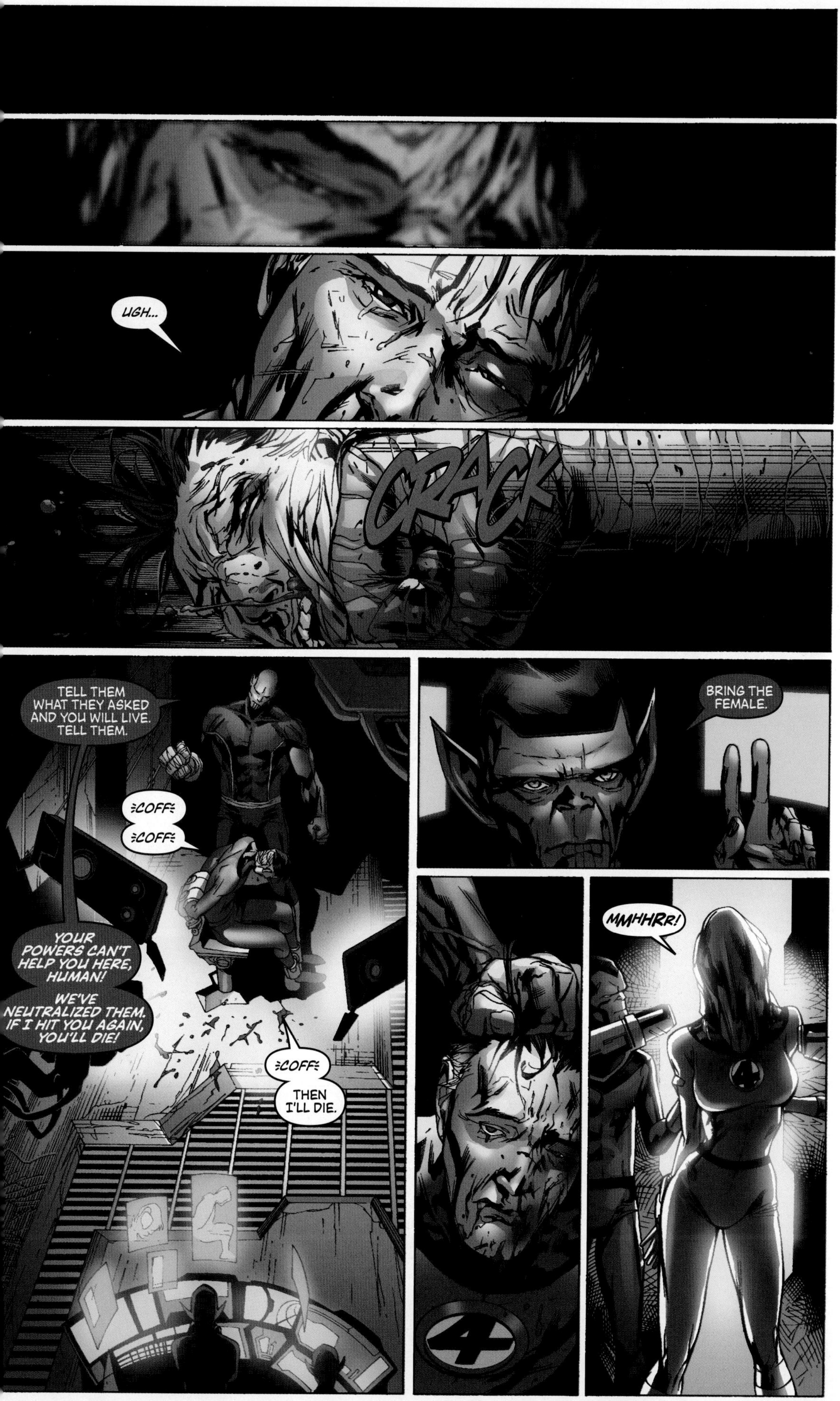
UGH...
CRACK
TELL THEM WHAT THEY ASKED AND YOU WILL LIVE. TELL THEM.
COFF
COFF
YOUR POWERS CAN'T HELP YOU HERE, HUMAN!
WE'VE NEUTRALIZED THEM. IF I HIT YOU AGAIN, YOU'LL DIE!
COFF
THEN I'LL DIE.
BRING THE FEMALE.
MMHHRR!

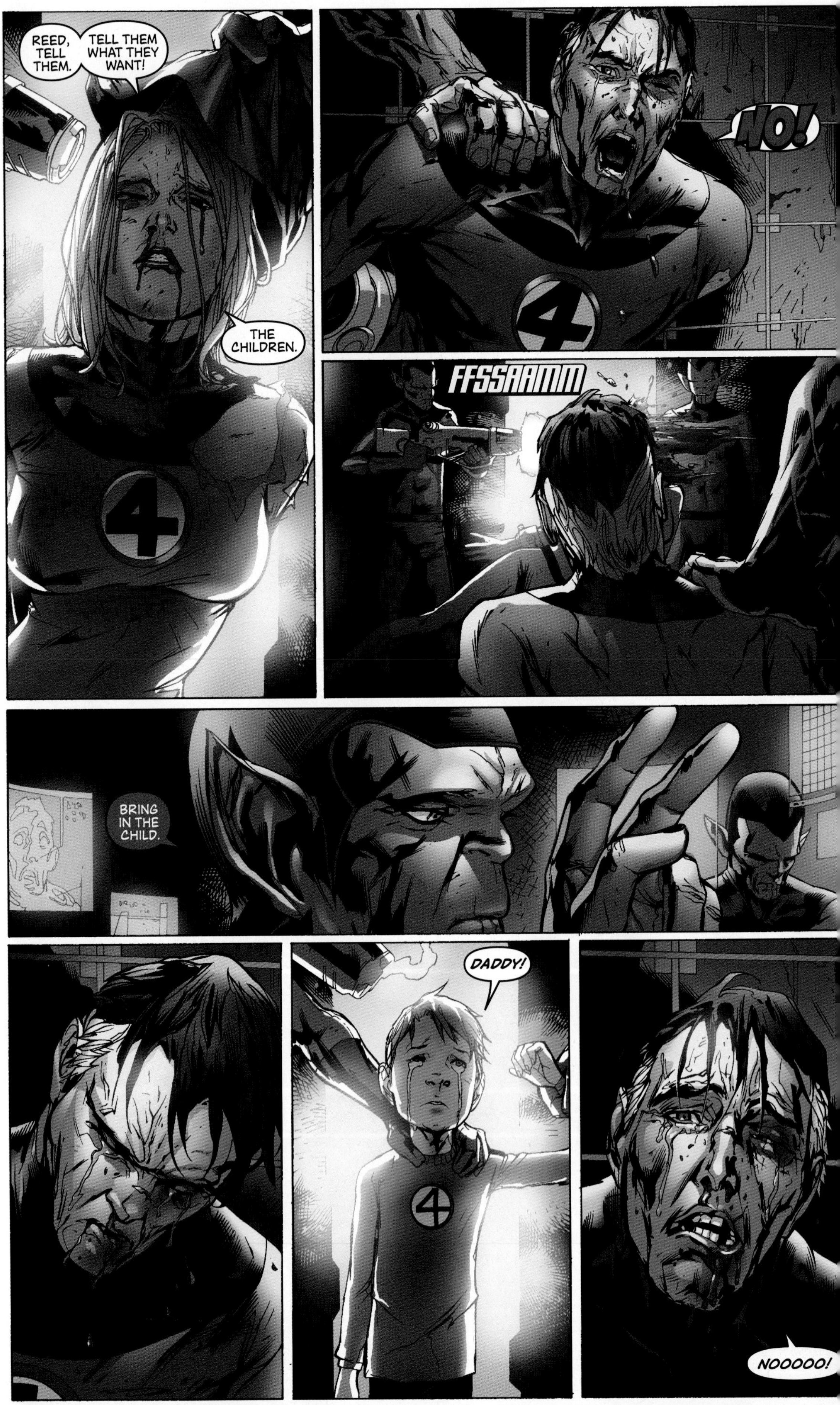

REED, TELL THEM.
TELL THEM WHAT THEY WANT!
THE CHILDREN.
NO!
FFSSAAMM
BRING IN THE CHILD.
DADDY!
NOOOOO!

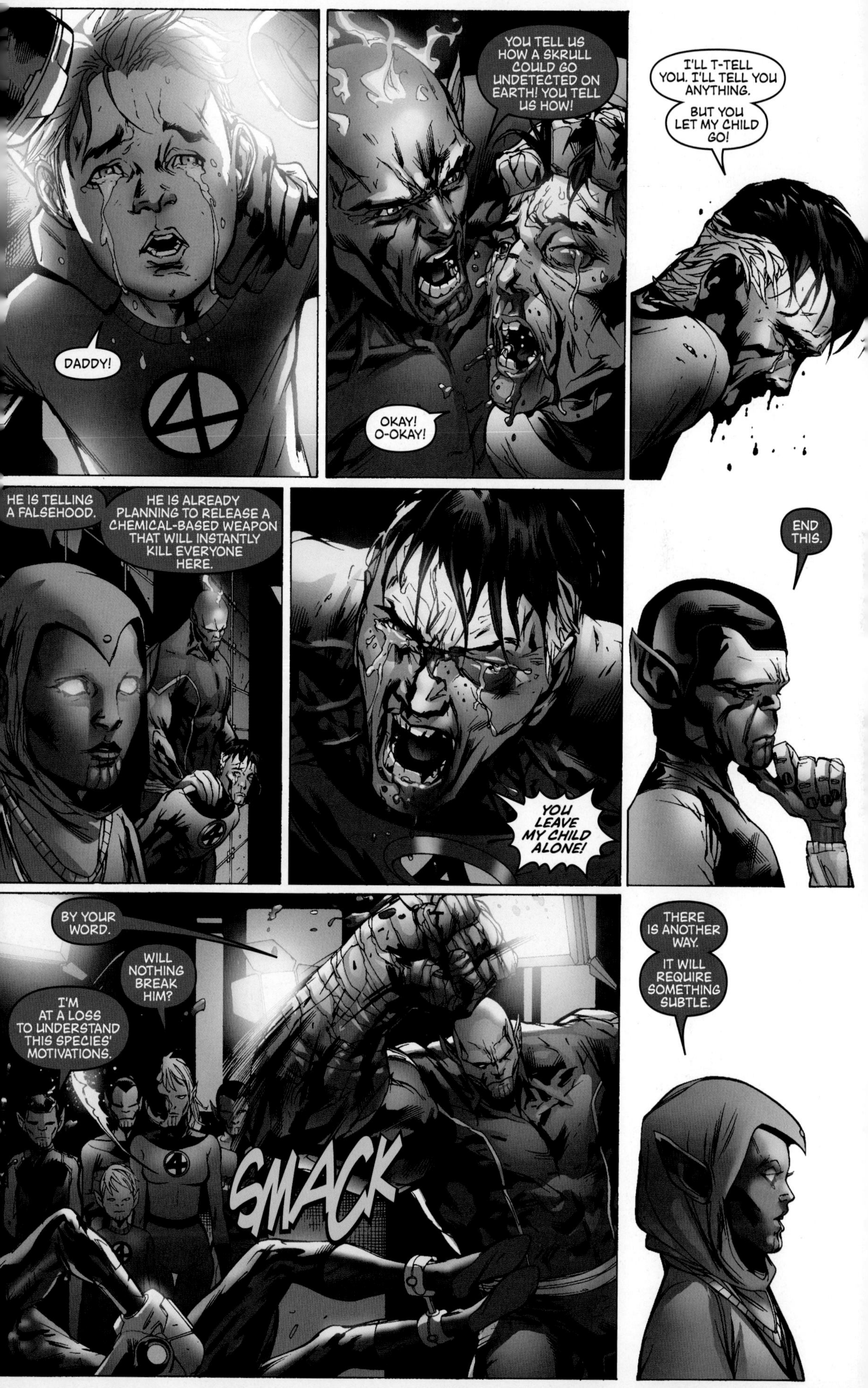
DADDY!
YOU TELL US HOW A SKRULL COULD GO UNDETECTED ON EARTH! YOU TELL US HOW!
OKAY! O-OKAY!
I'LL T-TELL YOU. I'LL TELL YOU ANYTHING.
BUT YOU LET MY CHILD GO!
HE IS TELLING A FALSEHOOD.
HE IS ALREADY PLANNING TO RELEASE A CHEMICAL-BASED WEAPON THAT WILL INSTANTLY KILL EVERYONE HERE.
YOU LEAVE MY CHILD ALONE!
END THIS.
BY YOUR WORD.
WILL NOTHING BREAK HIM?
I'M AT A LOSS TO UNDERSTAND THIS SPECIES' MOTIVATIONS.
SMACK
THERE IS ANOTHER WAY.
IT WILL REQUIRE SOMETHING SUBTLE.

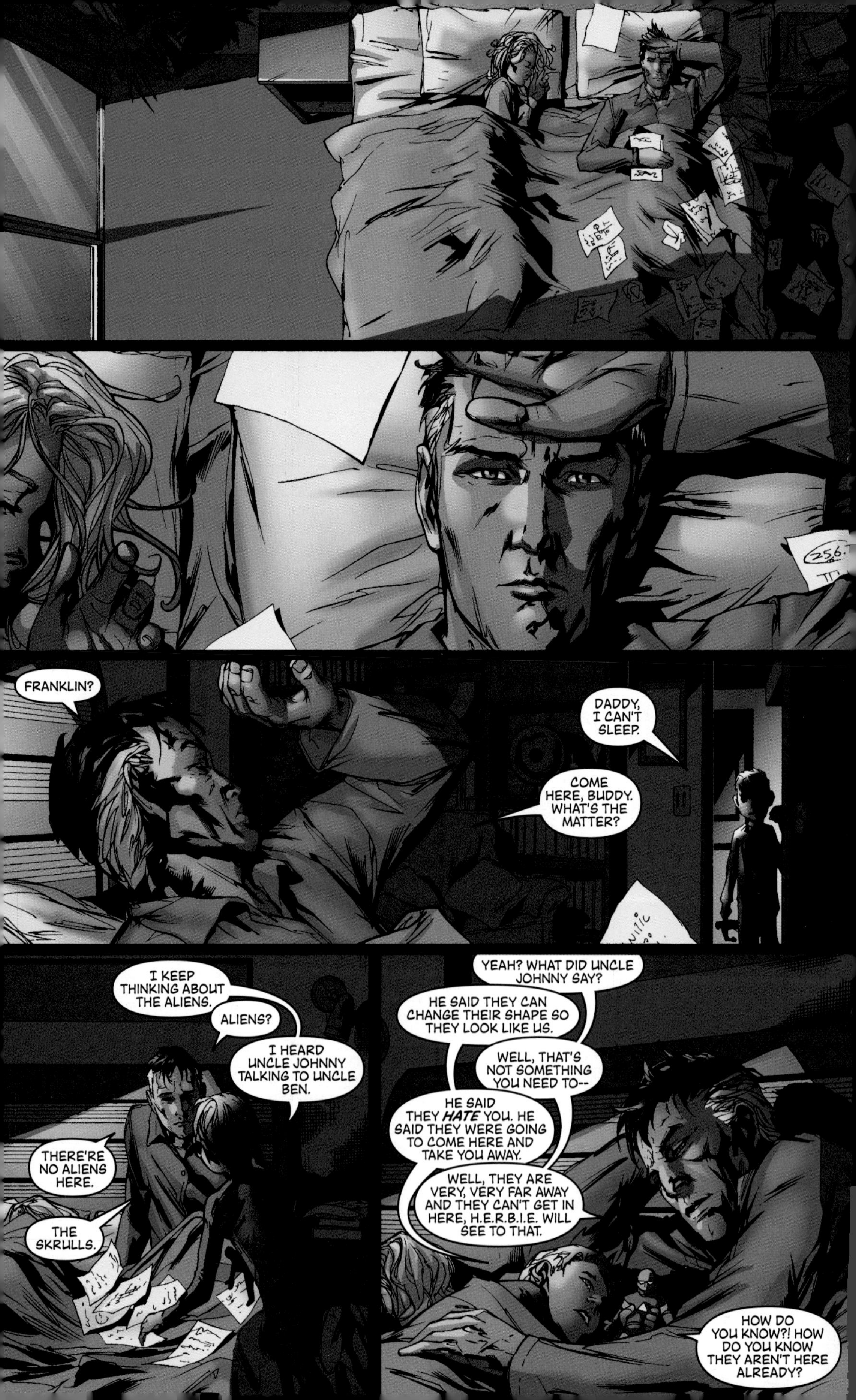
FRANKLIN?
DADDY, I CAN'T SLEEP.
COME HERE, BUDDY. WHAT'S THE MATTER?
I KEEP THINKING ABOUT THE ALIENS.
ALIENS?
I HEARD UNCLE JOHNNY TALKING TO UNCLE BEN.
THERE'RE NO ALIENS HERE.
THE SKRULLS.
YEAH? WHAT DID UNCLE JOHNNY SAY?
HE SAID THEY CAN CHANGE THEIR SHAPE SO THEY LOOK LIKE US.
WELL, THAT'S NOT SOMETHING YOU NEED TO--
HE SAID THEY HATE YOU. HE SAID THEY WERE GOING TO COME HERE AND TAKE YOU AWAY.
WELL, THEY ARE VERY, VERY FAR AWAY AND THEY CAN'T GET IN HERE, H.E.R.B.I.E. WILL SEE TO THAT.
HOW DO YOU KNOW?! HOW DO YOU KNOW THEY AREN'T HERE ALREADY?

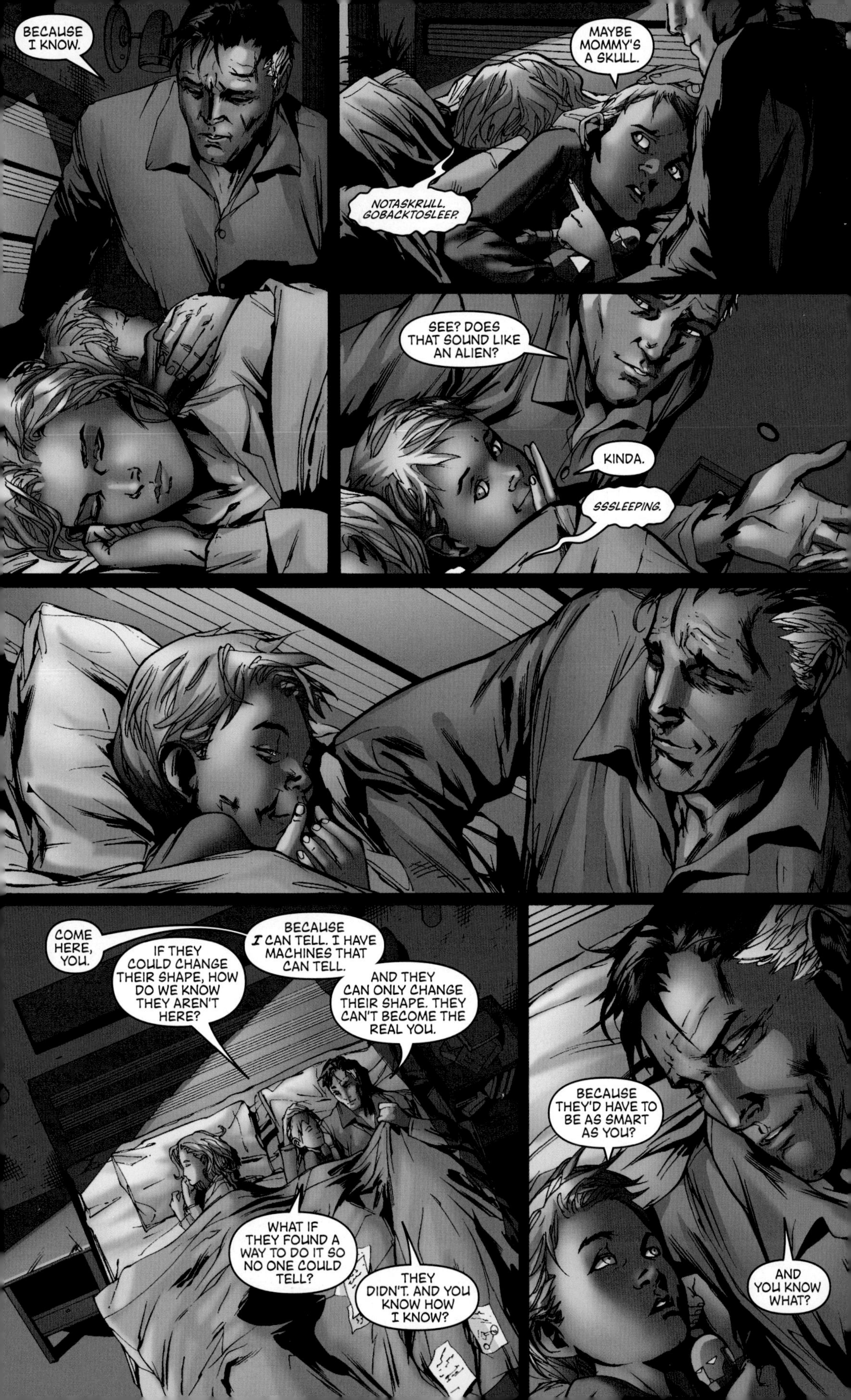
BECAUSE I KNOW.
MAYBE MOMMY'S A SKULL.
NOTASKRULL. GOBACKTOSLEEP.
SEE? DOES THAT SOUND LIKE AN ALIEN?
KINDA.
SSSLEEPING.
COME HERE, YOU.
IF THEY COULD CHANGE THEIR SHAPE, HOW DO WE KNOW THEY AREN'T HERE?
BECAUSE I CAN TELL. I HAVE MACHINES THAT CAN TELL.
AND THEY CAN ONLY CHANGE THEIR SHAPE. THEY CAN'T BECOME THE REAL YOU.
WHAT IF THEY FOUND A WAY TO DO IT SO NO ONE COULD TELL?
THEY DIDN'T. AND YOU KNOW HOW I KNOW?
BECAUSE THEY'D HAVE TO BE AS SMART AS YOU?
AND YOU KNOW WHAT?

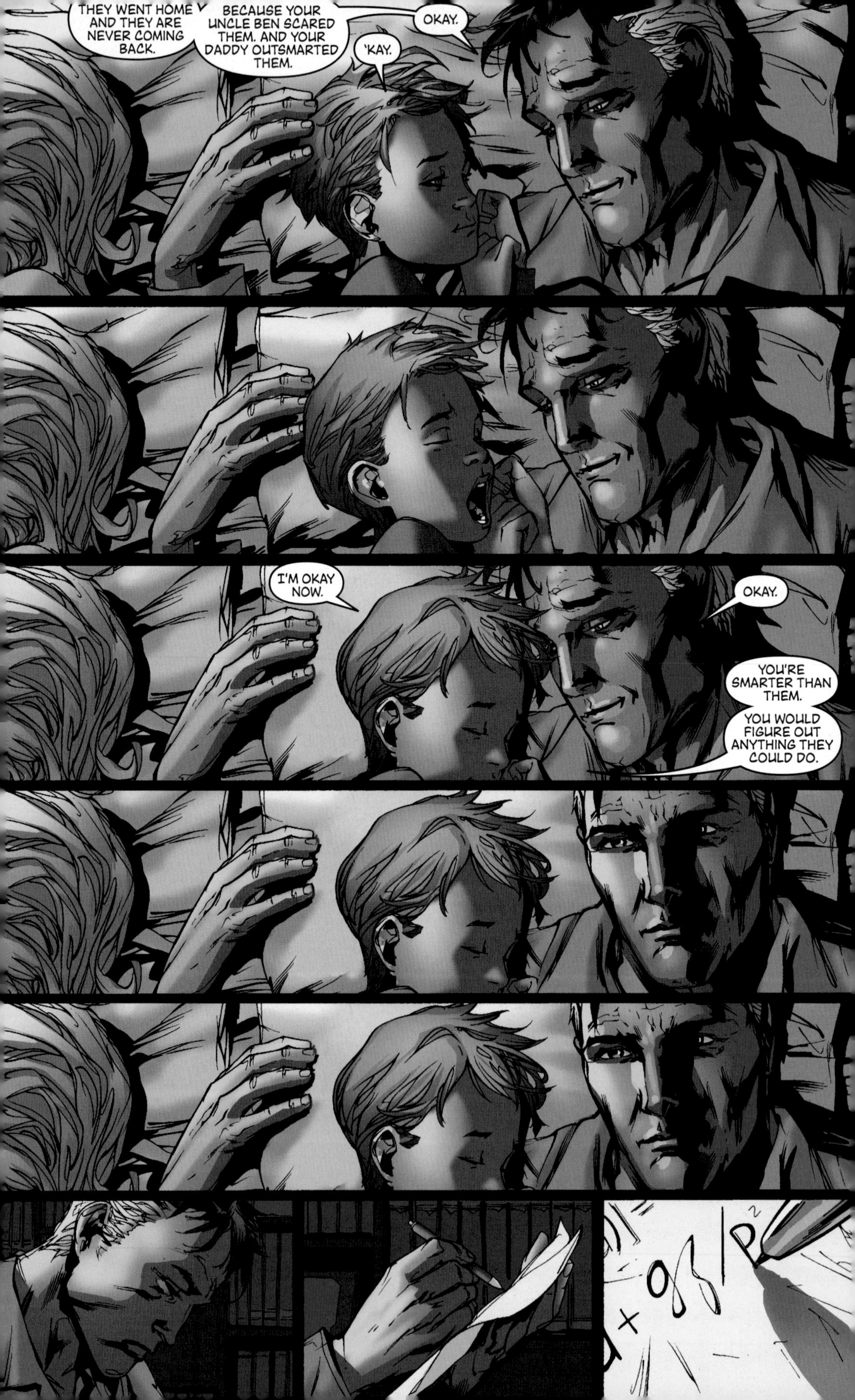
THEY WENT HOME AND THEY ARE NEVER COMING BACK.
BECAUSE YOUR UNCLE BEN SCARED THEM. AND YOUR DADDY OUTSMARTED THEM.
OKAY.
'KAY.
I'M OKAY NOW.
OKAY.
YOU'RE SMARTER THAN THEM.
YOU WOULD FIGURE OUT ANYTHING THEY COULD DO.

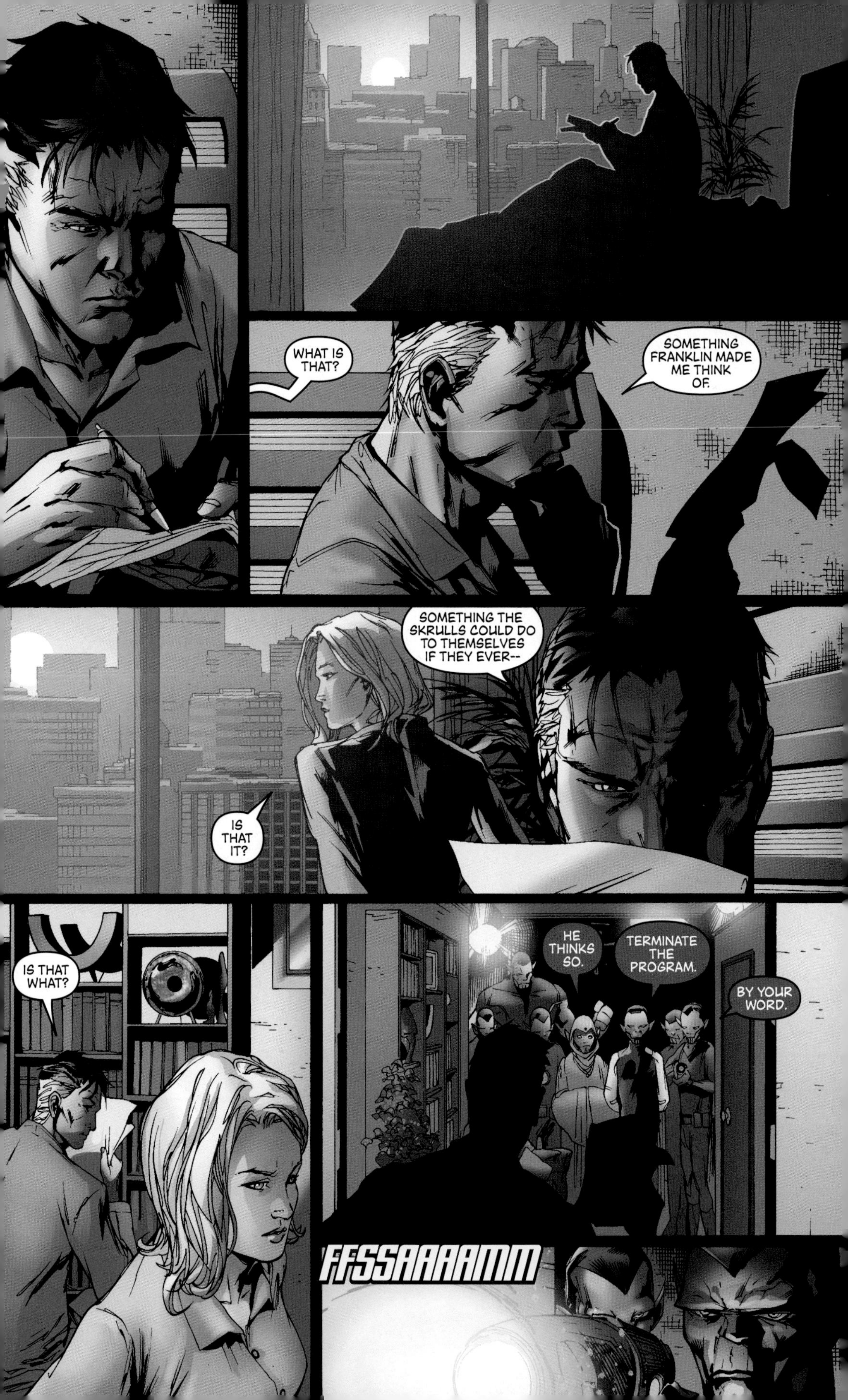

WHAT IS THAT?
SOMETHING FRANKLIN MADE ME THINK OF.
SOMETHING THE SKRULLS COULD DO TO THEMSELVES IF THEY EVER--
IS THAT IT?
IS THAT WHAT?
HE THINKS SO.
TERMINATE THE PROGRAM.
BY YOUR WORD.
FFSSAAAAAMM

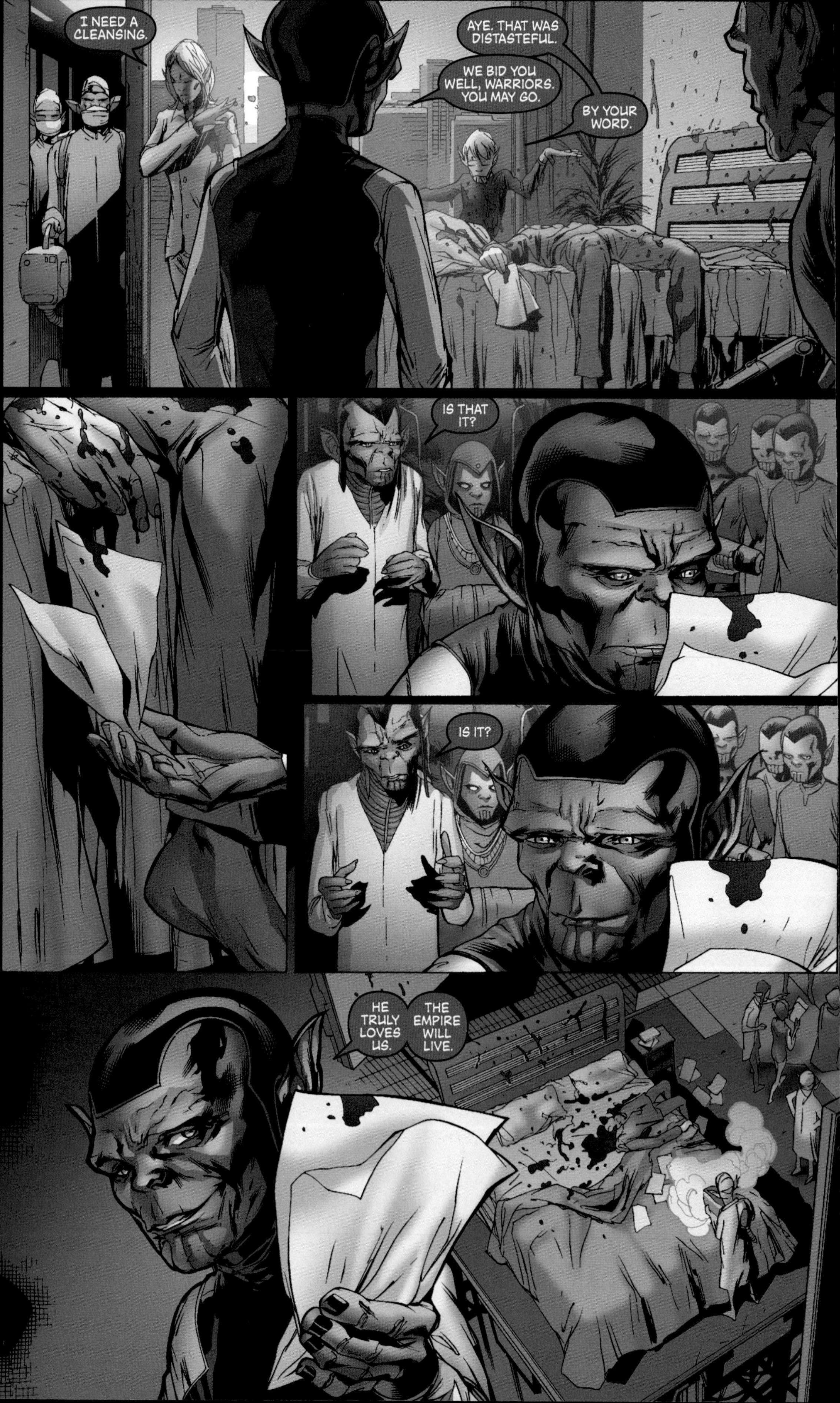
I NEED A CLEANSING.
AYE. THAT WAS DISTASTEFUL.
WE BID YOU WELL, WARRIORS. YOU MAY GO.
BY YOUR WORD.
IS THAT IT?
IS IT?
HE TRULY LOVES US.
THE EMPIRE WILL LIVE.

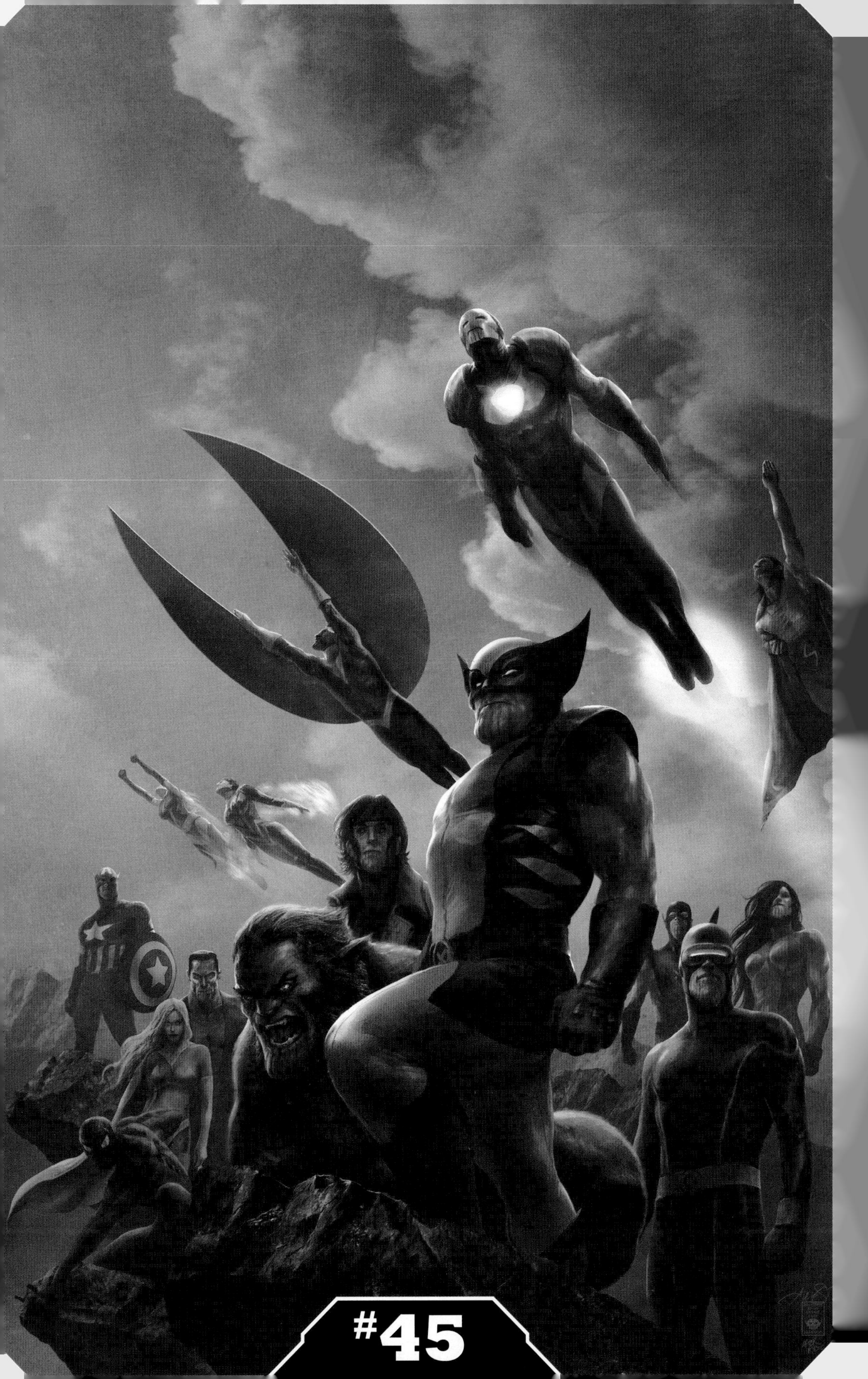
#45

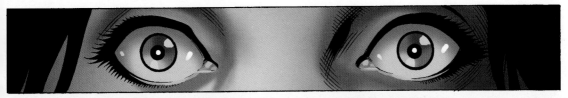

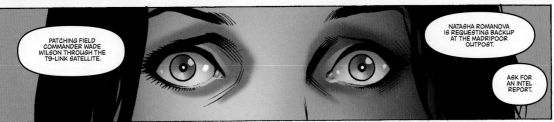

PATCHING FIELD COMMANDER WADE WILSON THROUGH THE T9-LINK SATELLITE.

NATASHA ROMANOVA IS REQUESTING BACKUP AT THE MADRIPOOR OUTPOST.

ASK FOR AN INTEL REPORT.

DIRECTOR SHAW HASN'T REPORTED IN YET.

SEND A B-TEAM OUT TO THE SAVAGE LAND AND SEE WHAT IS WHAT.

ANY WORD ON WEAPON XXXC?

SOME KIND OF FLUCTUATION.

LATVERIA HAS NO AMBASSADOR, HE'S LYING.

LATVERIA HAS NO AMBASSADOR? SINCE WHEN?

AGENT SITWELL IS CALLING IN?

THE BROOD SIGNAL IS STILL OFFLINE.

SEE WHAT YOU CAN DO WITH IT.

SERIOUSLY, SINCE WHEN?

HAVE WE GOTTEN AN UPDATE FROM GENOSHA'S OUTPOST?

GENOSHA, THIS IS HELICARRIER FIVE.

YOU'RE LATE WITH THE SCHEDULED UPDATE.

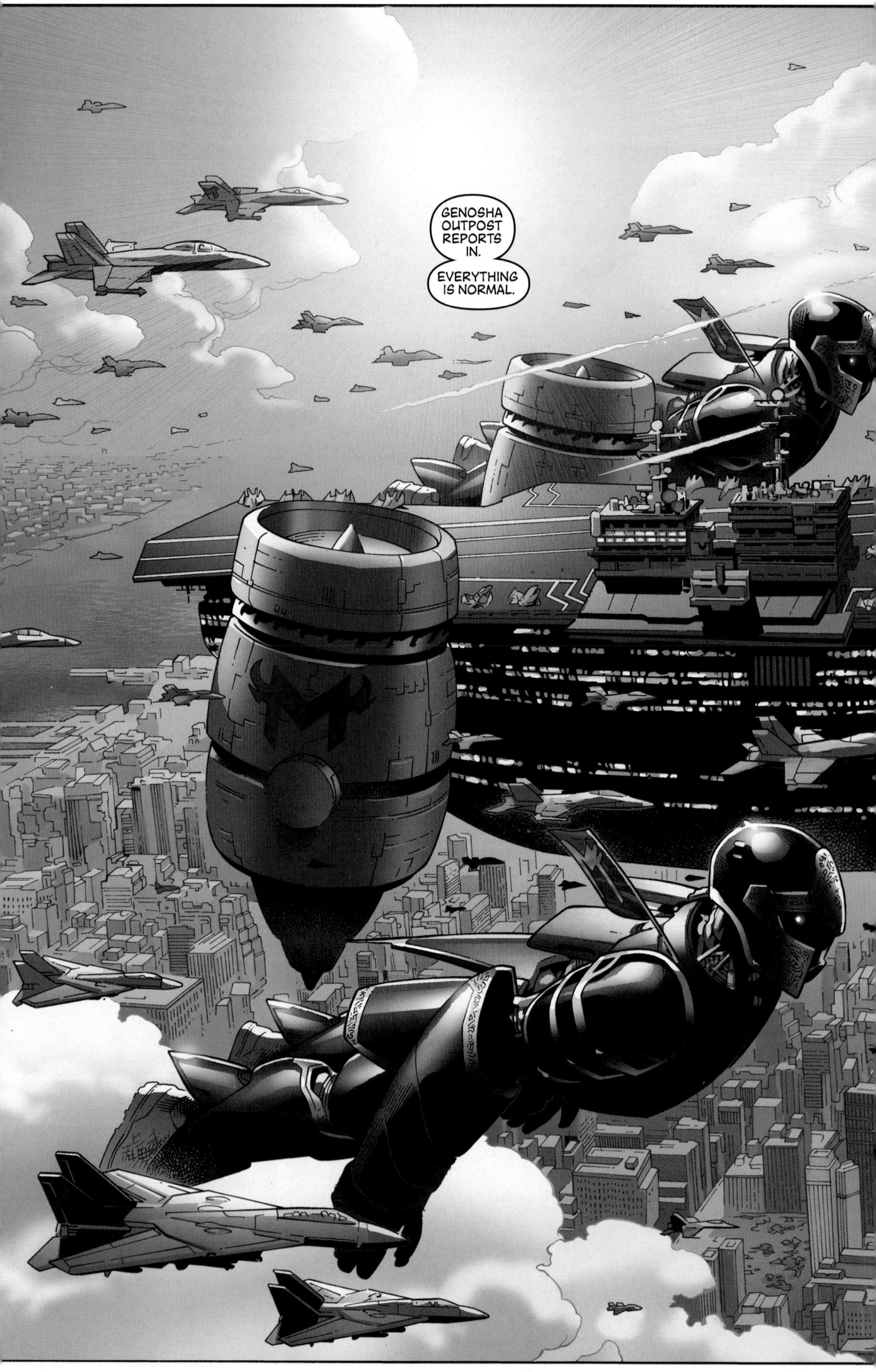
GENOSHA OUTPOST REPORTS IN.
EVERYTHING IS NORMAL.

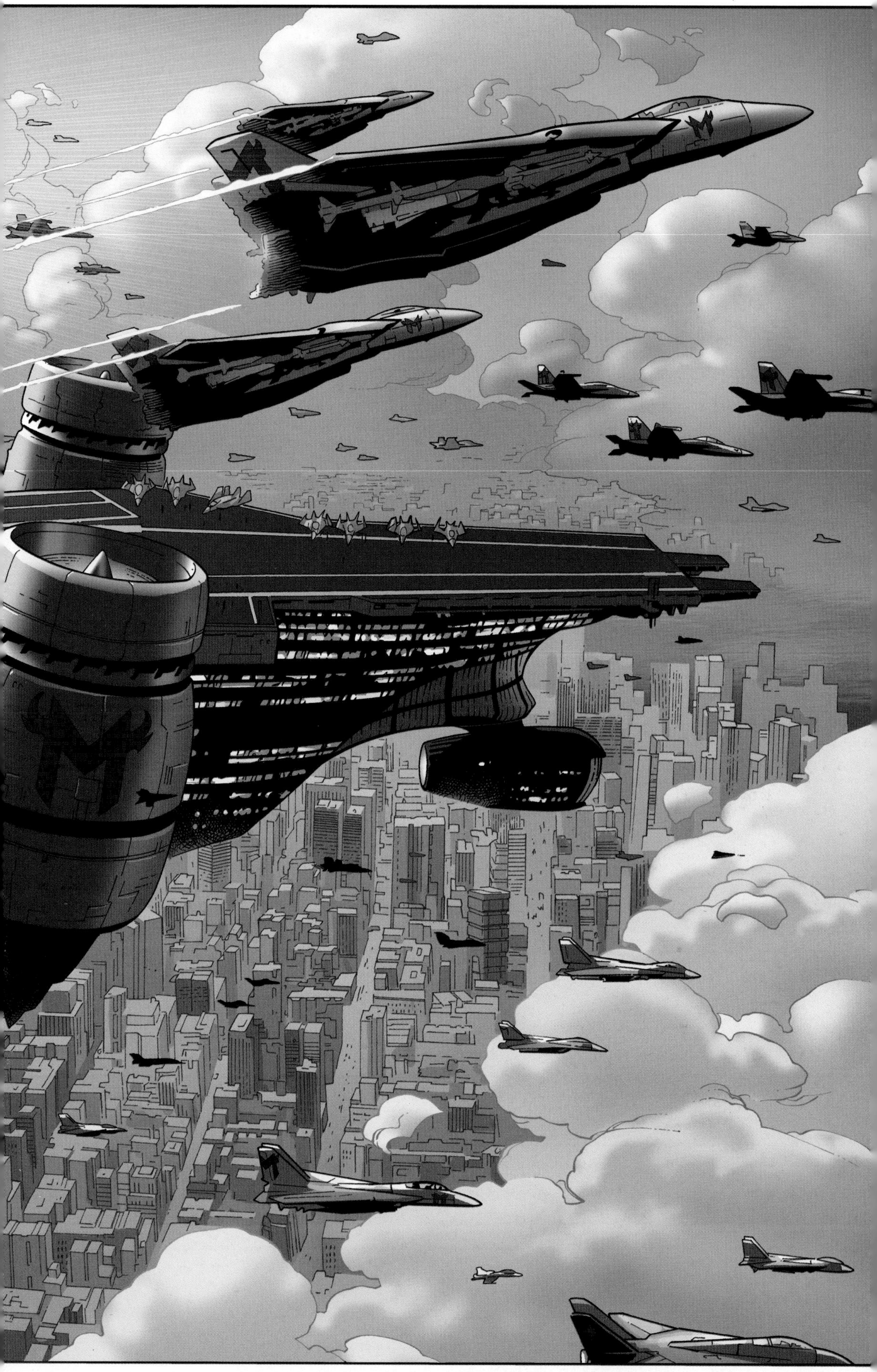

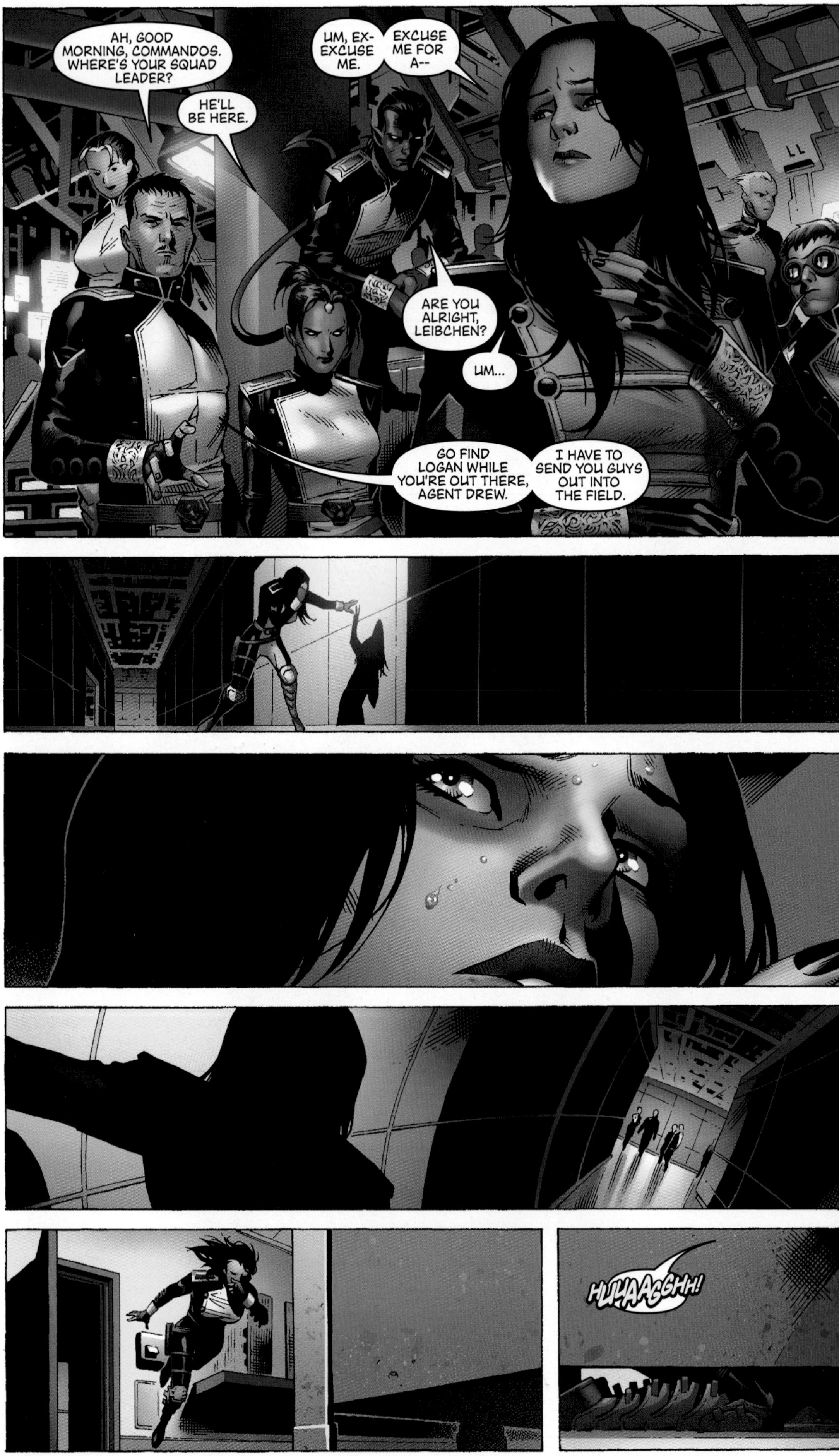
AH, GOOD MORNING, COMMANDOS. WHERE'S YOUR SQUAD LEADER?
HE'LL BE HERE.
UM, EX-EXCUSE ME.
EXCUSE ME FOR A--
ARE YOU ALRIGHT, LEIBCHEN?
UM...
I HAVE TO SEND YOU GUYS OUT INTO THE FIELD.
GO FIND LOGAN WHILE YOU'RE OUT THERE, AGENT DREW.
HUUAAGGHH!

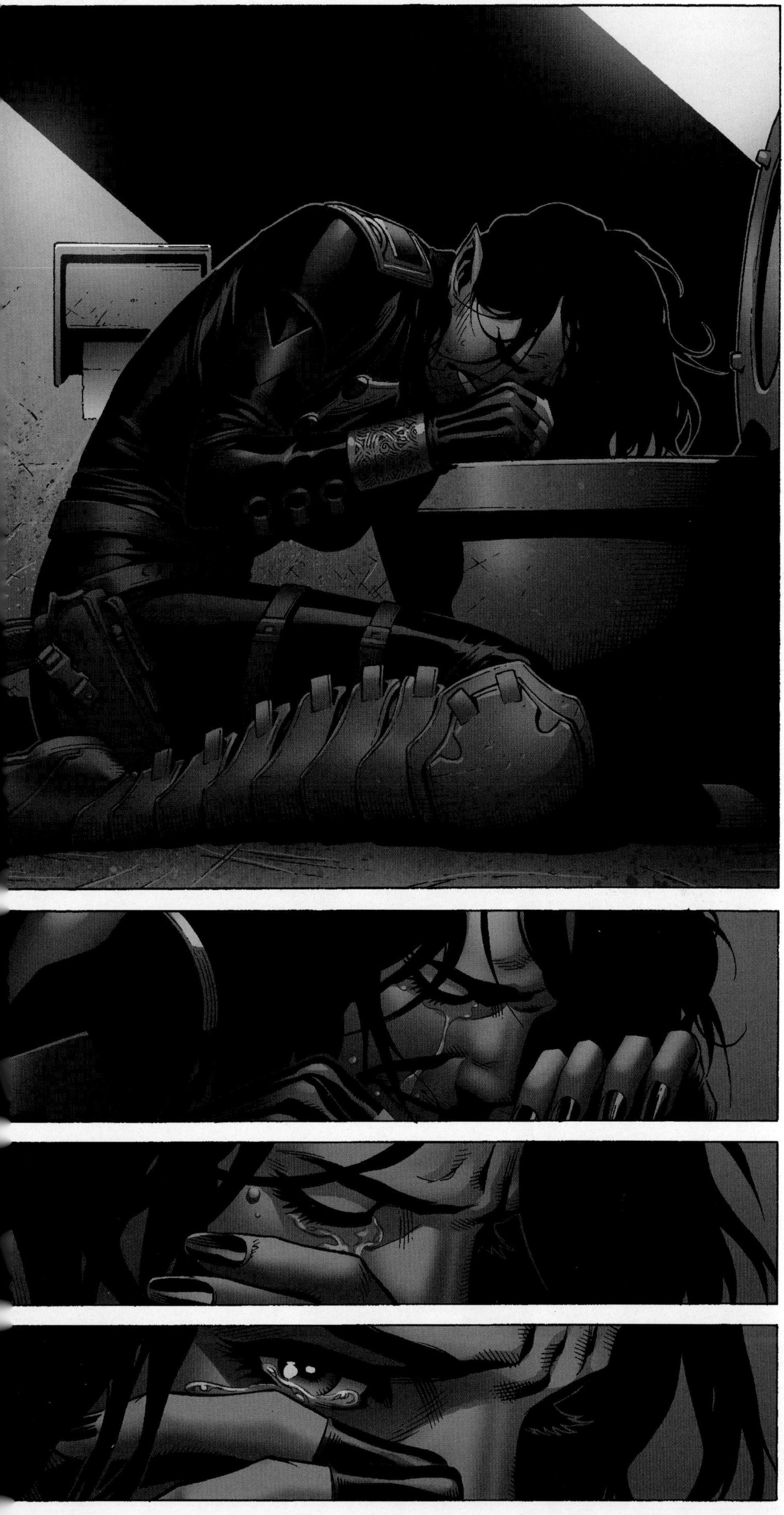

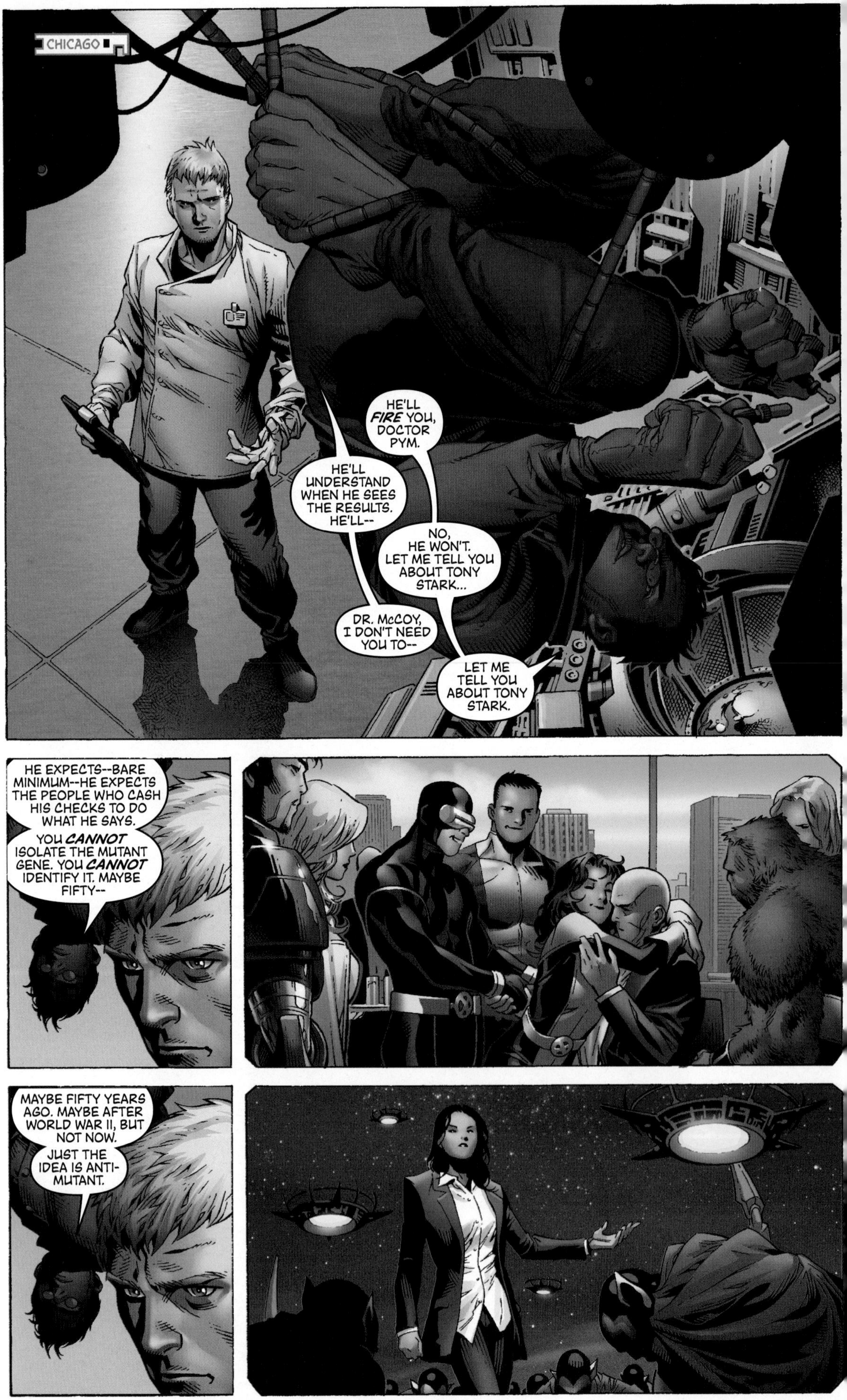
CHICAGO
HE'LL UNDERSTAND WHEN HE SEES THE RESULTS. HE'LL--
HE'LL FIRE YOU, DOCTOR PYM.
NO, HE WON'T. LET ME TELL YOU ABOUT TONY STARK...
DR. McCOY, I DON'T NEED YOU TO--
LET ME TELL YOU ABOUT TONY STARK.
HE EXPECTS--BARE MINIMUM--HE EXPECTS THE PEOPLE WHO CASH HIS CHECKS TO DO WHAT HE SAYS.
YOU CANNOT ISOLATE THE MUTANT GENE. YOU CANNOT IDENTIFY IT. MAYBE FIFTY--
MAYBE FIFTY YEARS AGO. MAYBE AFTER WORLD WAR II, BUT NOT NOW.
JUST THE IDEA IS ANTI-MUTANT.

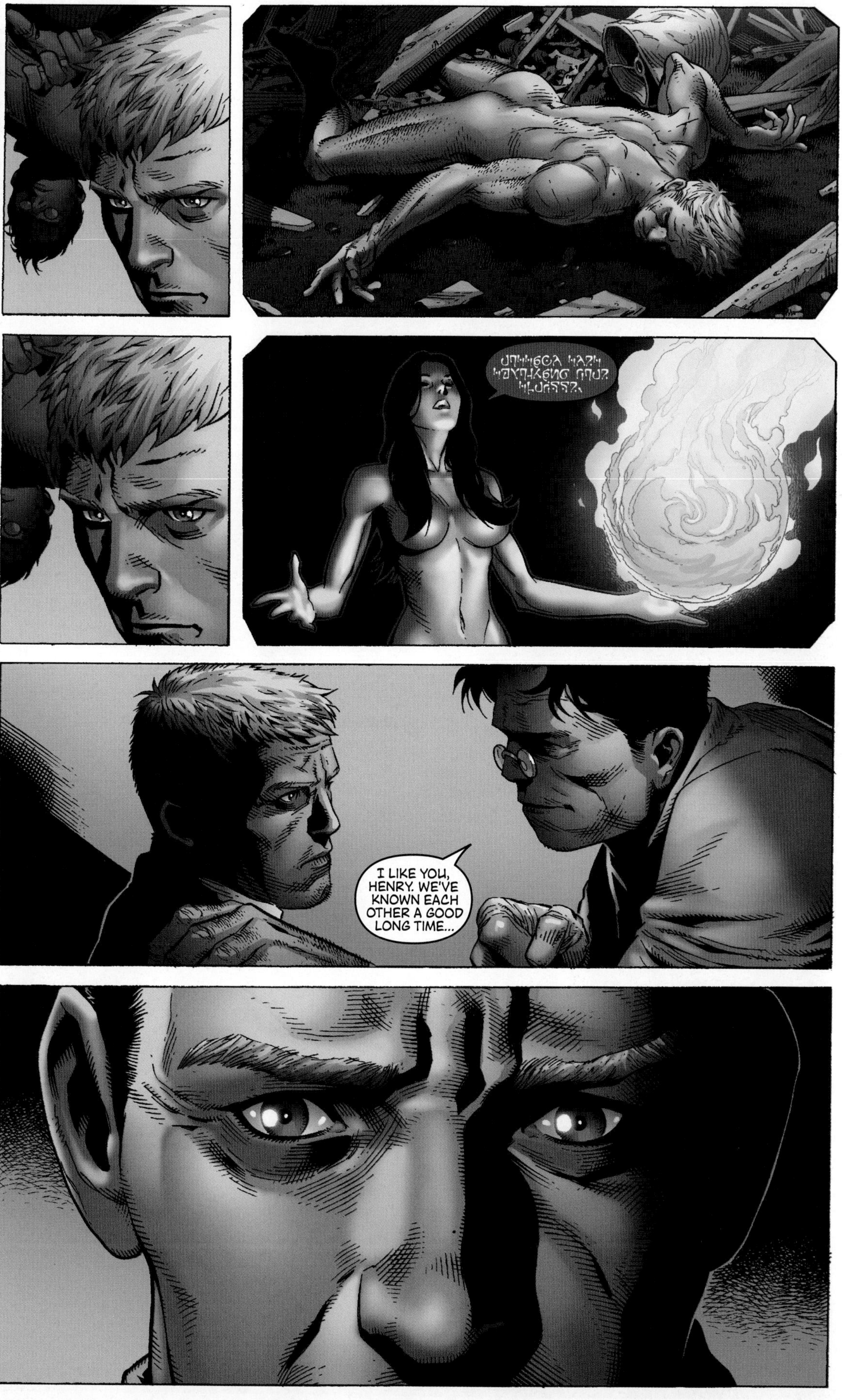
I LIKE YOU, HENRY. WE'VE KNOWN EACH OTHER A GOOD LONG TIME...

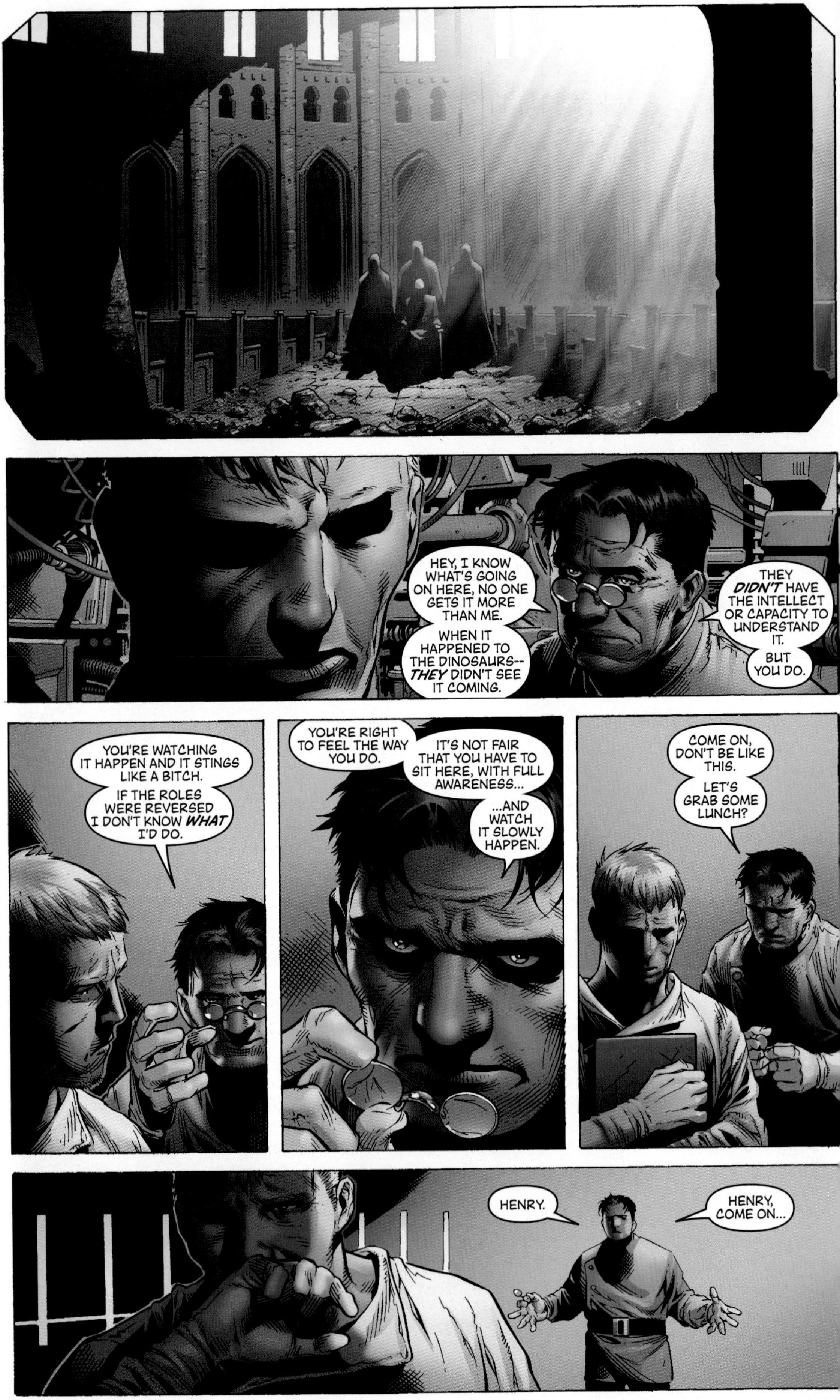
HEY, I KNOW WHAT'S GOING ON HERE, NO ONE GETS IT MORE THAN ME.
WHEN IT HAPPENED TO THE DINOSAURS-- *THEY* DIDN'T SEE IT COMING.
THEY *DIDN'T* HAVE THE INTELLECT OR CAPACITY TO UNDERSTAND IT.
BUT YOU DO.
YOU'RE WATCHING IT HAPPEN AND IT STINGS LIKE A BITCH.
IF THE ROLES WERE REVERSED I DON'T KNOW *WHAT* I'D DO.
YOU'RE RIGHT TO FEEL THE WAY YOU DO.
IT'S NOT FAIR THAT YOU HAVE TO SIT HERE, WITH FULL AWARENESS...
...AND WATCH IT SLOWLY HAPPEN.
COME ON, DON'T BE LIKE THIS.
LET'S GRAB SOME LUNCH?
HENRY.
HENRY, COME ON...

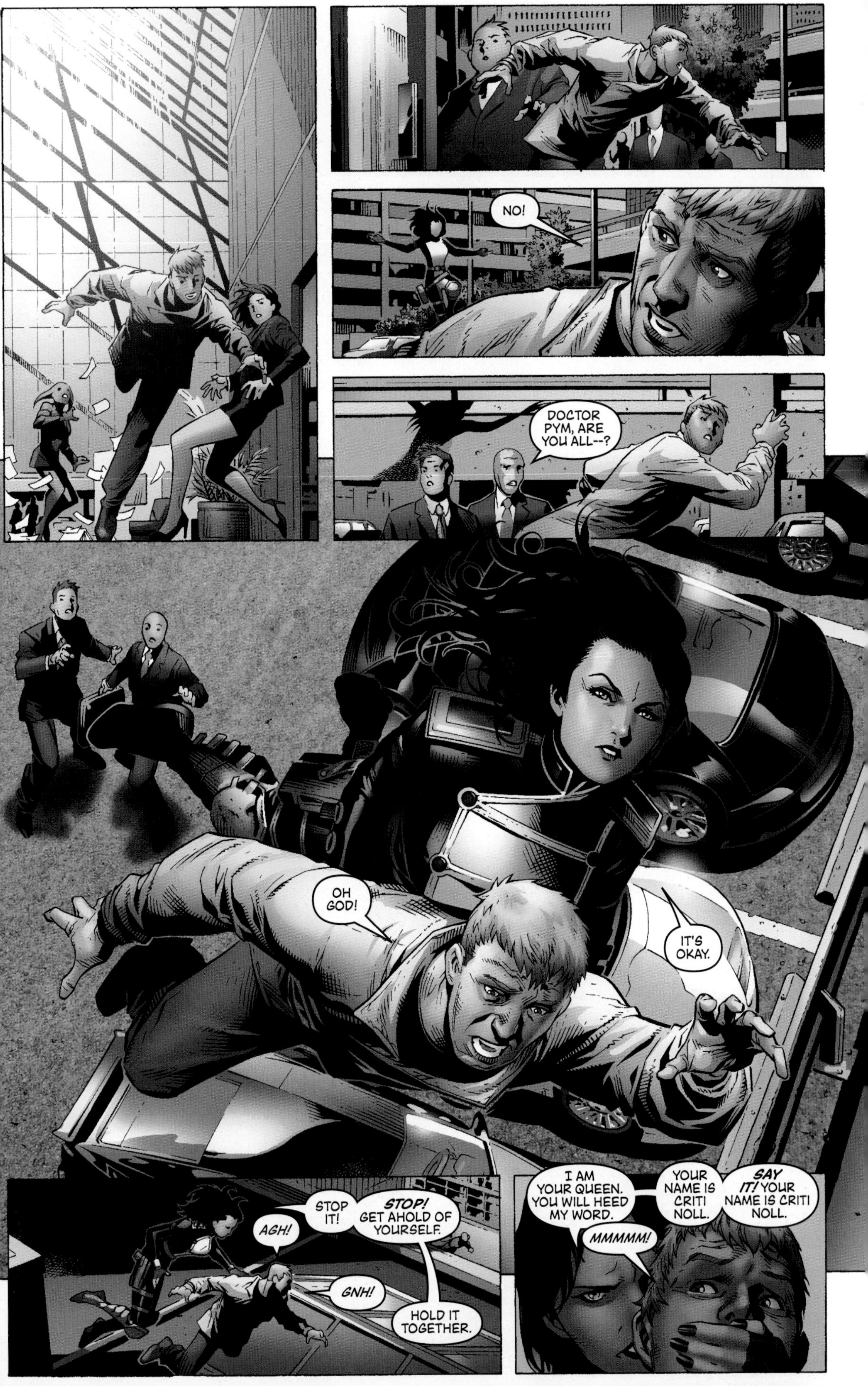
NO!
DOCTOR PYM, ARE YOU ALL--?
OH GOD!
IT'S OKAY.
STOP IT!
STOP! GET AHOLD OF YOURSELF.
AGH!
GNH!
HOLD IT TOGETHER.
I AM YOUR QUEEN. YOU WILL HEED MY WORD.
YOUR NAME IS CRITI NOLL.
SAY IT! YOUR NAME IS CRITI NOLL.
MMMMM!

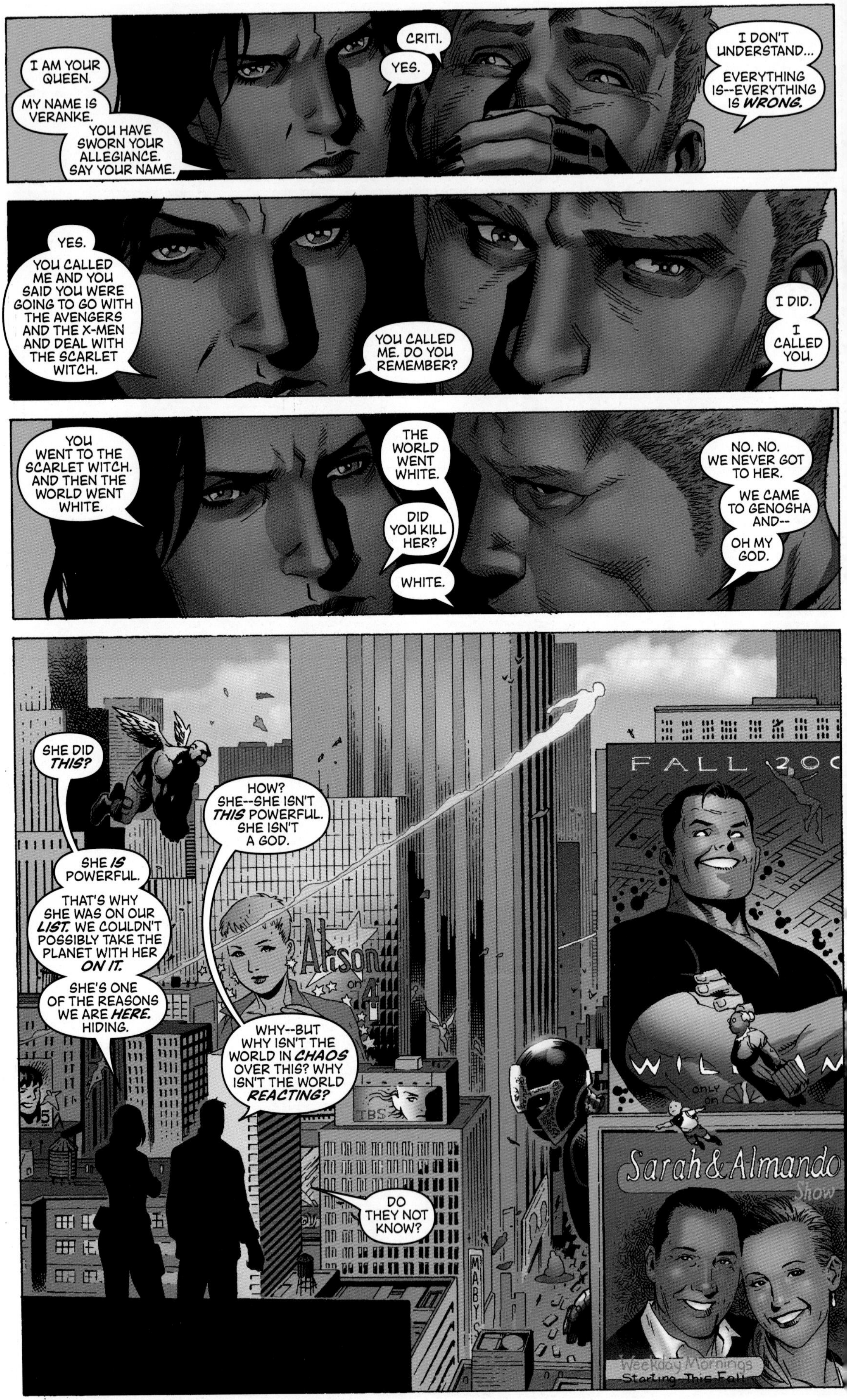
I AM YOUR QUEEN.
MY NAME IS VERANKE.
YOU HAVE SWORN YOUR ALLEGIANCE. SAY YOUR NAME.
CRITI.
YES.
I DON'T UNDERSTAND...
EVERYTHING IS--EVERYTHING IS *WRONG.*
YES.
YOU CALLED ME AND YOU SAID YOU WERE GOING TO GO WITH THE AVENGERS AND THE X-MEN AND DEAL WITH THE SCARLET WITCH.
YOU CALLED ME. DO YOU REMEMBER?
I DID.
I CALLED YOU.
YOU WENT TO THE SCARLET WITCH. AND THEN THE WORLD WENT WHITE.
THE WORLD WENT WHITE.
DID YOU KILL HER?
WHITE.
NO. NO. WE NEVER GOT TO HER.
WE CAME TO GENOSHA AND--
OH MY GOD.
SHE DID *THIS?*
HOW? SHE--SHE ISN'T *THIS* POWERFUL. SHE ISN'T A GOD.
SHE *IS* POWERFUL.
THAT'S WHY SHE WAS ON OUR *LIST.* WE COULDN'T POSSIBLY TAKE THE PLANET WITH HER *ON IT.*
SHE'S ONE OF THE REASONS WE ARE *HERE.* HIDING.
WHY--BUT WHY ISN'T THE WORLD IN *CHAOS* OVER THIS? WHY ISN'T THE WORLD *REACTING?*
DO THEY NOT KNOW?
FALL 20
Alison on 4
TBS
ONLY ON
Sarah & Almando Show
Weekday Mornings
Starting This Fall

LOOK. THEY LIVE HAPPILY. SATIATED.

THIS MANY MUTANTS. THE SKRULL ARMADA CAN'T BATTLE AGAINST **THIS.** THIS IS THE **OPPOSITE** OF WHAT WE WERE SENT HERE TO DO.

LISTEN TO ME... I SAW WITH MY OWN EYES THAT WOLVERINE, LOGAN, SAW RIGHT THROUGH THIS ILLUSION.

THEY SENT US TO HUNT HIM. THERE ARE OTHERS. THERE HAVE TO BE.

LIKE US.

THE ILLUSION IS-- IT FEELS PAPER THIN. IT HAS CRACKS IN IT. WE--**WE** ARE THE CRACKS IN IT.

THIS **WILL** CRUMBLE AND WORD WILL GET OUT. WE'LL MAKE **SURE** THE WORD GETS OUT THAT A **MUTANT** DID THIS. AND **WHEN** THE WORD GETS OUT, A WAR AGAINST THE MUTANTS WILL BE **IMMEDIATE** AND **FIERCE.**

THE MUTANTS WILL BE DECIMATED AND IMPRISONED... THE SCARLET WITCH WILL BE EXECUTED... AND THEN WE WILL KNOW IT IS OUR TIME.

AND IF THIS PROVES ANYTHING, ANYTHING AT ALL... IT'S THAT AS LONG AS THEY ARE LEFT ALONE TO EAT, SLEEP, WATCH THEIR TV AND FORNICATE, MOST OF THE HUMAN RACE WILL GO ALONG WITH WHATEVER THEY ARE TOLD TO DO.

THEY WILL EASILY BUCKLE TO THE WILL OF THE SKRULL EMPIRE.

YOU--YOU ARE REALLY LOOKING AT THIS IN AN OPTIMISTIC LIGHT. I CAN'T SEE HOW YOU CAN JUST--

I HAVE TO--AND I DO BELIEVE MY WORDS. I KNOW MY JOB HERE IS CLEAR.

YOUR JOB?

FIND WANDA MAXIMOFF AND BLOW HER BRAINS OUT.

SHE'S IN GENOSHA. IT'S NOT A SECRET.

THEN I FIND AN OPENING AND I TAKE IT.

WE'LL GO TOGETHER.

NO.

BUT MAGNETO--

YOU'LL STAY HERE. YOU'LL DO NOTHING. SOMEONE HAS TO TAKE OVER THE OPERATIONS IF I DON'T MAKE IT BACK.

HOW WILL YOU GET TO GENOSHA?

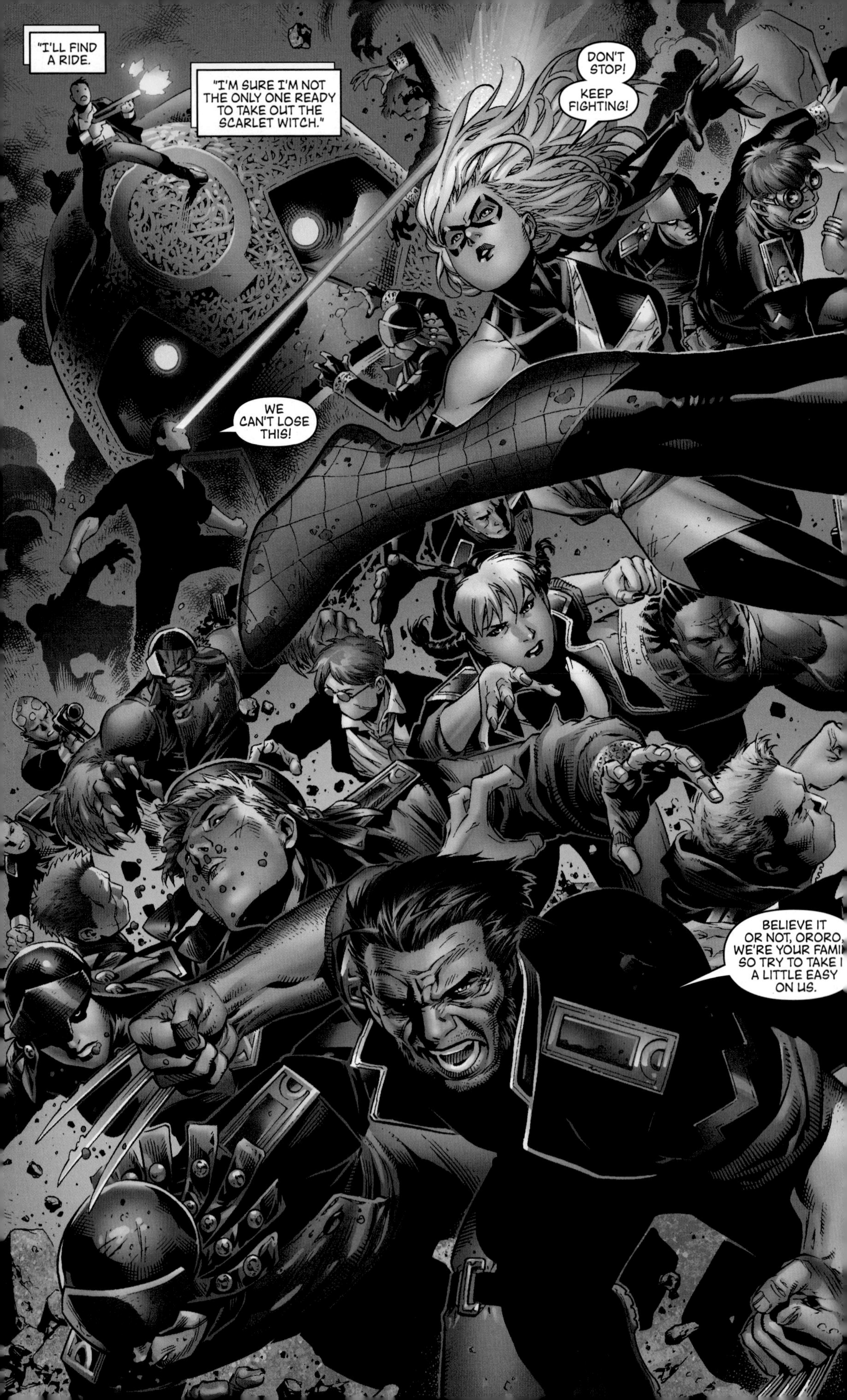
"I'LL FIND A RIDE.
"I'M SURE I'M NOT THE ONLY ONE READY TO TAKE OUT THE SCARLET WITCH."
DON'T STOP!
KEEP FIGHTING!
WE CAN'T LOSE THIS!
BELIEVE IT OR NOT, ORORO, WE'RE YOUR FAMI SO TRY TO TAKE I A LITTLE EASY ON US.

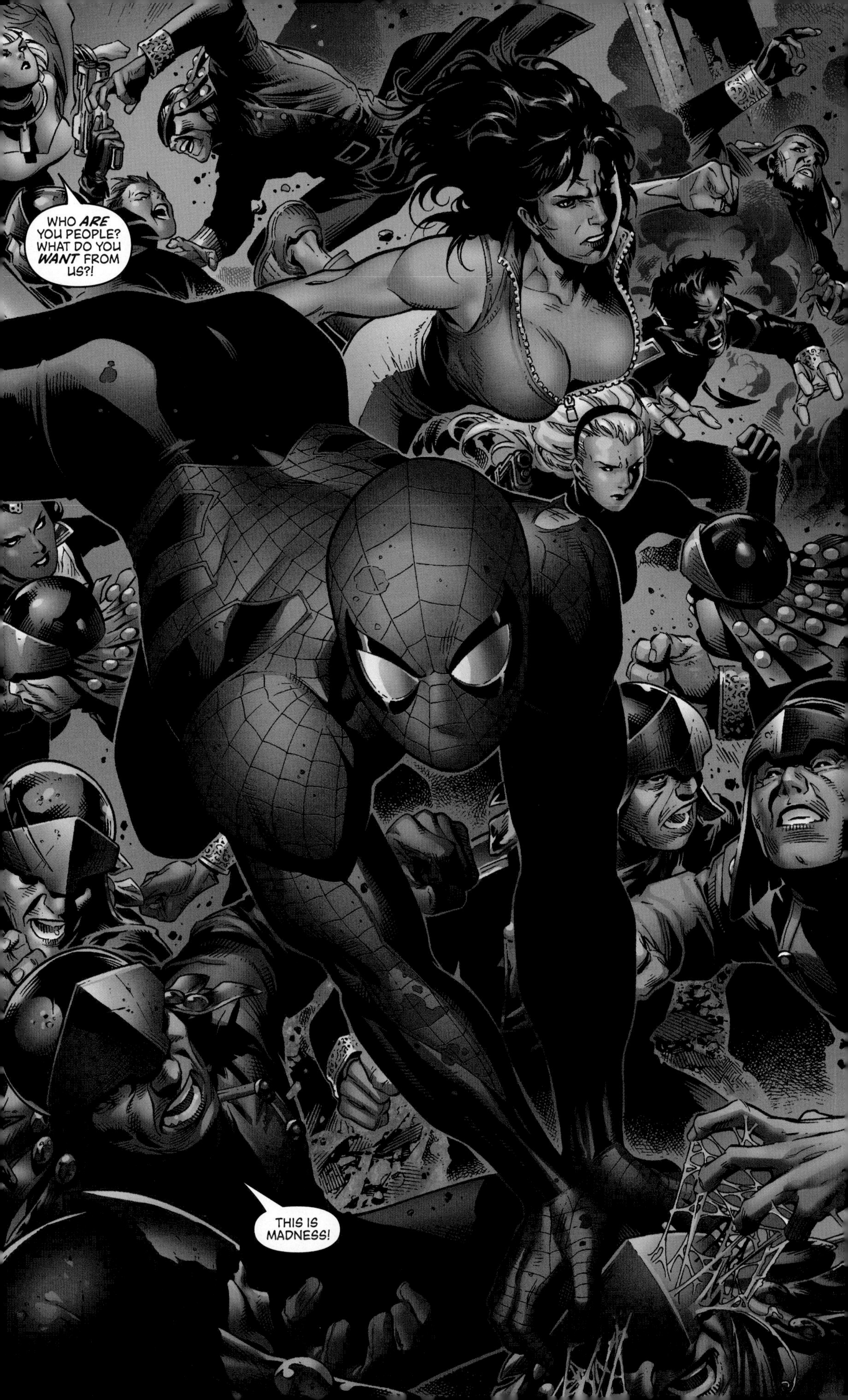

WHO **ARE** YOU PEOPLE? WHAT DO YOU ***WANT*** FROM US?!
THIS IS MADNESS!

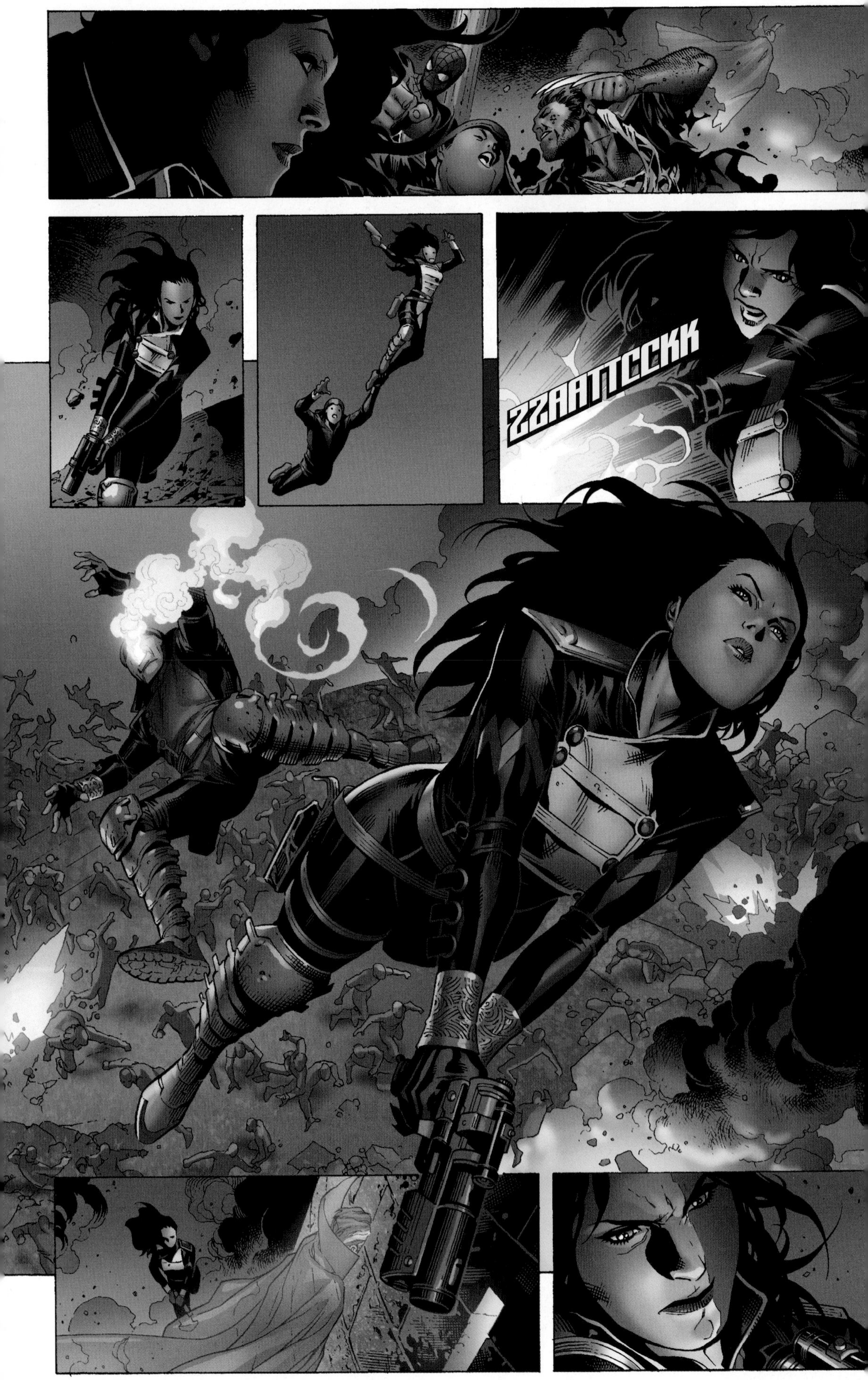
ZZAATTCCKK

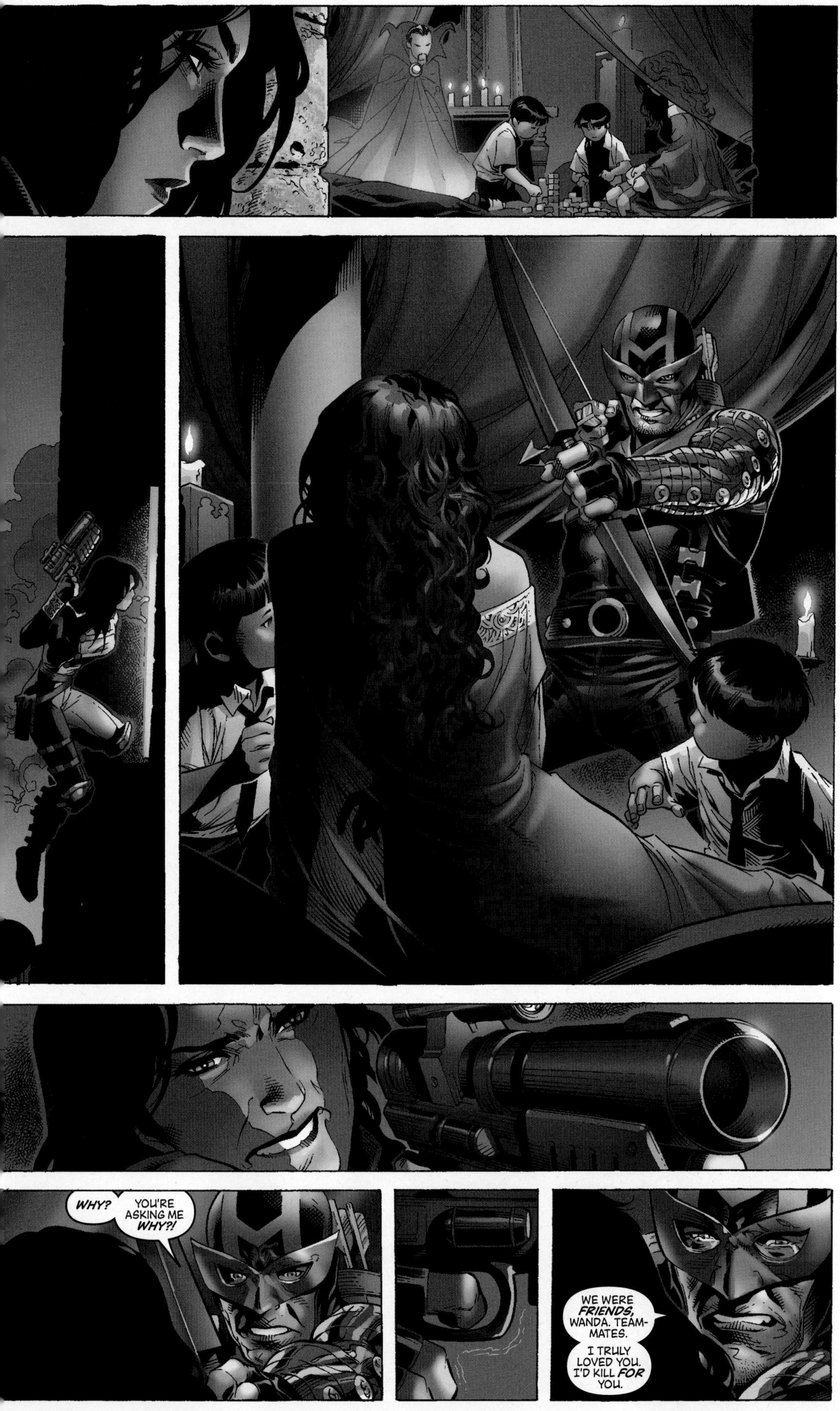
WHY?
YOU'RE ASKING ME WHY?!
WE WERE FRIENDS, WANDA. TEAM-MATES.
I TRULY LOVED YOU. I'D KILL FOR YOU.

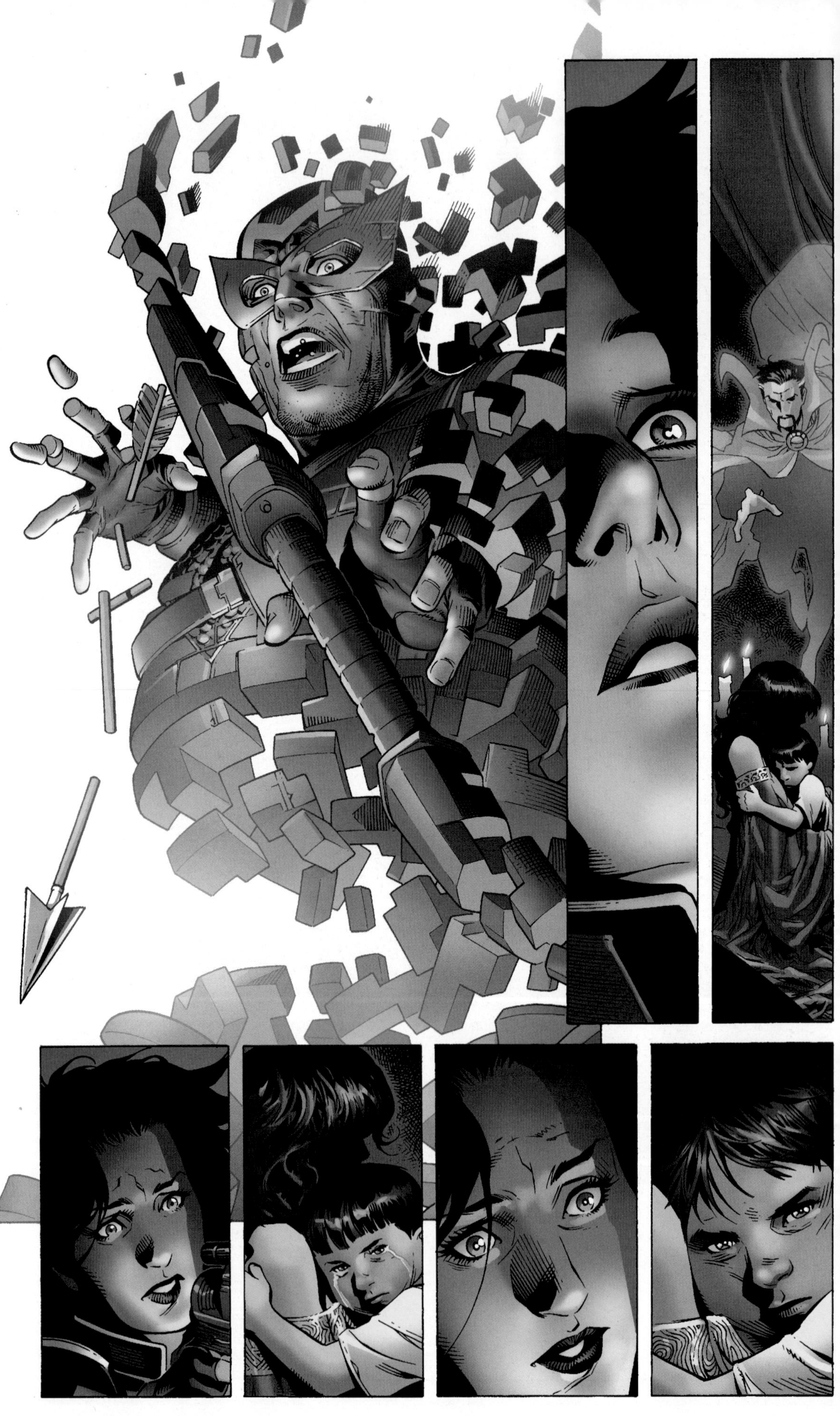

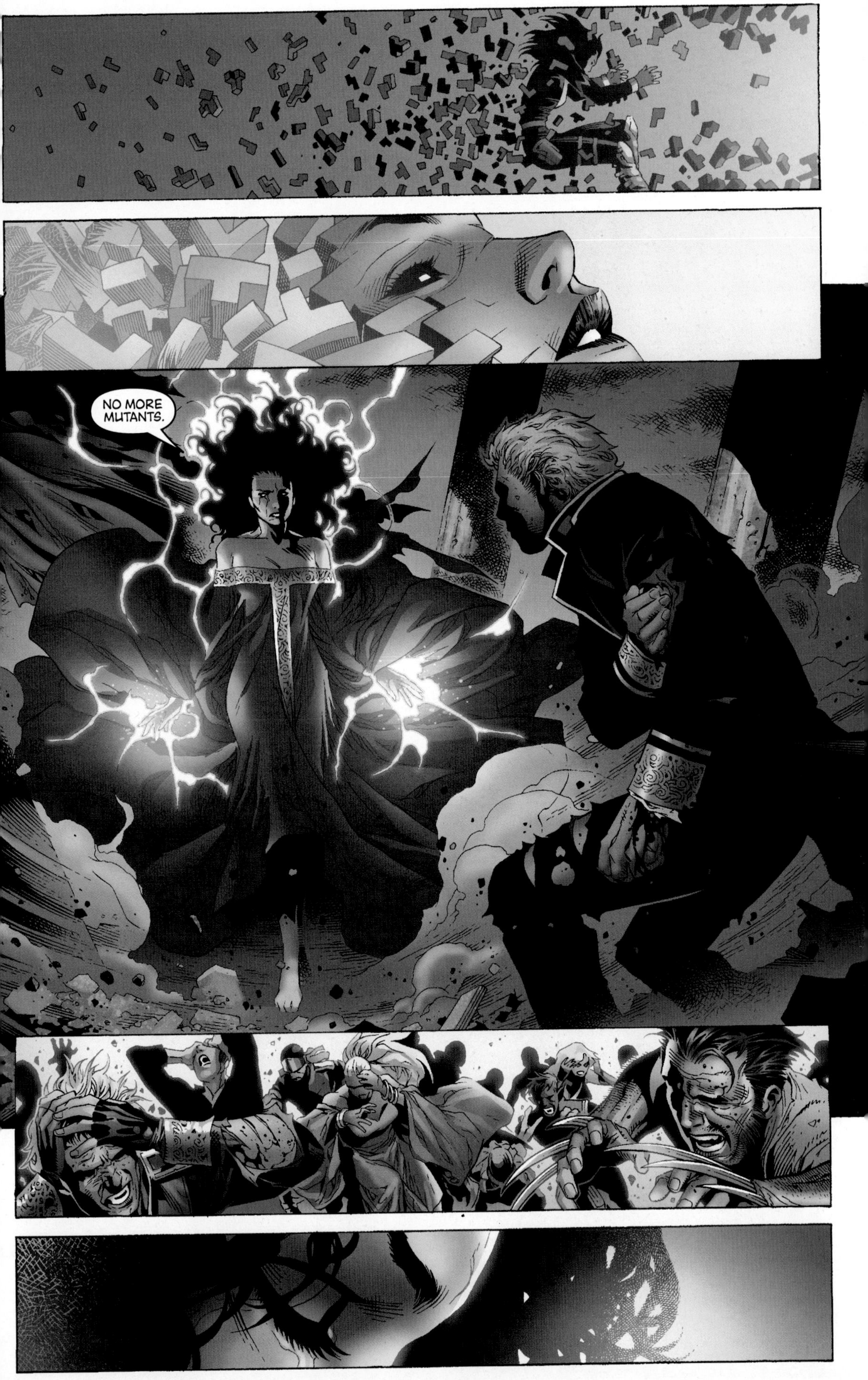
NO MORE MUTANTS.

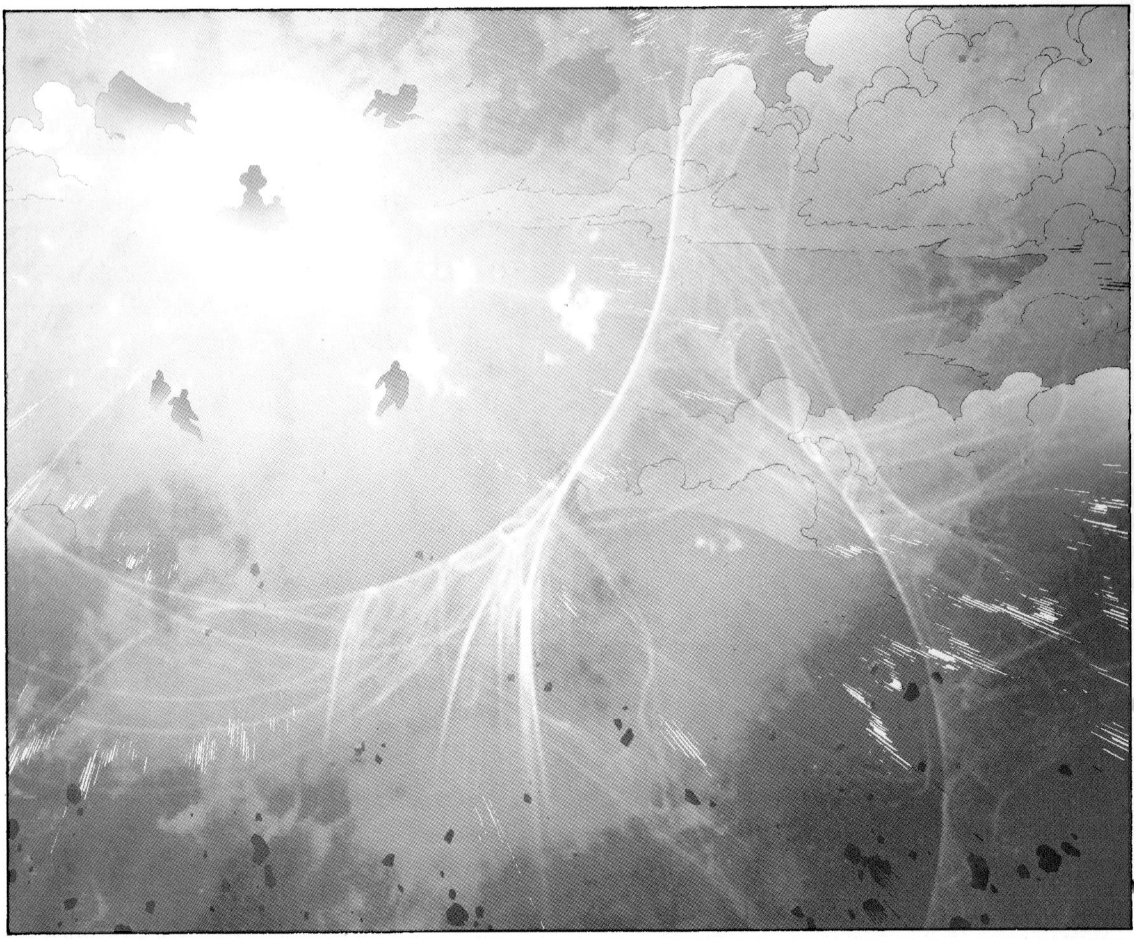

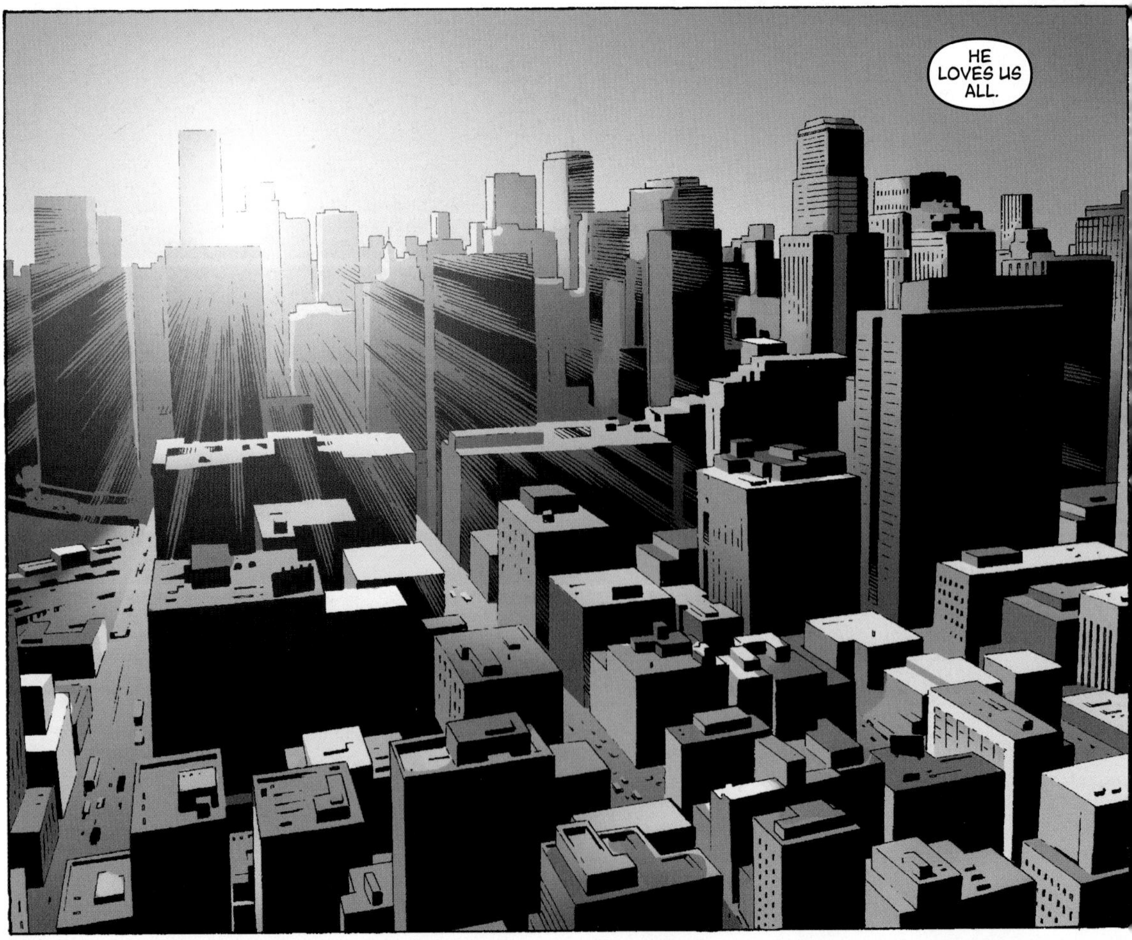
HE LOVES US ALL.

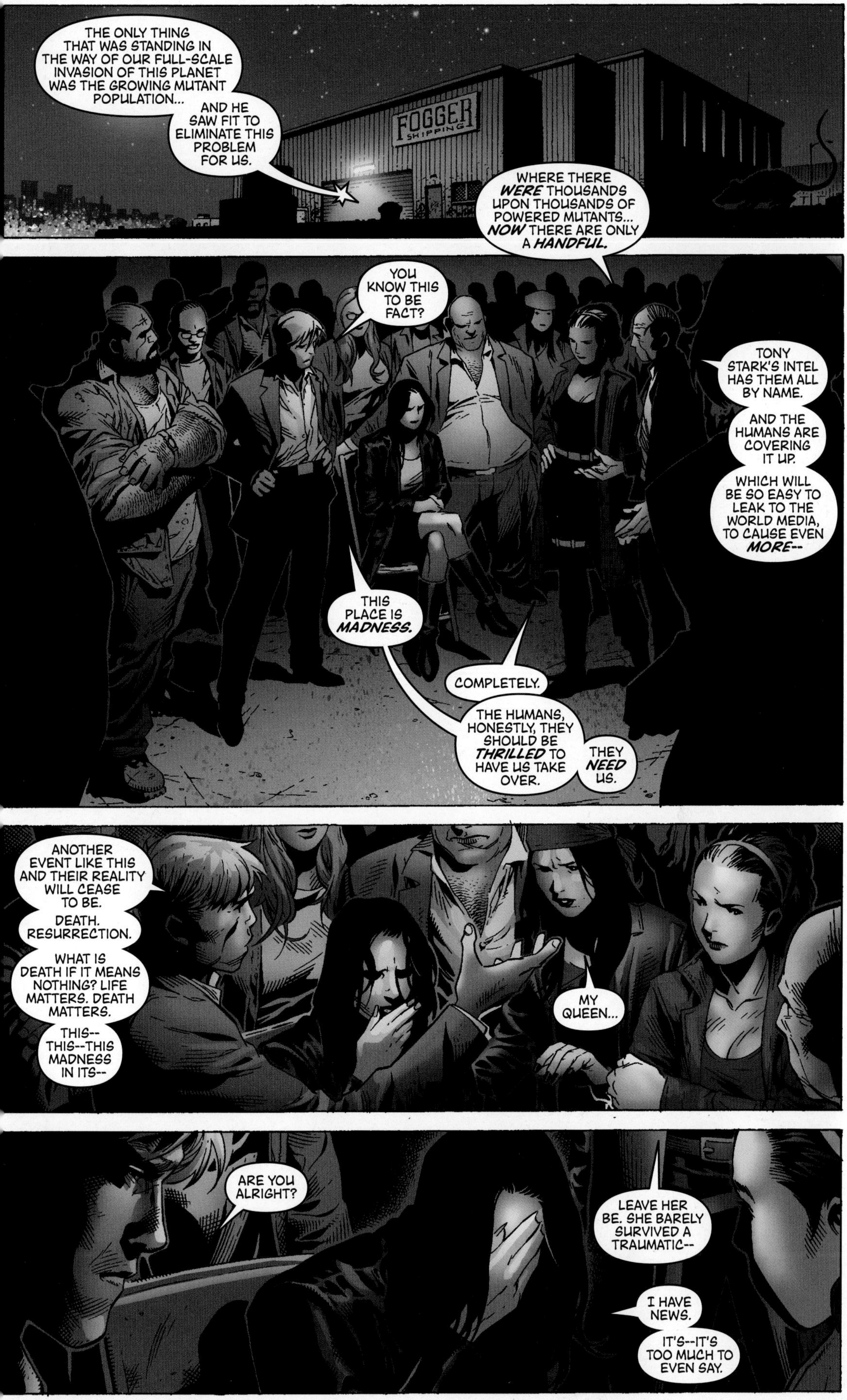
THE ONLY THING THAT WAS STANDING IN THE WAY OF OUR FULL-SCALE INVASION OF THIS PLANET WAS THE GROWING MUTANT POPULATION...
AND HE SAW FIT TO ELIMINATE THIS PROBLEM FOR US.
FOGGER SHIPPING
WHERE THERE *WERE* THOUSANDS UPON THOUSANDS OF POWERED MUTANTS... *NOW* THERE ARE ONLY A *HANDFUL.*
YOU KNOW THIS TO BE FACT?
TONY STARK'S INTEL HAS THEM ALL BY NAME.
AND THE HUMANS ARE COVERING IT UP.
WHICH WILL BE SO EASY TO LEAK TO THE WORLD MEDIA, TO CAUSE EVEN *MORE--*
THIS PLACE IS *MADNESS.*
COMPLETELY.
THE HUMANS, HONESTLY, THEY SHOULD BE *THRILLED* TO HAVE US TAKE OVER.
THEY *NEED* US.
ANOTHER EVENT LIKE THIS AND THEIR REALITY WILL CEASE TO BE.
DEATH. RESURRECTION.
WHAT IS DEATH IF IT MEANS NOTHING? LIFE MATTERS. DEATH MATTERS.
THIS-- THIS--THIS MADNESS IN ITS--
MY QUEEN...
ARE YOU ALRIGHT?
LEAVE HER BE. SHE BARELY SURVIVED A TRAUMATIC--
I HAVE NEWS.
IT'S--IT'S TOO MUCH TO EVEN SAY.

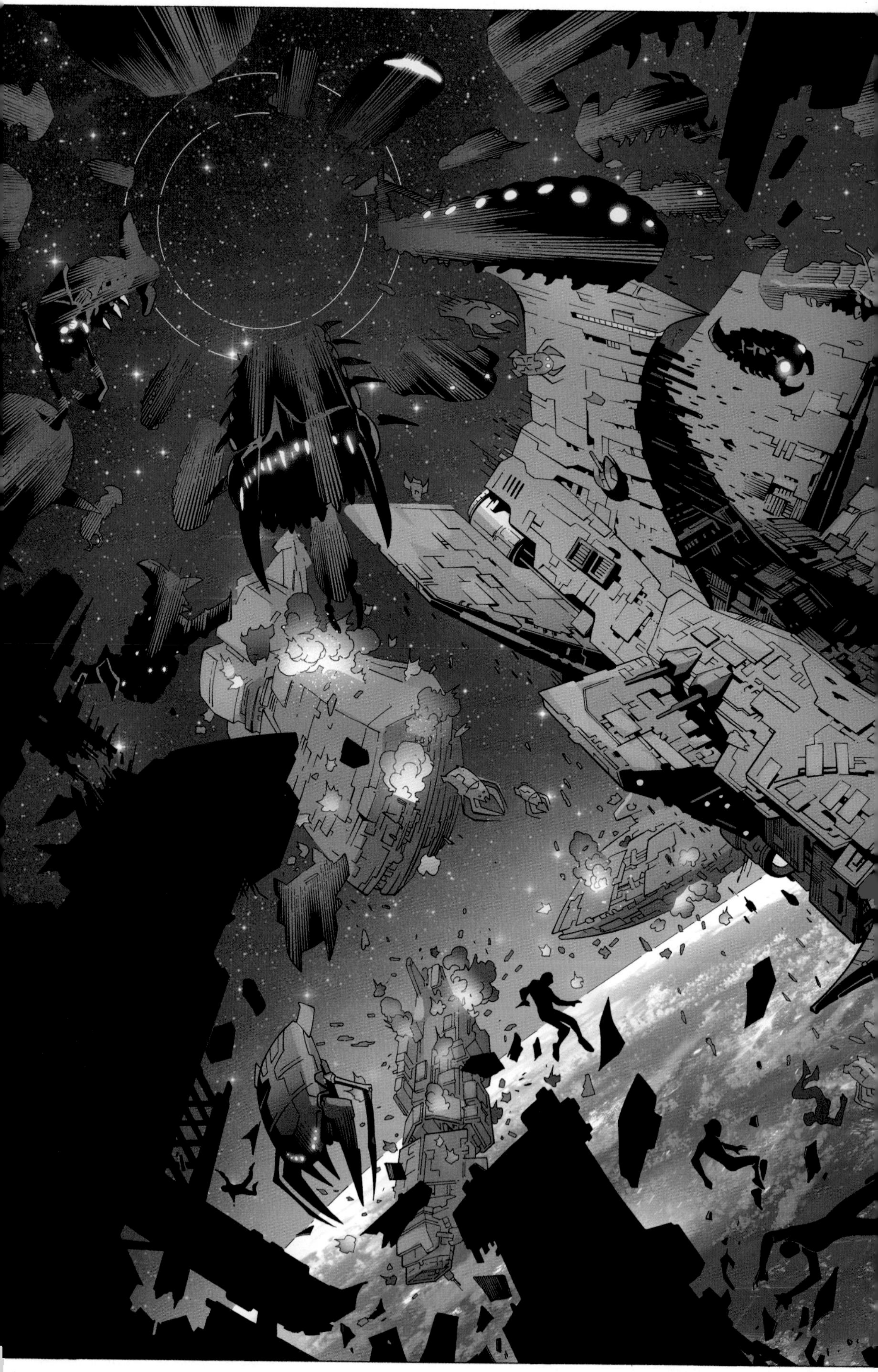

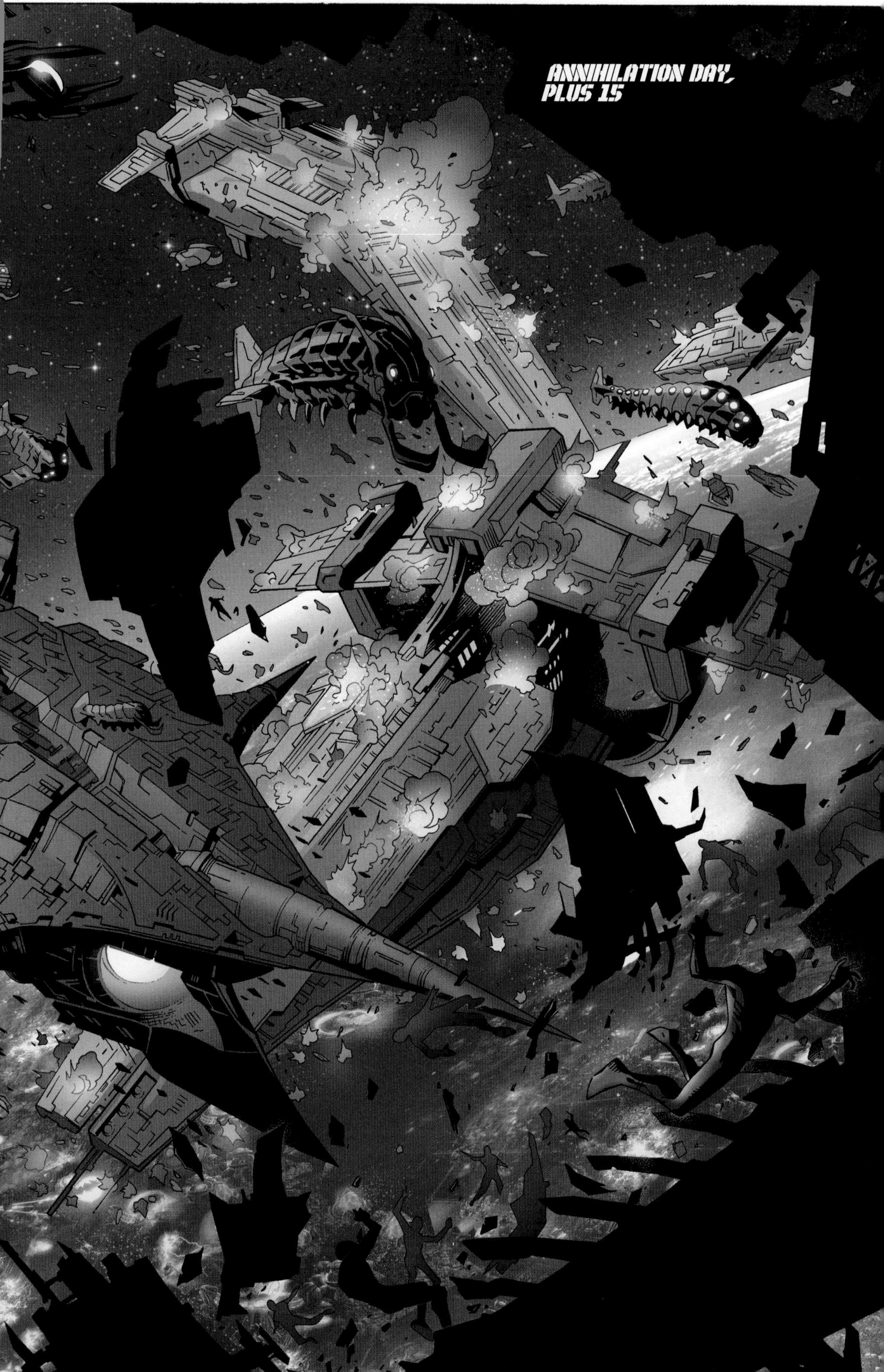
ANNIHILATION DAY,
PLUS 15

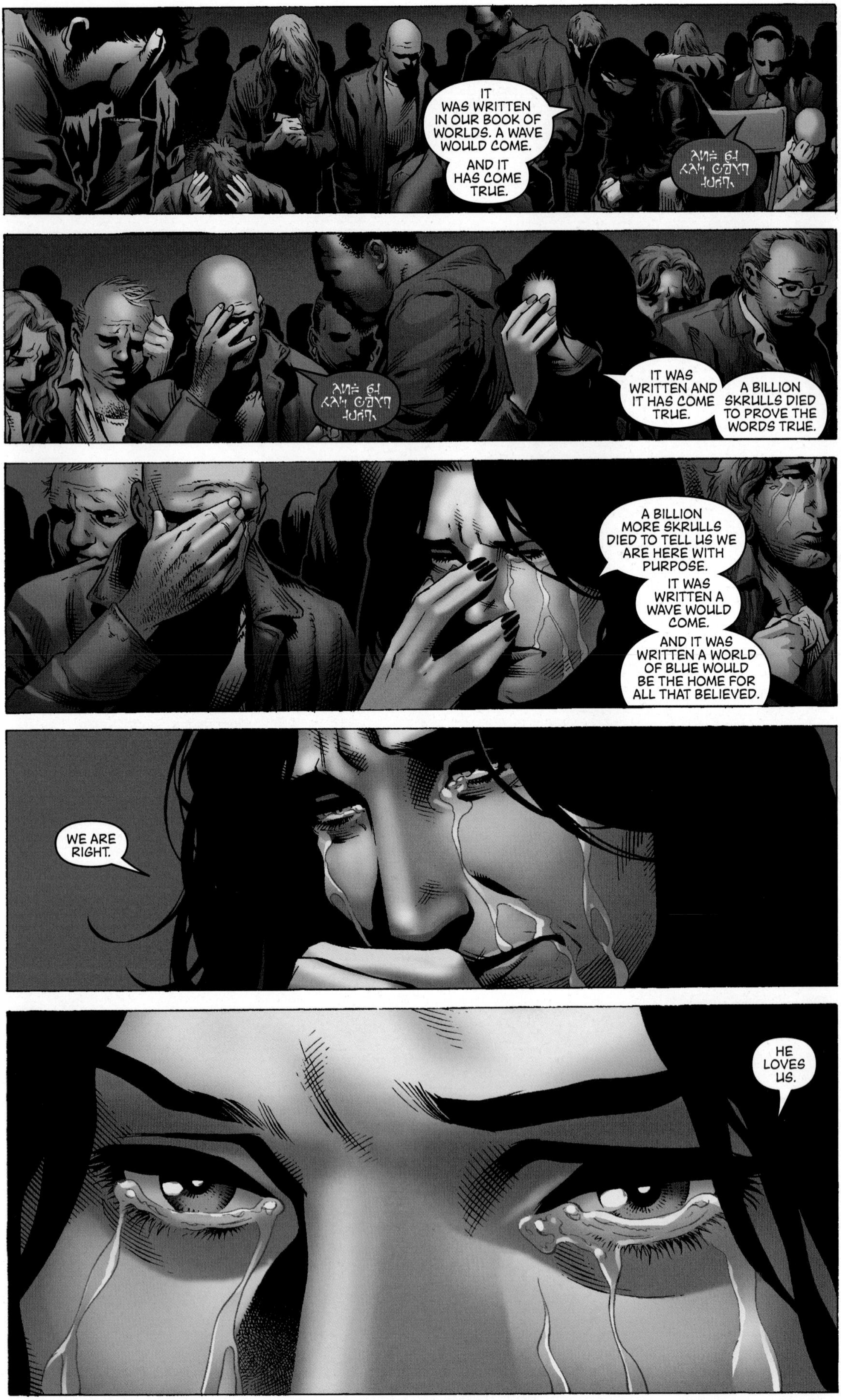
IT WAS WRITTEN IN OUR BOOK OF WORLDS. A WAVE WOULD COME.
AND IT HAS COME TRUE.
IT WAS WRITTEN AND IT HAS COME TRUE.
A BILLION SKRULLS DIED TO PROVE THE WORDS TRUE.
A BILLION MORE SKRULLS DIED TO TELL US WE ARE HERE WITH PURPOSE.
IT WAS WRITTEN A WAVE WOULD COME.
AND IT WAS WRITTEN A WORLD OF BLUE WOULD BE THE HOME FOR ALL THAT BELIEVED.
WE ARE RIGHT.
HE LOVES US.

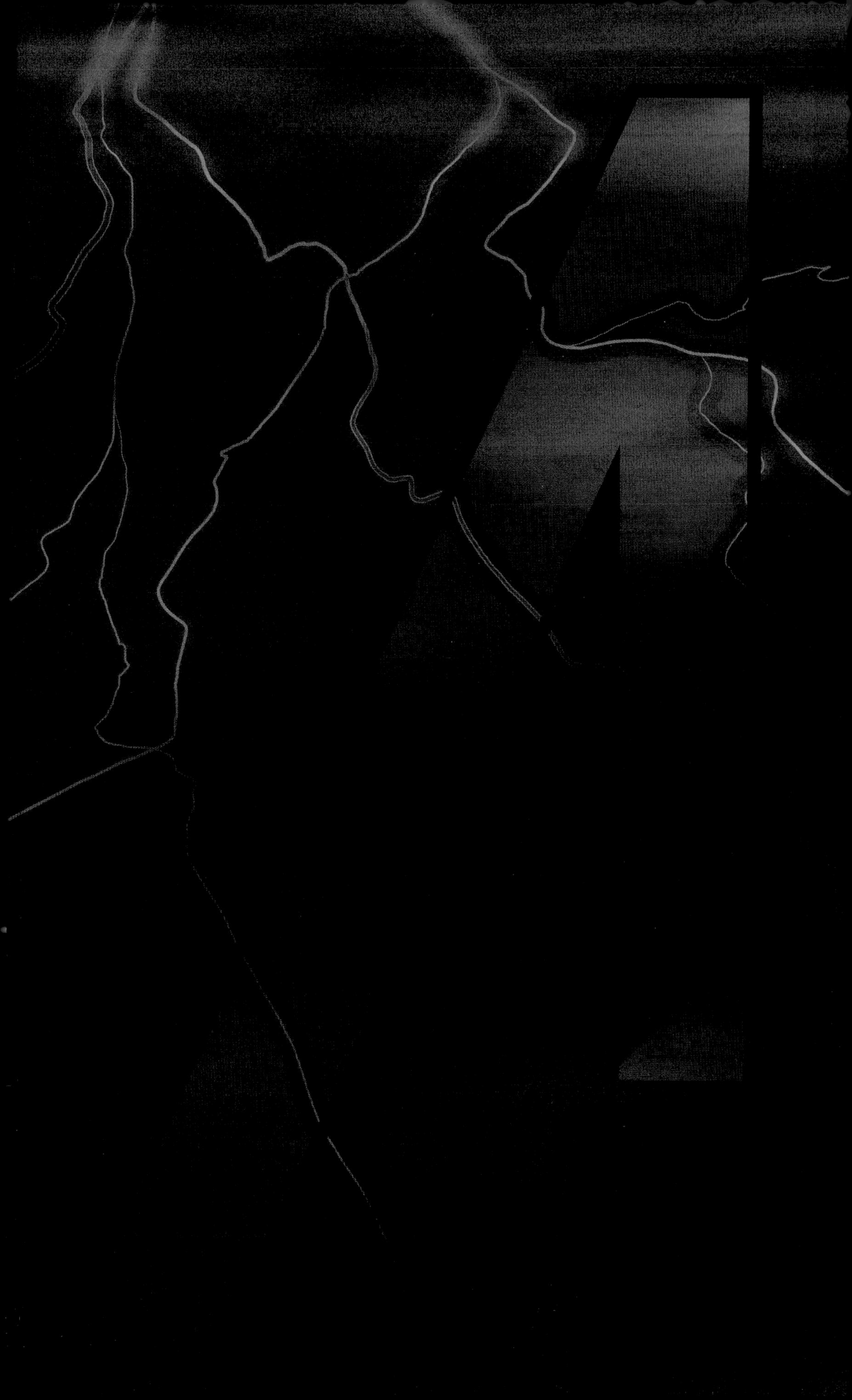

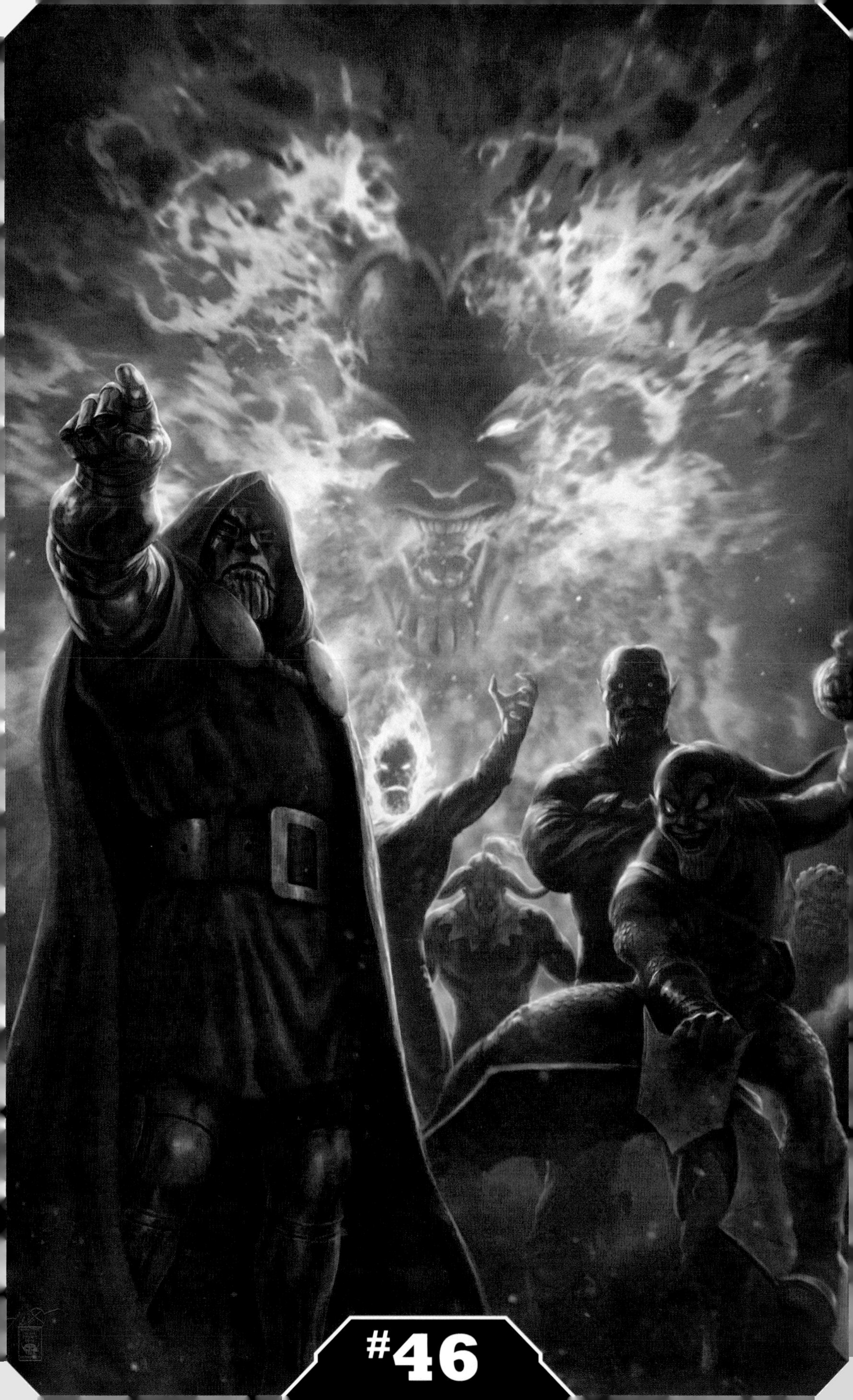
#46

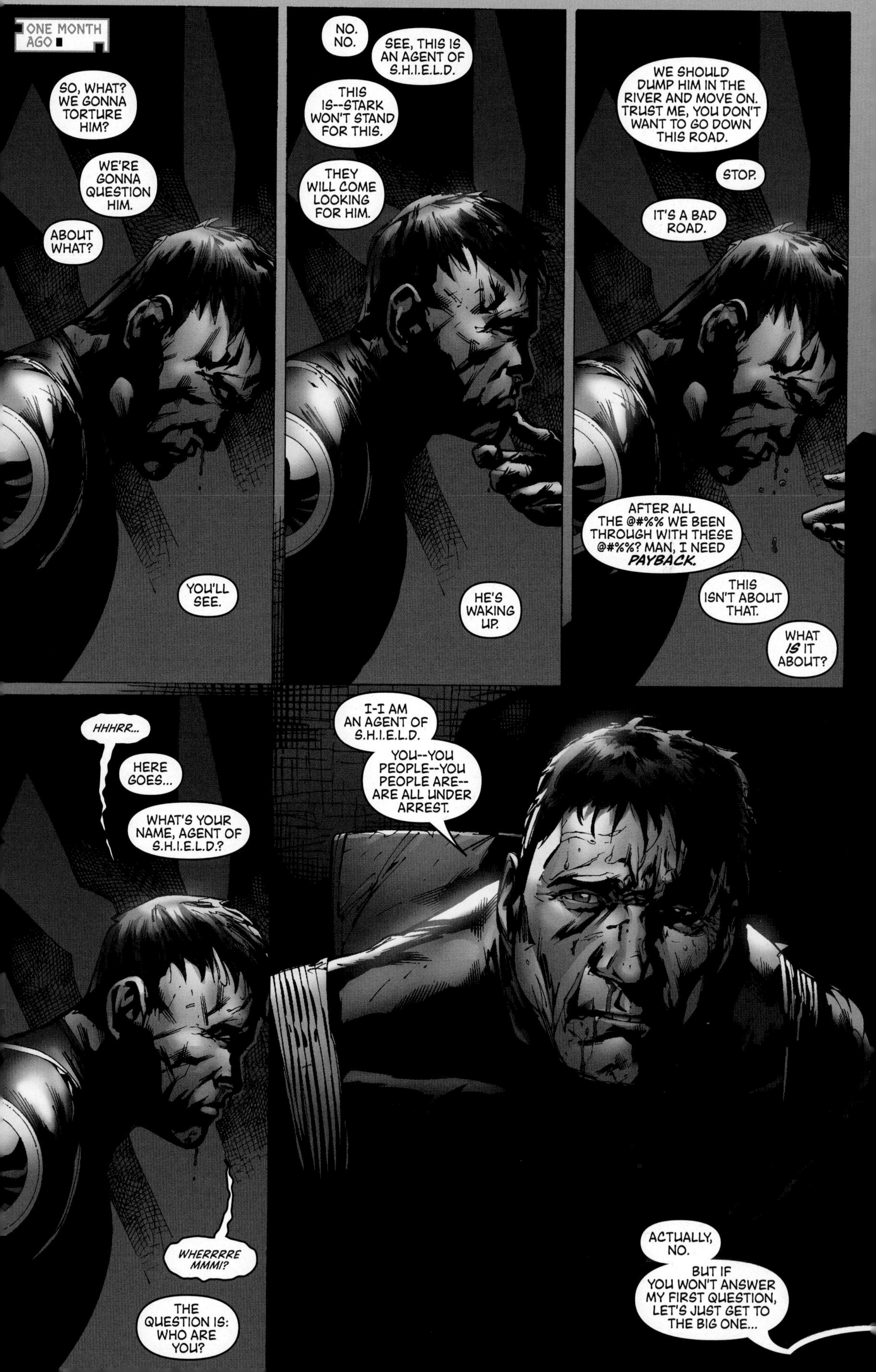
ONE MONTH AGO
SO, WHAT? WE GONNA TORTURE HIM?
WE'RE GONNA QUESTION HIM.
ABOUT WHAT?
YOU'LL SEE.
NO. NO.
SEE, THIS IS AN AGENT OF S.H.I.E.L.D.
THIS IS--STARK WON'T STAND FOR THIS.
THEY WILL COME LOOKING FOR HIM.
HE'S WAKING UP.
WE SHOULD DUMP HIM IN THE RIVER AND MOVE ON. TRUST ME, YOU DON'T WANT TO GO DOWN THIS ROAD.
STOP.
IT'S A BAD ROAD.
AFTER ALL THE @#%% WE BEEN THROUGH WITH THESE @#%%? MAN, I NEED *PAYBACK.*
THIS ISN'T ABOUT THAT.
WHAT *IS* IT ABOUT?
HHHRR...
HERE GOES...
WHAT'S YOUR NAME, AGENT OF S.H.I.E.L.D.?
WHERRRRE MMMI?
THE QUESTION IS: WHO ARE YOU?
I-I AM AN AGENT OF S.H.I.E.L.D.
YOU--YOU PEOPLE--YOU PEOPLE ARE--ARE ALL UNDER ARREST.
ACTUALLY, NO.
BUT IF YOU WON'T ANSWER MY FIRST QUESTION, LET'S JUST GET TO THE BIG ONE...

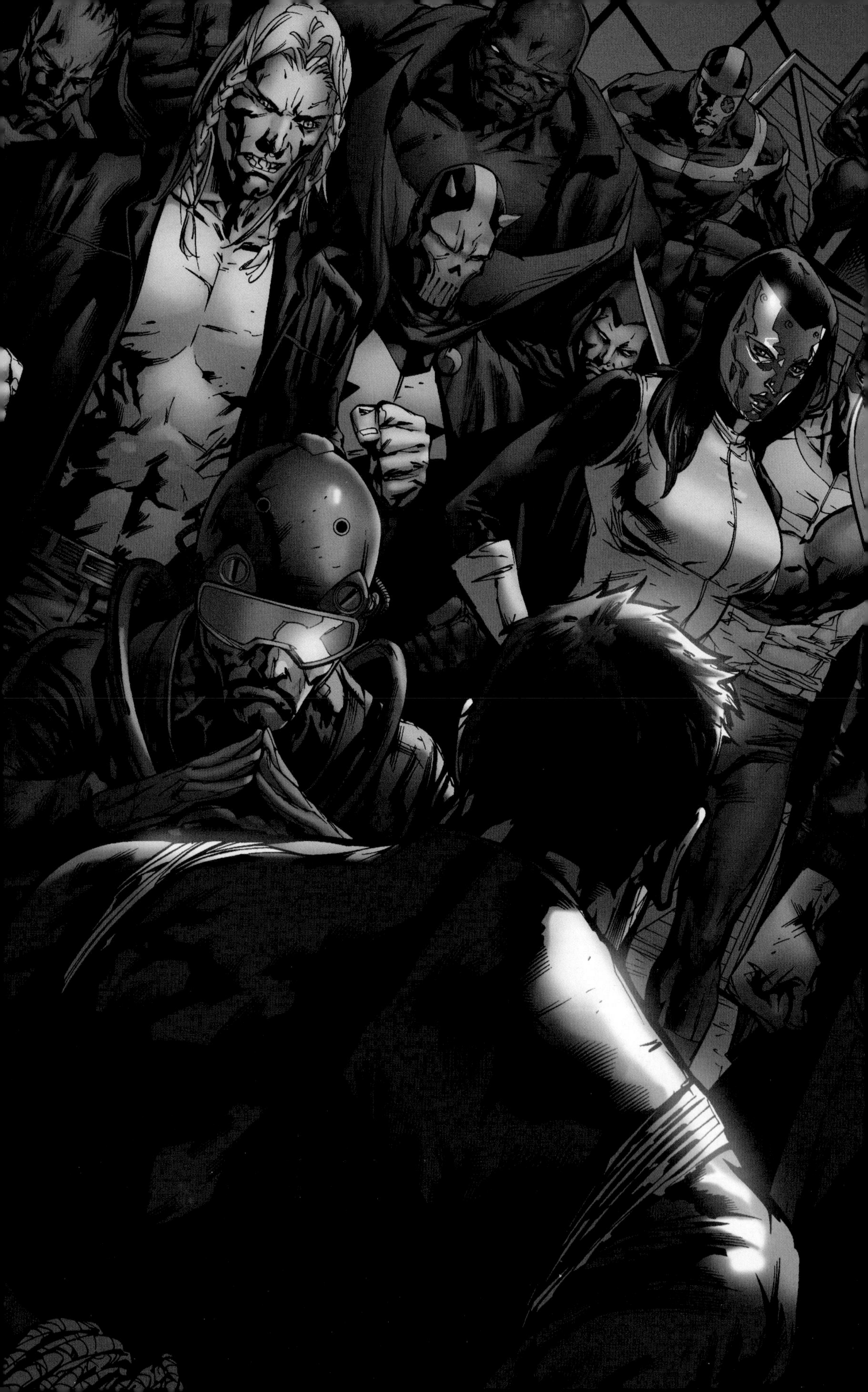

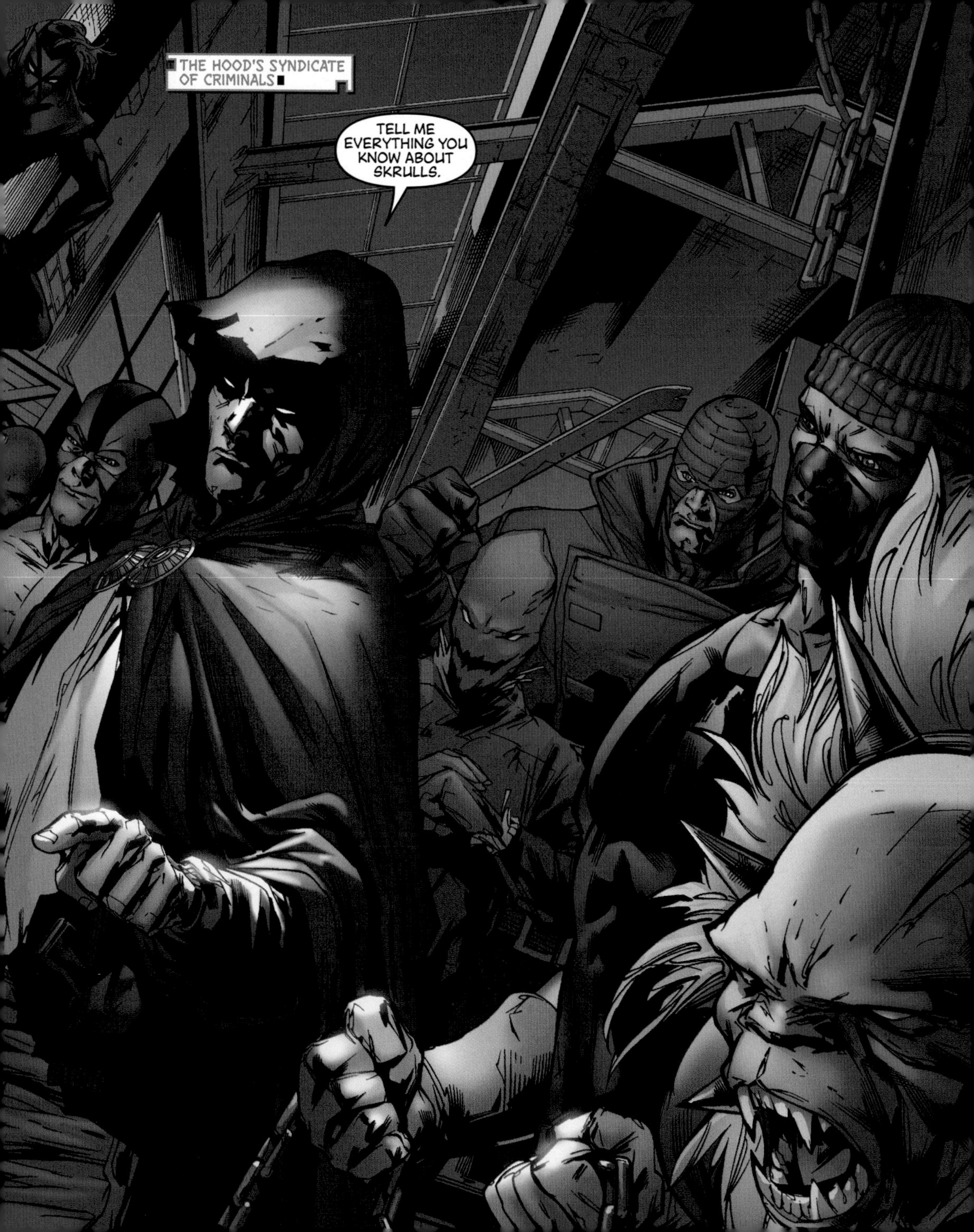
THE HOOD'S SYNDICATE OF CRIMINALS
TELL ME EVERYTHING YOU KNOW ABOUT SKRULLS.

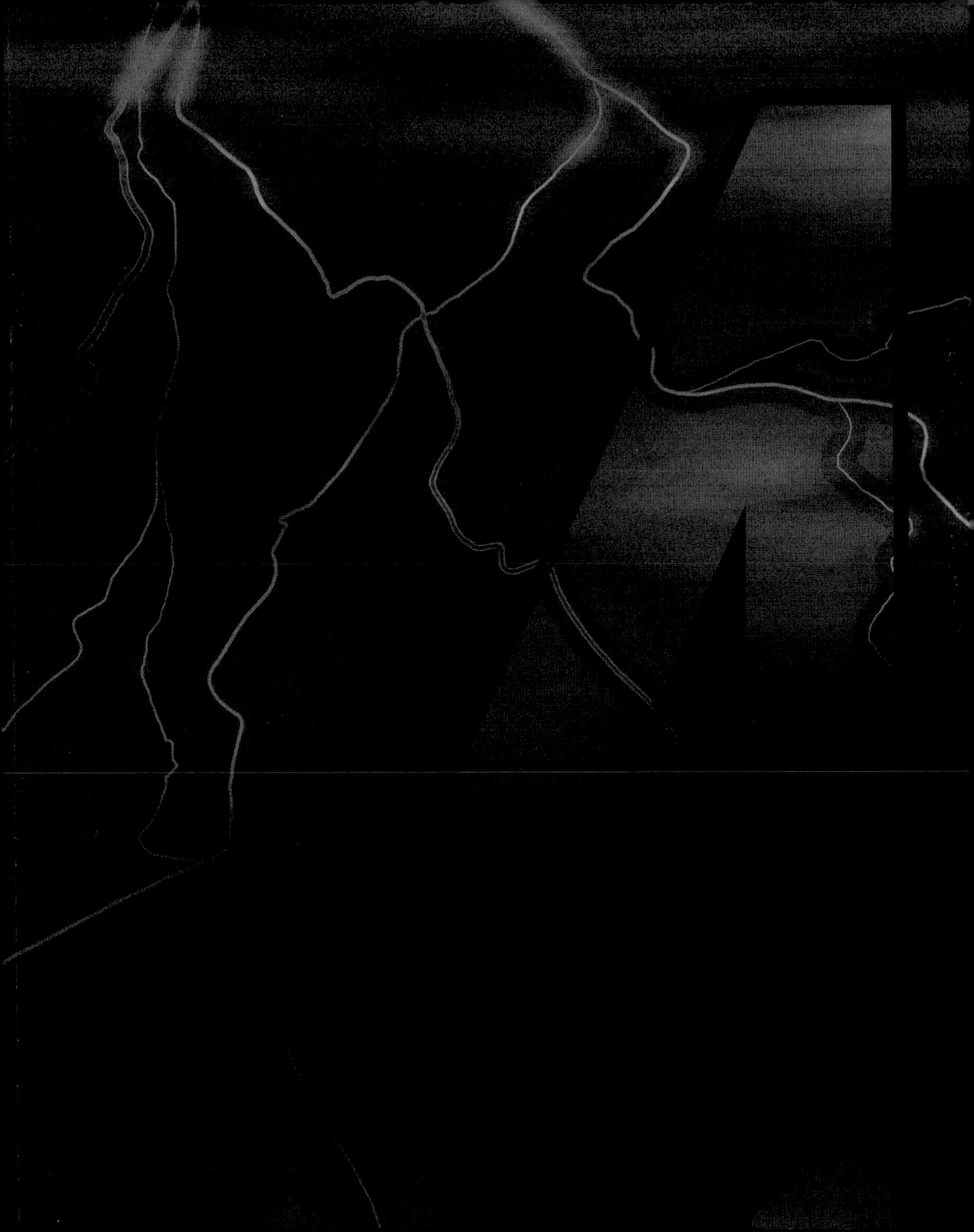

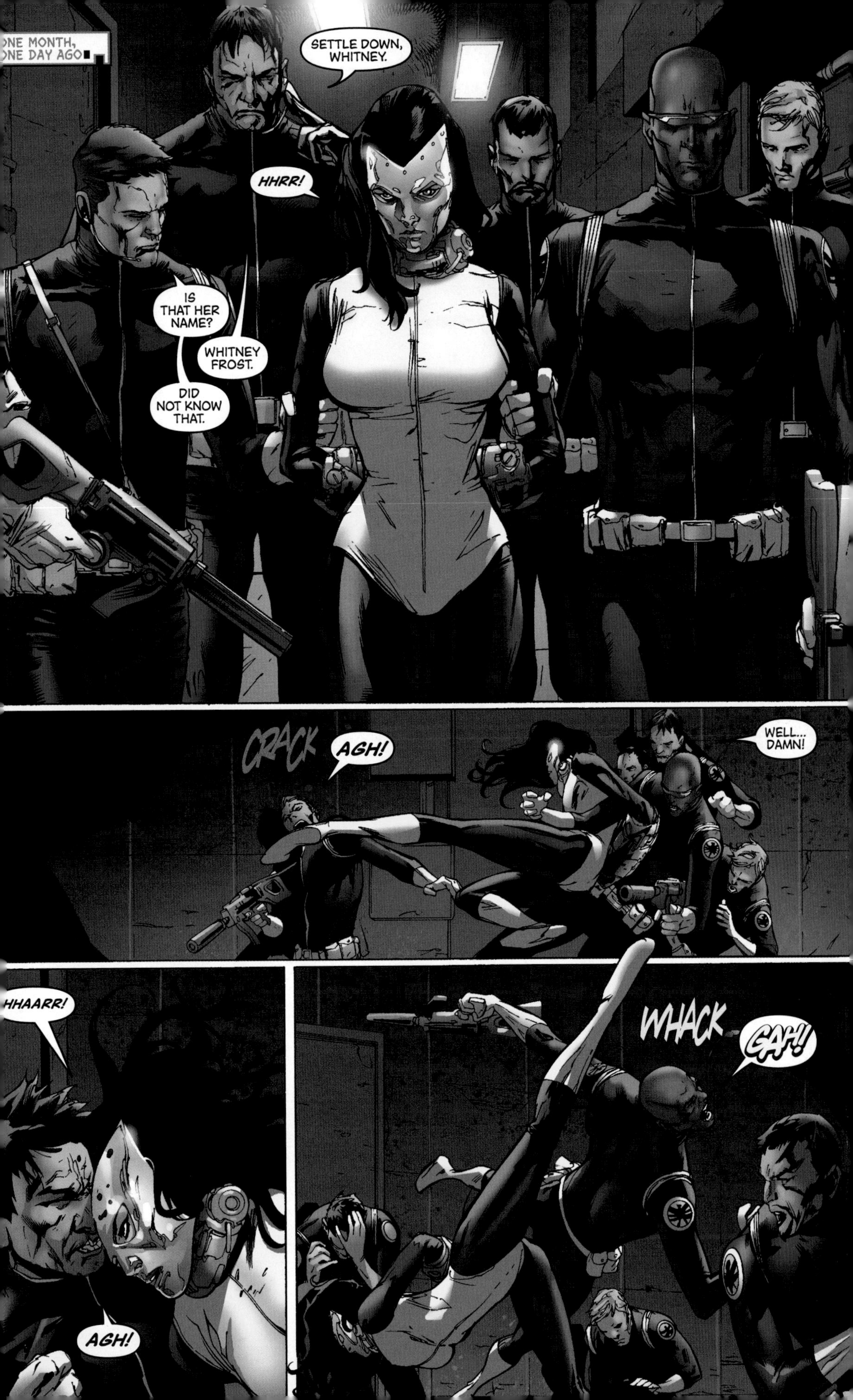
ONE MONTH, ONE DAY AGO
SETTLE DOWN, WHITNEY.
HHRR!
IS THAT HER NAME?
WHITNEY FROST.
DID NOT KNOW THAT.
CRACK
AGH!
WELL... DAMN!
HHAARR!
AGH!
WHACK
GAH!!

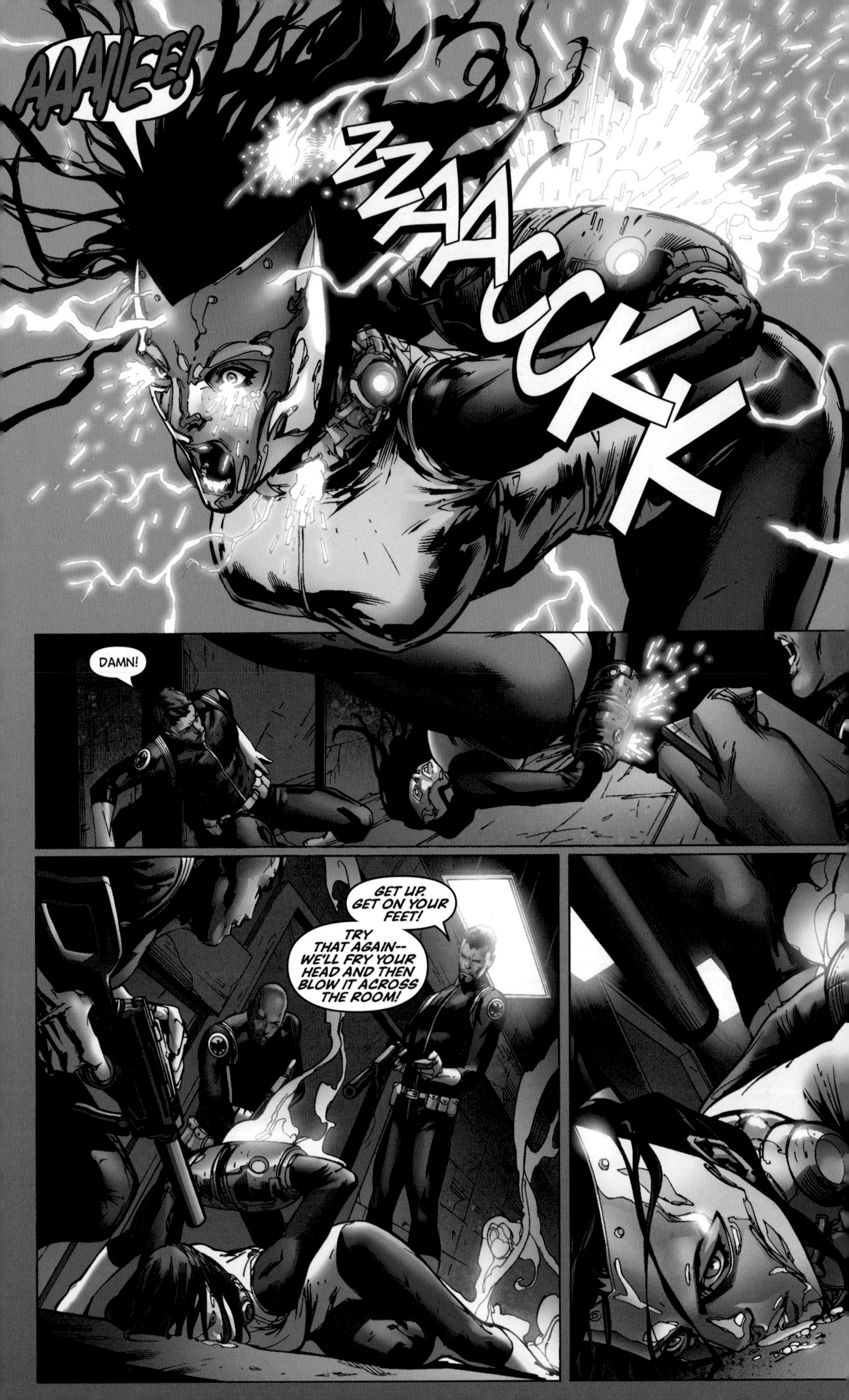
AAAIIEEE!
ZZAACCKK
DAMN!
GET UP. GET ON YOUR FEET!
TRY THAT AGAIN-- WE'LL FRY YOUR HEAD AND THEN BLOW IT ACROSS THE ROOM!

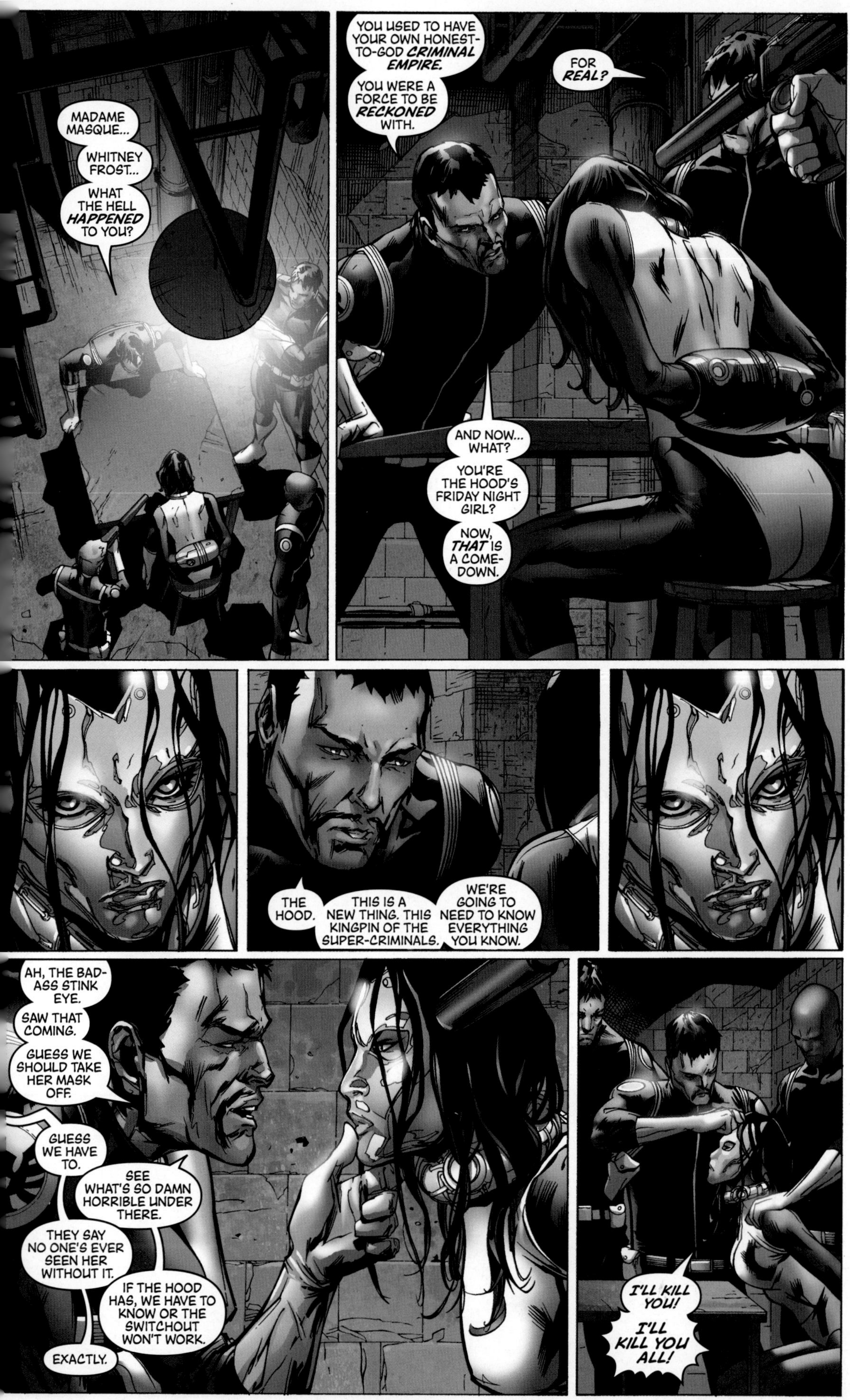

MADAME MASQUE...
WHITNEY FROST...
WHAT THE HELL HAPPENED TO YOU?
YOU USED TO HAVE YOUR OWN HONEST-TO-GOD CRIMINAL EMPIRE.
YOU WERE A FORCE TO BE RECKONED WITH.
FOR REAL?
AND NOW... WHAT?
YOU'RE THE HOOD'S FRIDAY NIGHT GIRL?
NOW, THAT IS A COME-DOWN.
THE HOOD.
THIS IS A NEW THING. THIS KINGPIN OF THE SUPER-CRIMINALS.
WE'RE GOING TO NEED TO KNOW EVERYTHING YOU KNOW.
AH, THE BAD-ASS STINK EYE.
SAW THAT COMING.
GUESS WE SHOULD TAKE HER MASK OFF.
GUESS WE HAVE TO.
SEE WHAT'S SO DAMN HORRIBLE UNDER THERE.
THEY SAY NO ONE'S EVER SEEN HER WITHOUT IT.
IF THE HOOD HAS, WE HAVE TO KNOW OR THE SWITCHOUT WON'T WORK.
EXACTLY.
I'LL KILL YOU!
I'LL KILL YOU ALL!

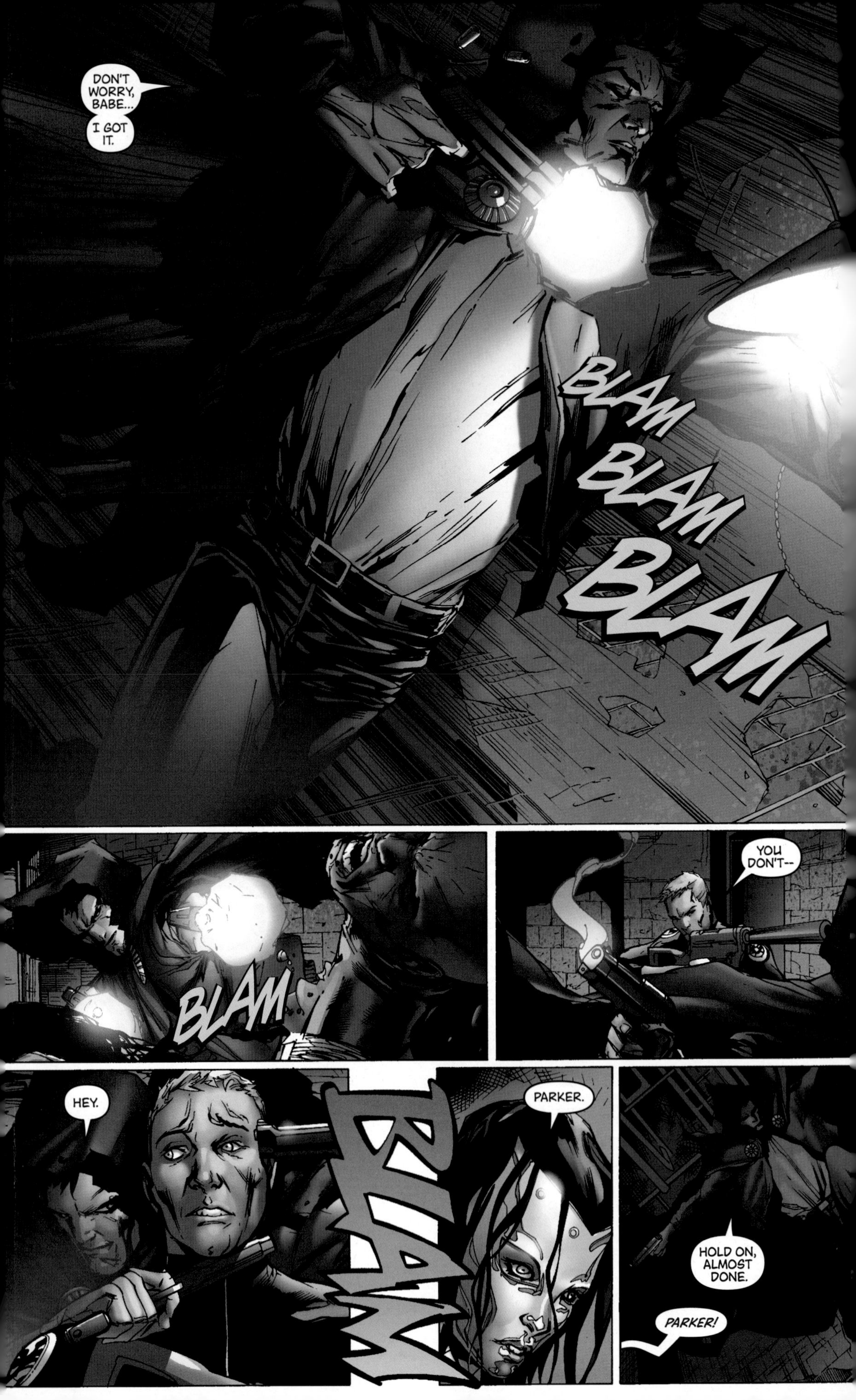
DON'T WORRY, BABE...
I GOT IT.
BLAM BLAM BLAM
BLAM
YOU DON'T--
HEY.
PARKER.
BLAM
HOLD ON, ALMOST DONE.
PARKER!

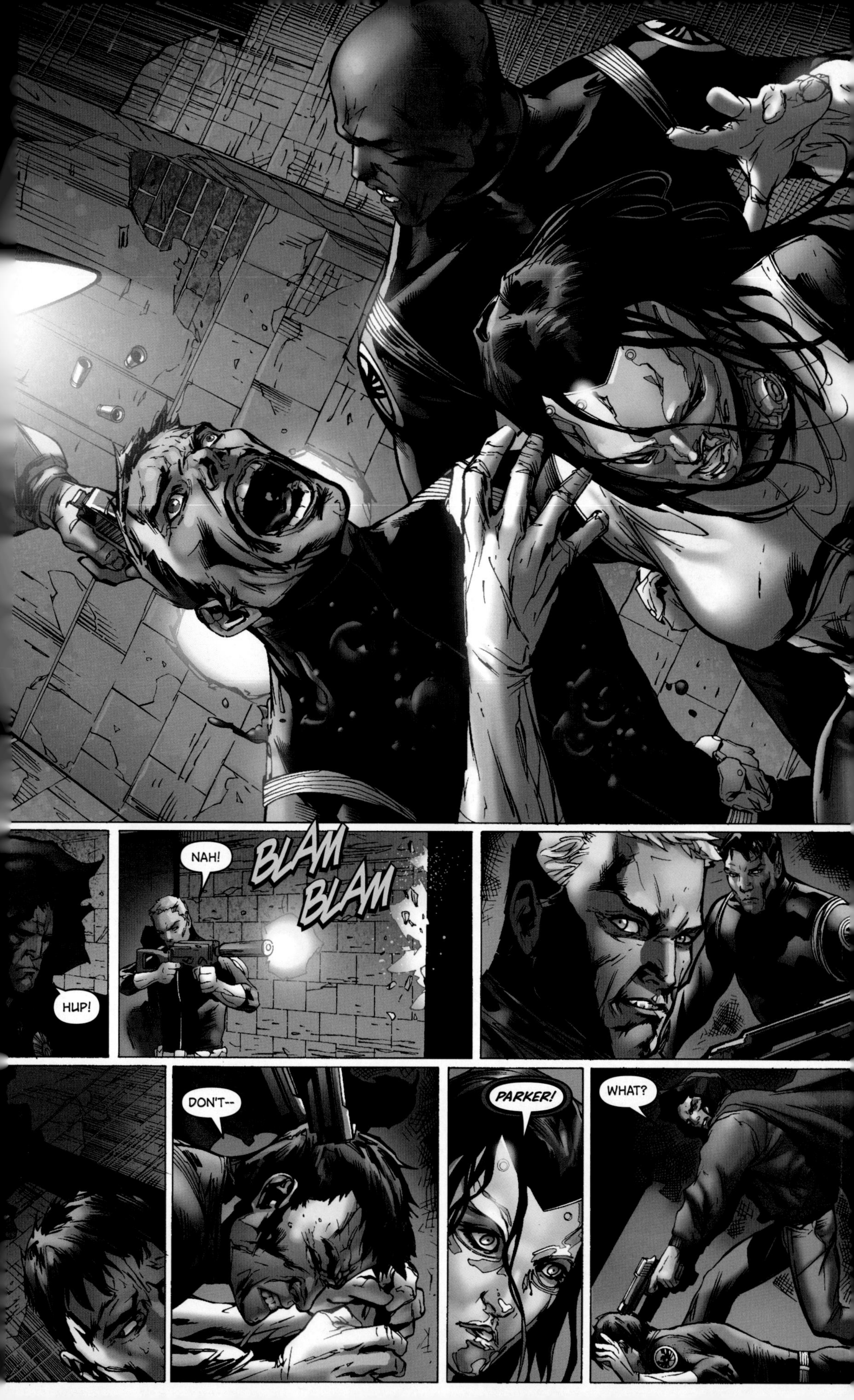
HUP!
NAH!
BLAM
BLAM
DON'T--
PARKER!
WHAT?

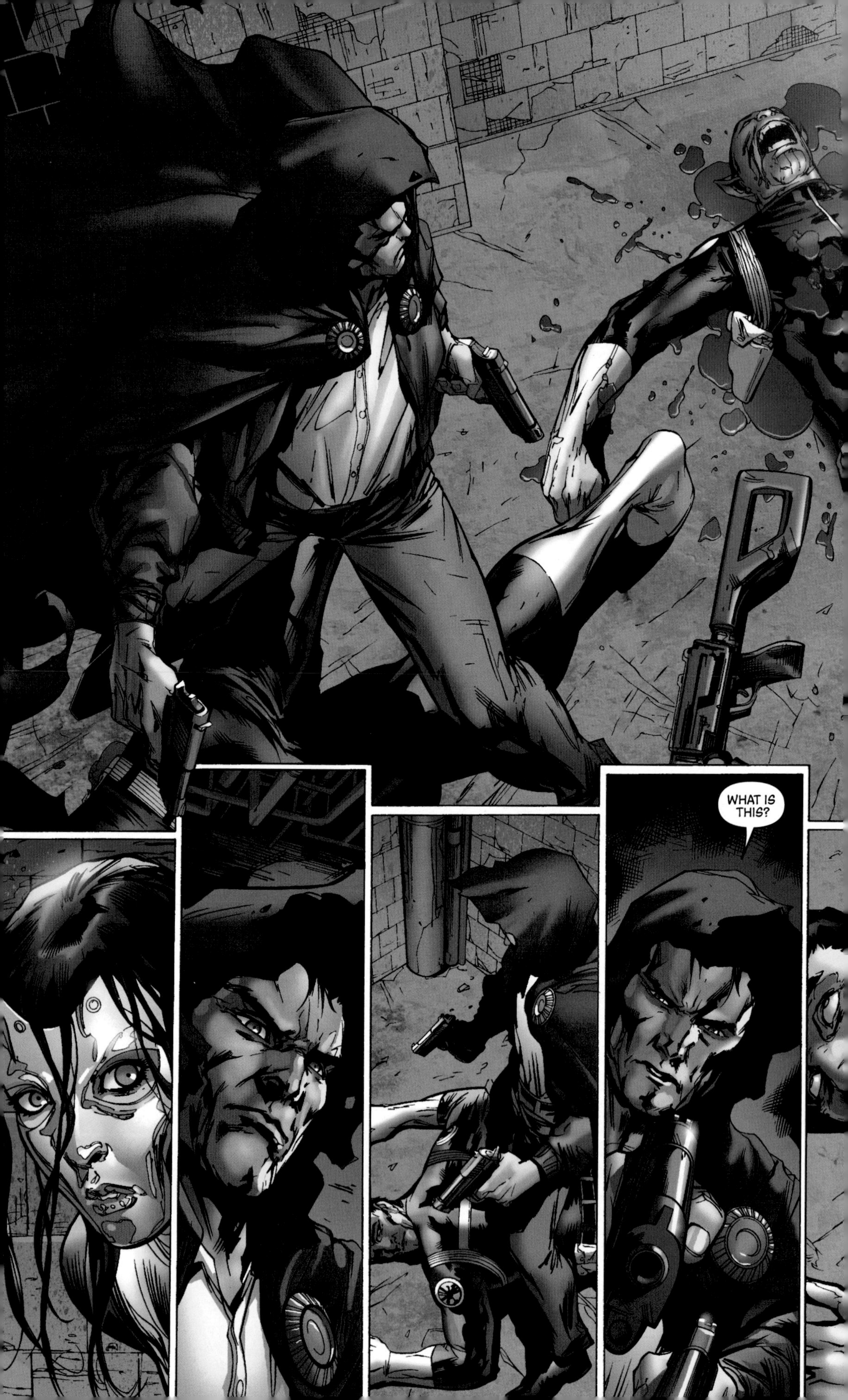
WHAT IS THIS?

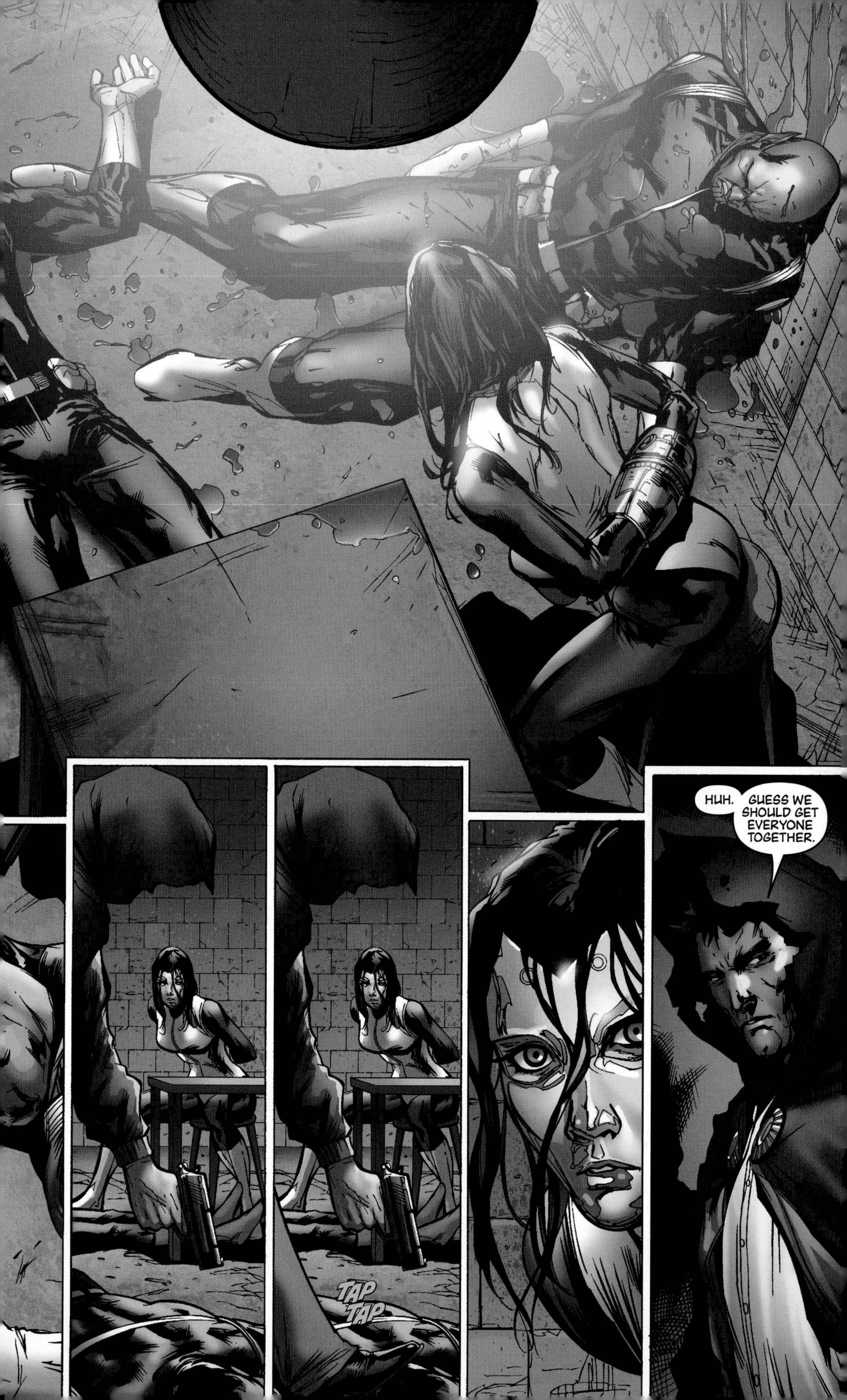
TAP
TAP
HUH.
GUESS WE SHOULD GET EVERYONE TOGETHER.

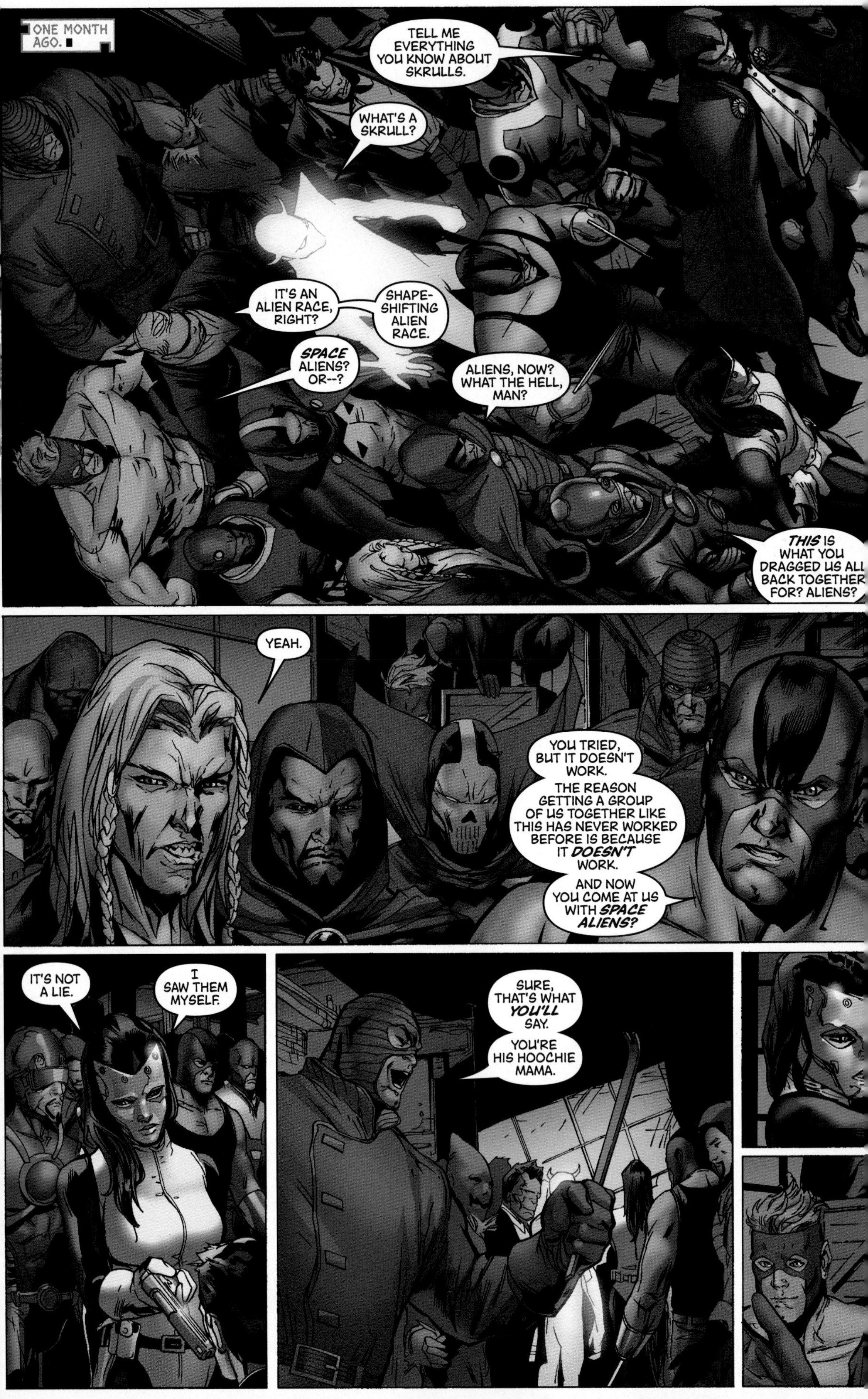
ONE MONTH AGO.
TELL ME EVERYTHING YOU KNOW ABOUT SKRULLS.
WHAT'S A SKRULL?
IT'S AN ALIEN RACE, RIGHT?
SHAPE-SHIFTING ALIEN RACE.
SPACE ALIENS? OR--?
ALIENS, NOW? WHAT THE HELL, MAN?
THIS IS WHAT YOU DRAGGED US ALL BACK TOGETHER FOR? ALIENS?
YEAH.
YOU TRIED, BUT IT DOESN'T WORK.
THE REASON GETTING A GROUP OF US TOGETHER LIKE THIS HAS NEVER WORKED BEFORE IS BECAUSE IT DOESN'T WORK.
AND NOW YOU COME AT US WITH SPACE ALIENS?
IT'S NOT A LIE.
I SAW THEM MYSELF.
SURE, THAT'S WHAT YOU'LL SAY.
YOU'RE HIS HOOCHIE MAMA.

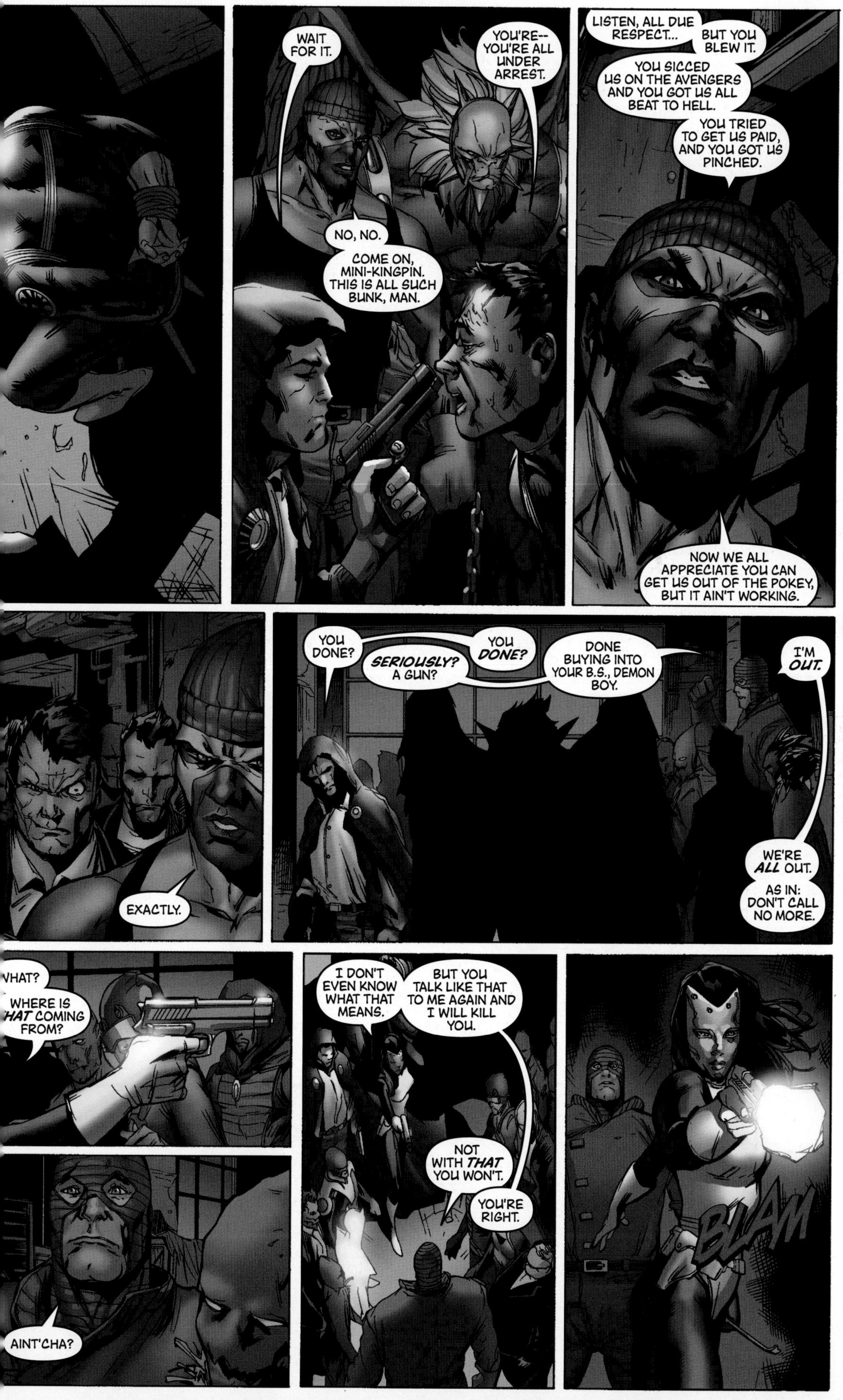
WAIT FOR IT.
YOU'RE-- YOU'RE ALL UNDER ARREST.
NO, NO.
COME ON, MINI-KINGPIN. THIS IS ALL SUCH BUNK, MAN.
LISTEN, ALL DUE RESPECT...
BUT YOU BLEW IT.
YOU SICCED US ON THE AVENGERS AND YOU GOT US ALL BEAT TO HELL.
YOU TRIED TO GET US PAID, AND YOU GOT US PINCHED.
NOW WE ALL APPRECIATE YOU CAN GET US OUT OF THE POKEY, BUT IT AIN'T WORKING.
EXACTLY.
YOU DONE?
SERIOUSLY? A GUN?
YOU DONE?
DONE BUYING INTO YOUR B.S., DEMON BOY.
I'M OUT.
WE'RE ALL OUT.
AS IN: DON'T CALL NO MORE.
WHAT?
WHERE IS THAT COMING FROM?
AINT'CHA?
I DON'T EVEN KNOW WHAT THAT MEANS.
BUT YOU TALK LIKE THAT TO ME AGAIN AND I WILL KILL YOU.
NOT WITH THAT YOU WON'T.
YOU'RE RIGHT.
BLAM

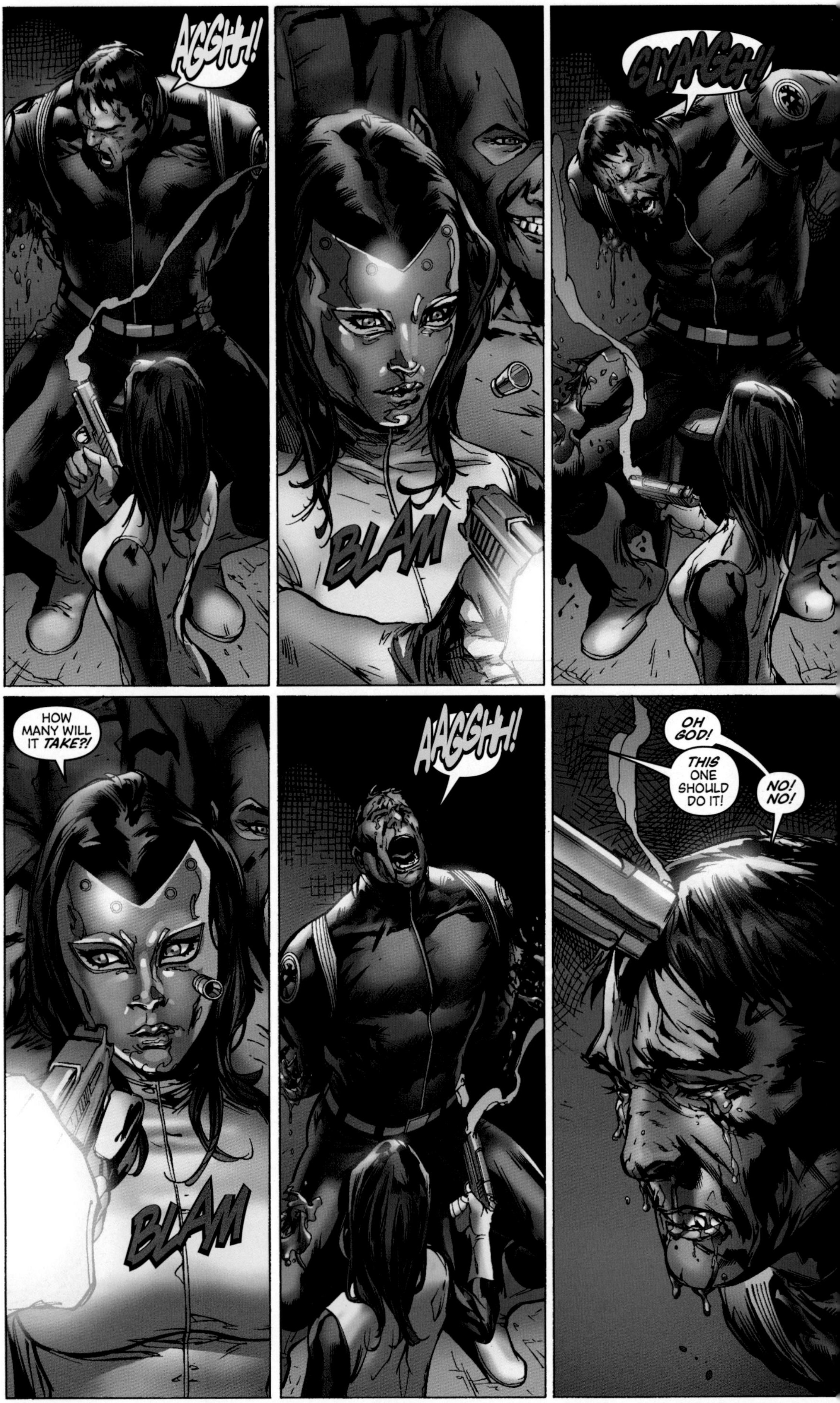
AGGHH!
BLAM
GLYAAGGH!
HOW MANY WILL IT TAKE?!
BLAM
AAGGHH!
OH GOD!
THIS ONE SHOULD DO IT!
NO! NO!

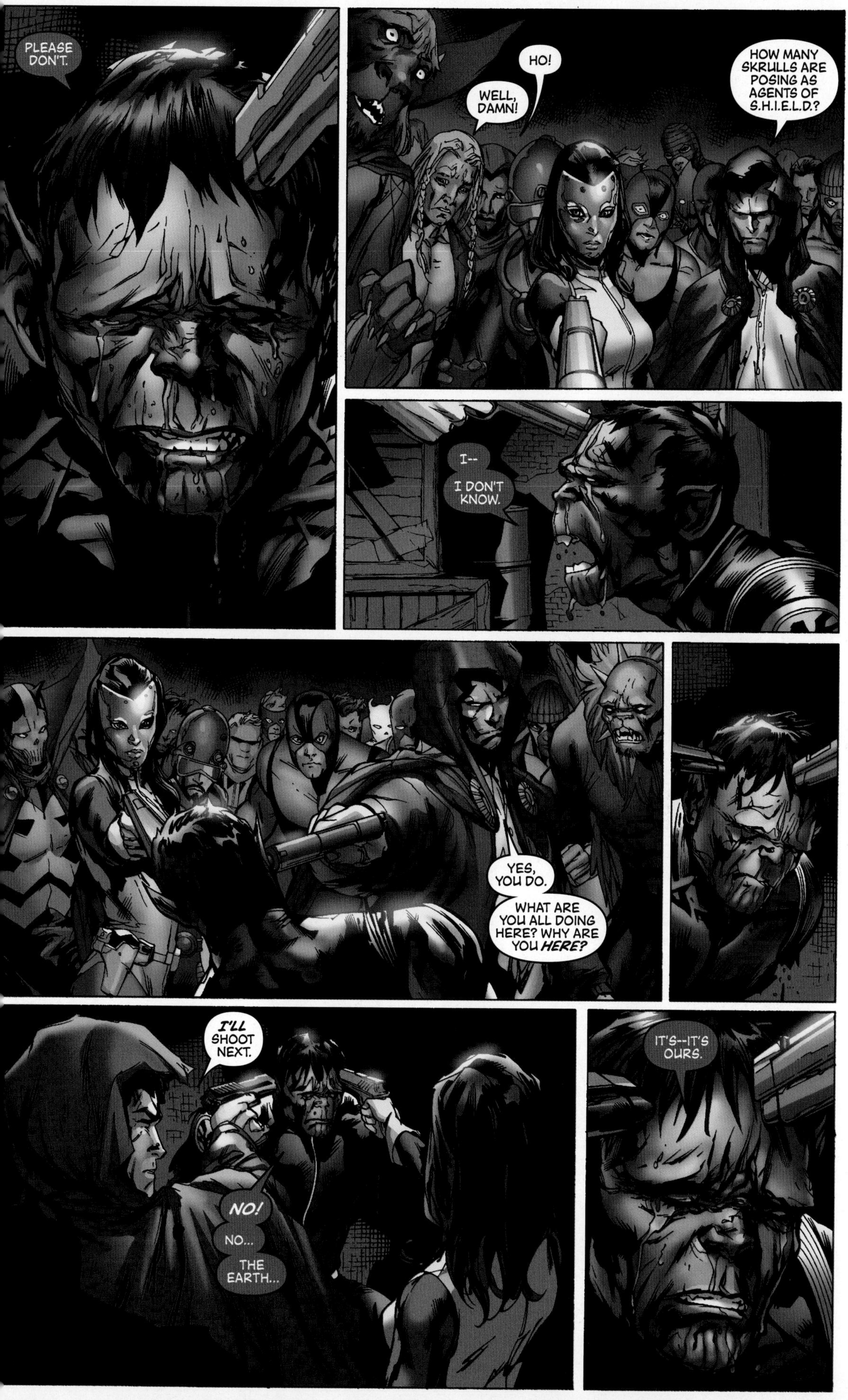
PLEASE DON'T.
WELL, DAMN!
HO!
HOW MANY SKRULLS ARE POSING AS AGENTS OF S.H.I.E.L.D.?
I--
I DON'T KNOW.
YES, YOU DO.
WHAT ARE YOU ALL DOING HERE? WHY ARE YOU *HERE?*
I'LL SHOOT NEXT.
NO!
NO...
THE EARTH...
IT'S--IT'S OURS.

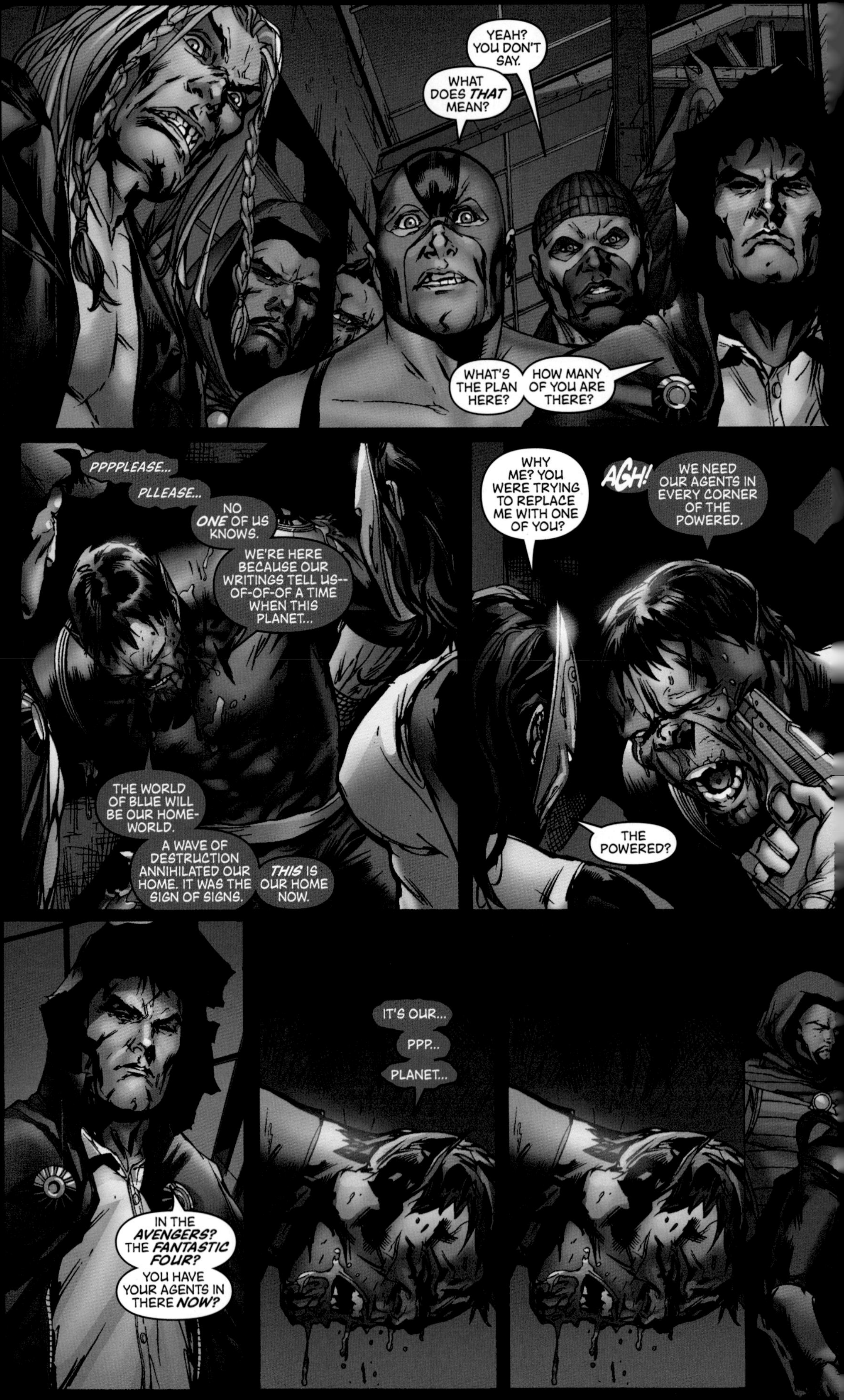
YEAH? YOU DON'T SAY.
WHAT DOES THAT MEAN?
WHAT'S THE PLAN HERE?
HOW MANY OF YOU ARE THERE?
PPPPLEASE...
PLLEASE...
NO ONE OF US KNOWS.
WE'RE HERE BECAUSE OUR WRITINGS TELL US-- OF-OF-OF A TIME WHEN THIS PLANET...
THE WORLD OF BLUE WILL BE OUR HOME-WORLD.
A WAVE OF DESTRUCTION ANNIHILATED OUR HOME. IT WAS THE SIGN OF SIGNS.
THIS IS OUR HOME NOW.
WHY ME? YOU WERE TRYING TO REPLACE ME WITH ONE OF YOU?
AGH!
WE NEED OUR AGENTS IN EVERY CORNER OF THE POWERED.
THE POWERED?
IN THE AVENGERS? THE FANTASTIC FOUR? YOU HAVE YOUR AGENTS IN THERE NOW?
IT'S OUR...
PPP...
PLANET...

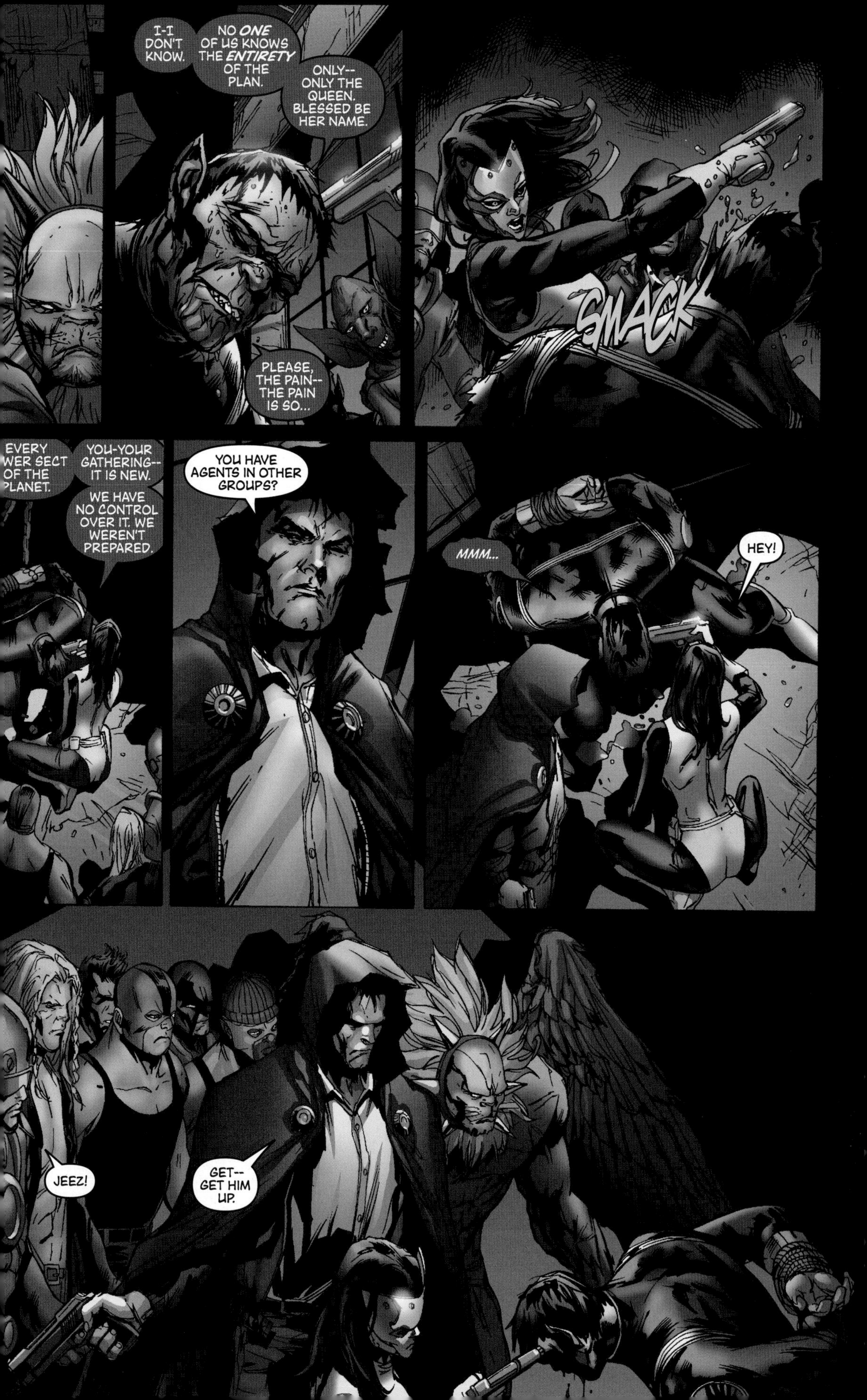
I-I DON'T KNOW.
NO ONE OF US KNOWS THE ENTIRETY OF THE PLAN.
ONLY-- ONLY THE QUEEN. BLESSED BE HER NAME.
PLEASE, THE PAIN-- THE PAIN IS SO...
SMACK
EVERY WER SECT OF THE PLANET.
YOU-YOUR GATHERING-- IT IS NEW.
WE HAVE NO CONTROL OVER IT. WE WEREN'T PREPARED.
YOU HAVE AGENTS IN OTHER GROUPS?
MMM...
HEY!
JEEZ!
GET-- GET HIM UP.

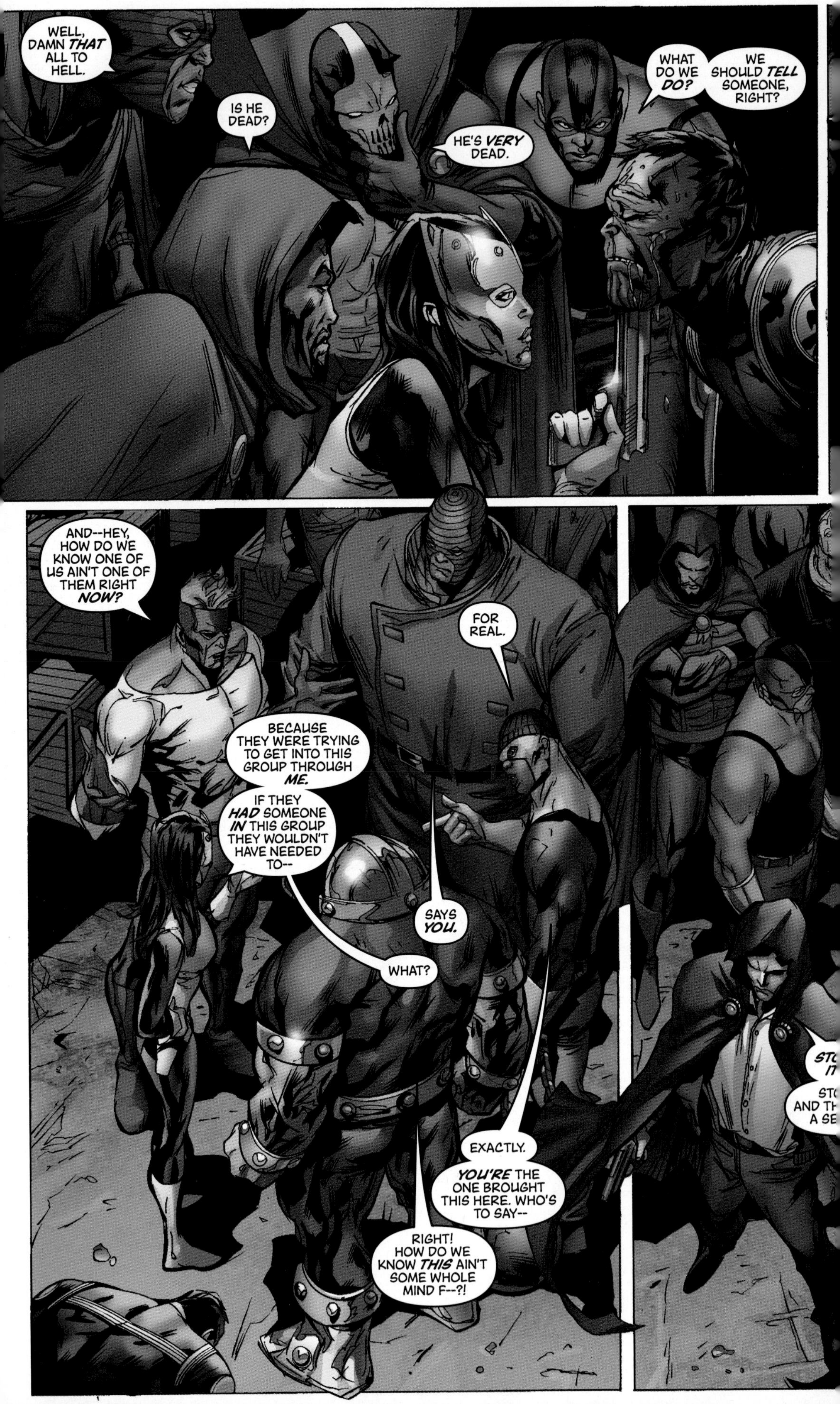
WELL, DAMN THAT ALL TO HELL.
IS HE DEAD?
HE'S VERY DEAD.
WHAT DO WE DO?
WE SHOULD TELL SOMEONE, RIGHT?
AND--HEY, HOW DO WE KNOW ONE OF US AIN'T ONE OF THEM RIGHT NOW?
FOR REAL.
BECAUSE THEY WERE TRYING TO GET INTO THIS GROUP THROUGH ME.
IF THEY HAD SOMEONE IN THIS GROUP THEY WOULDN'T HAVE NEEDED TO--
SAYS YOU.
WHAT?
EXACTLY.
YOU'RE THE ONE BROUGHT THIS HERE. WHO'S TO SAY--
RIGHT! HOW DO WE KNOW THIS AIN'T SOME WHOLE MIND F--?!

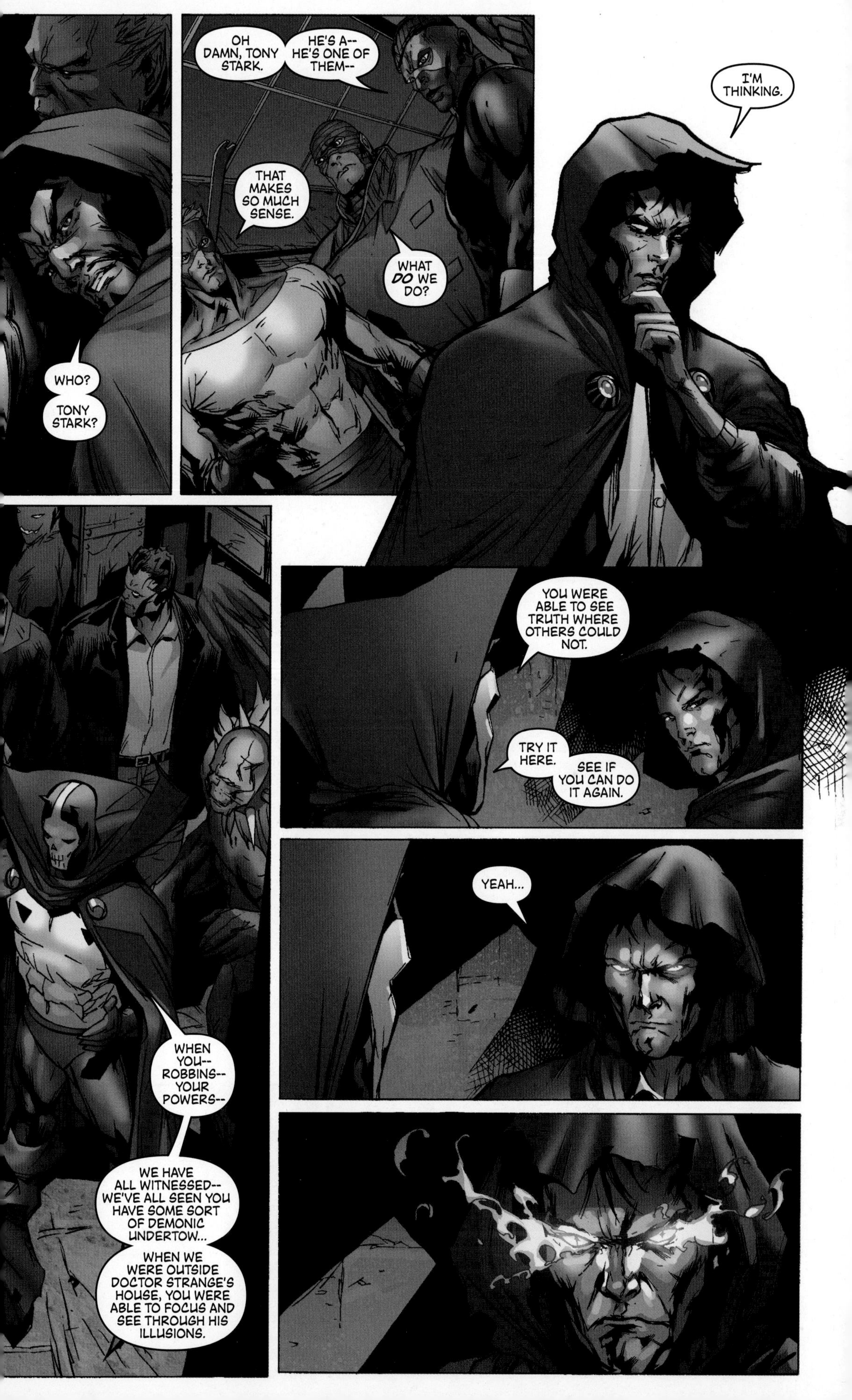

OH DAMN, TONY STARK.
HE'S A-- HE'S ONE OF THEM--
THAT MAKES SO MUCH SENSE.
WHAT DO WE DO?
WHO?
TONY STARK?
I'M THINKING.
WHEN YOU-- ROBBINS-- YOUR POWERS--
WE HAVE ALL WITNESSED-- WE'VE ALL SEEN YOU HAVE SOME SORT OF DEMONIC UNDERTOW...
WHEN WE WERE OUTSIDE DOCTOR STRANGE'S HOUSE, YOU WERE ABLE TO FOCUS AND SEE THROUGH HIS ILLUSIONS.
YOU WERE ABLE TO SEE TRUTH WHERE OTHERS COULD NOT.
TRY IT HERE.
SEE IF YOU CAN DO IT AGAIN.
YEAH...

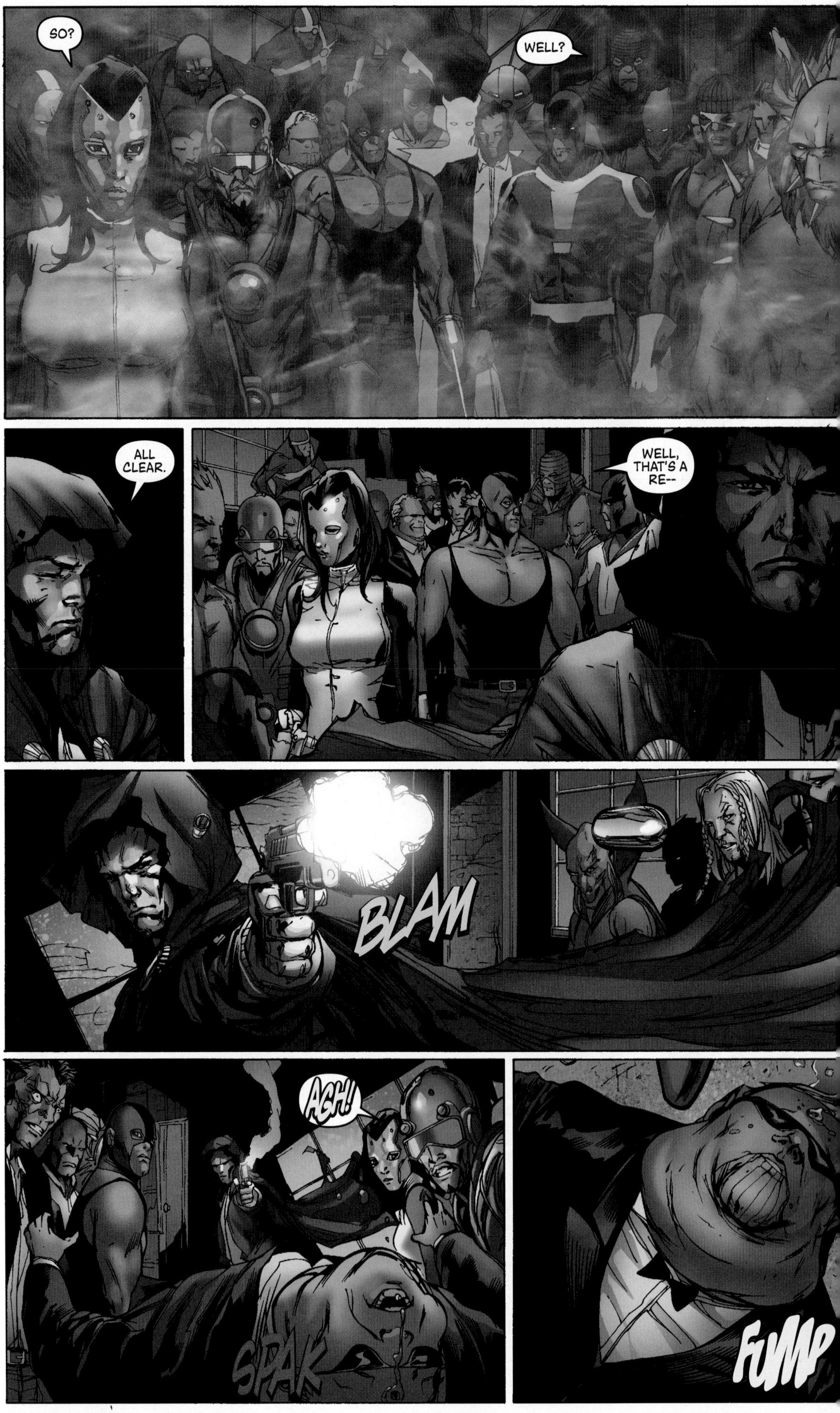
SO?
WELL?
ALL CLEAR.
WELL, THAT'S A RE--
BLAM
AGH!
SPAK
FUMP

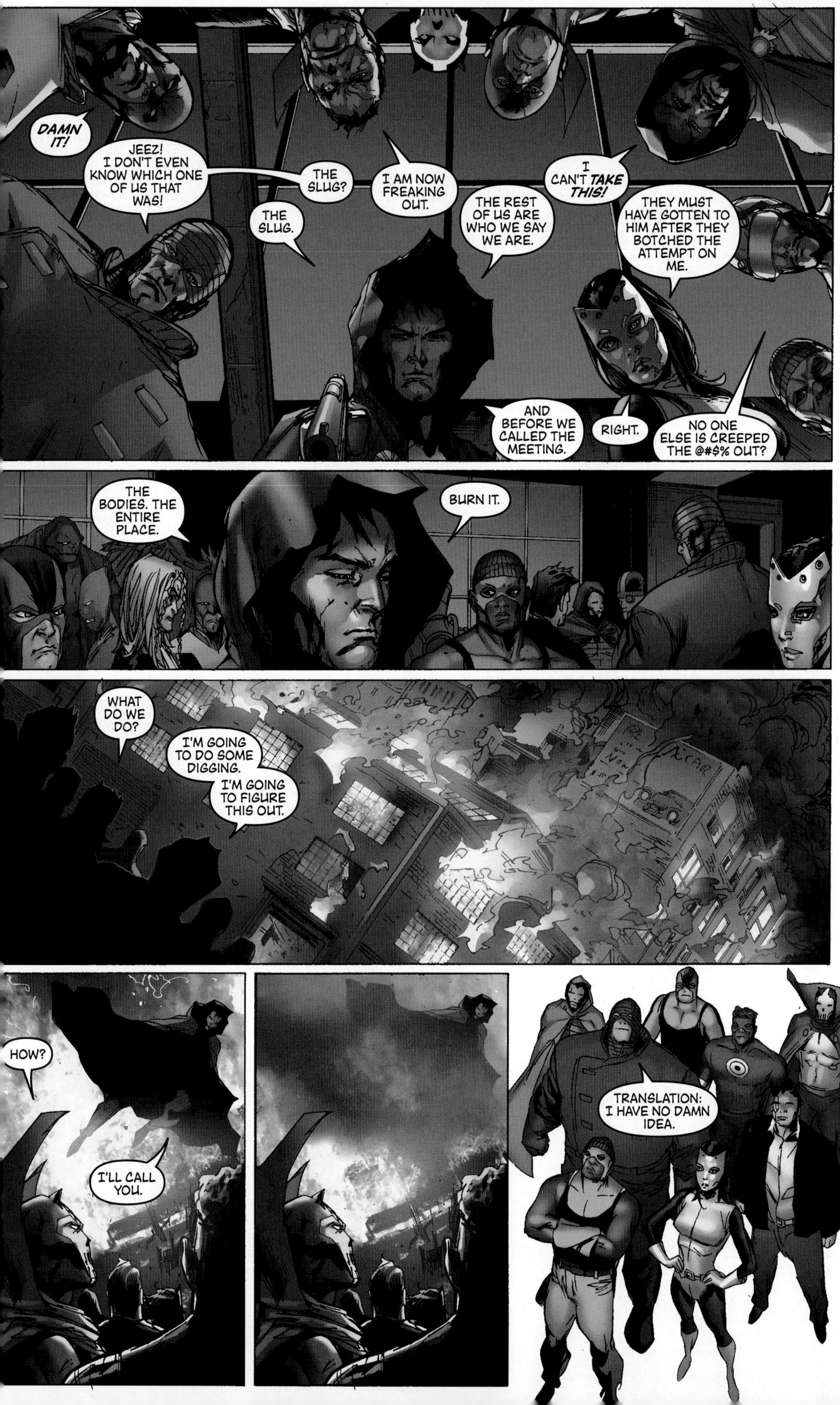
DAMN IT!
JEEZ! I DON'T EVEN KNOW WHICH ONE OF US THAT WAS!
THE SLUG?
THE SLUG.
I AM NOW FREAKING OUT.
THE REST OF US ARE WHO WE SAY WE ARE.
I CAN'T TAKE THIS!
THEY MUST HAVE GOTTEN TO HIM AFTER THEY BOTCHED THE ATTEMPT ON ME.
AND BEFORE WE CALLED THE MEETING.
RIGHT.
NO ONE ELSE IS CREEPED THE @#$% OUT?
THE BODIES. THE ENTIRE PLACE.
BURN IT.
WHAT DO WE DO?
I'M GOING TO DO SOME DIGGING.
I'M GOING TO FIGURE THIS OUT.
HOW?
I'LL CALL YOU.
TRANSLATION: I HAVE NO DAMN IDEA.

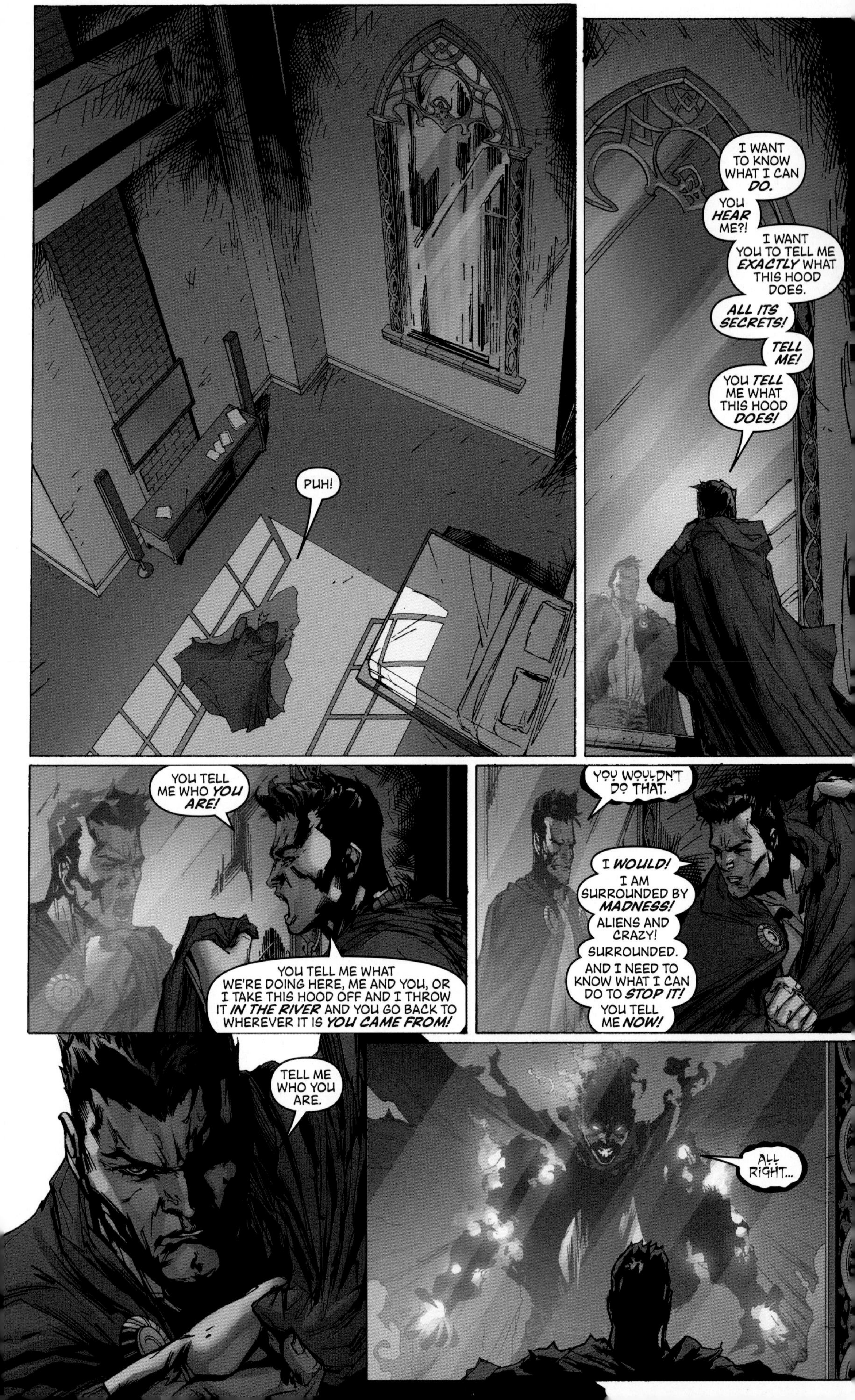
PUH!
I WANT TO KNOW WHAT I CAN DO.
YOU HEAR ME?!
I WANT YOU TO TELL ME EXACTLY WHAT THIS HOOD DOES.
ALL ITS SECRETS!
TELL ME!
YOU TELL ME WHAT THIS HOOD DOES!
YOU TELL ME WHO YOU ARE!
YOU TELL ME WHAT WE'RE DOING HERE, ME AND YOU, OR I TAKE THIS HOOD OFF AND I THROW IT IN THE RIVER AND YOU GO BACK TO WHEREVER IT IS YOU CAME FROM!
YOU WOULDN'T DO THAT.
I WOULD!
I AM SURROUNDED BY MADNESS!
ALIENS AND CRAZY!
SURROUNDED.
AND I NEED TO KNOW WHAT I CAN DO TO STOP IT!
YOU TELL ME NOW!
TELL ME WHO YOU ARE.
ALL RIGHT...

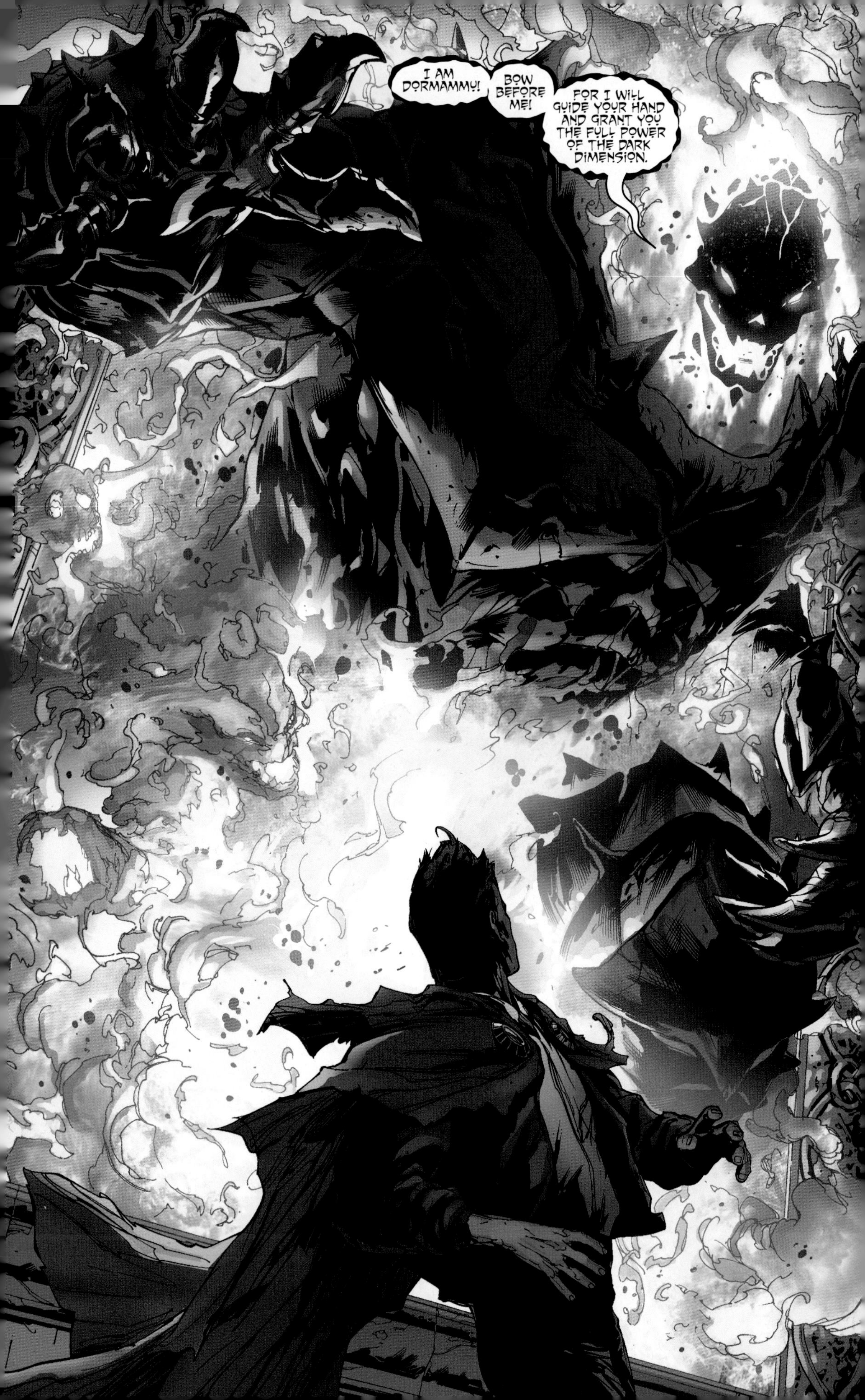
I AM DORMAMMU!
BOW BEFORE ME!
FOR I WILL GUIDE YOUR HAND AND GRANT YOU THE FULL POWER OF THE DARK DIMENSION.

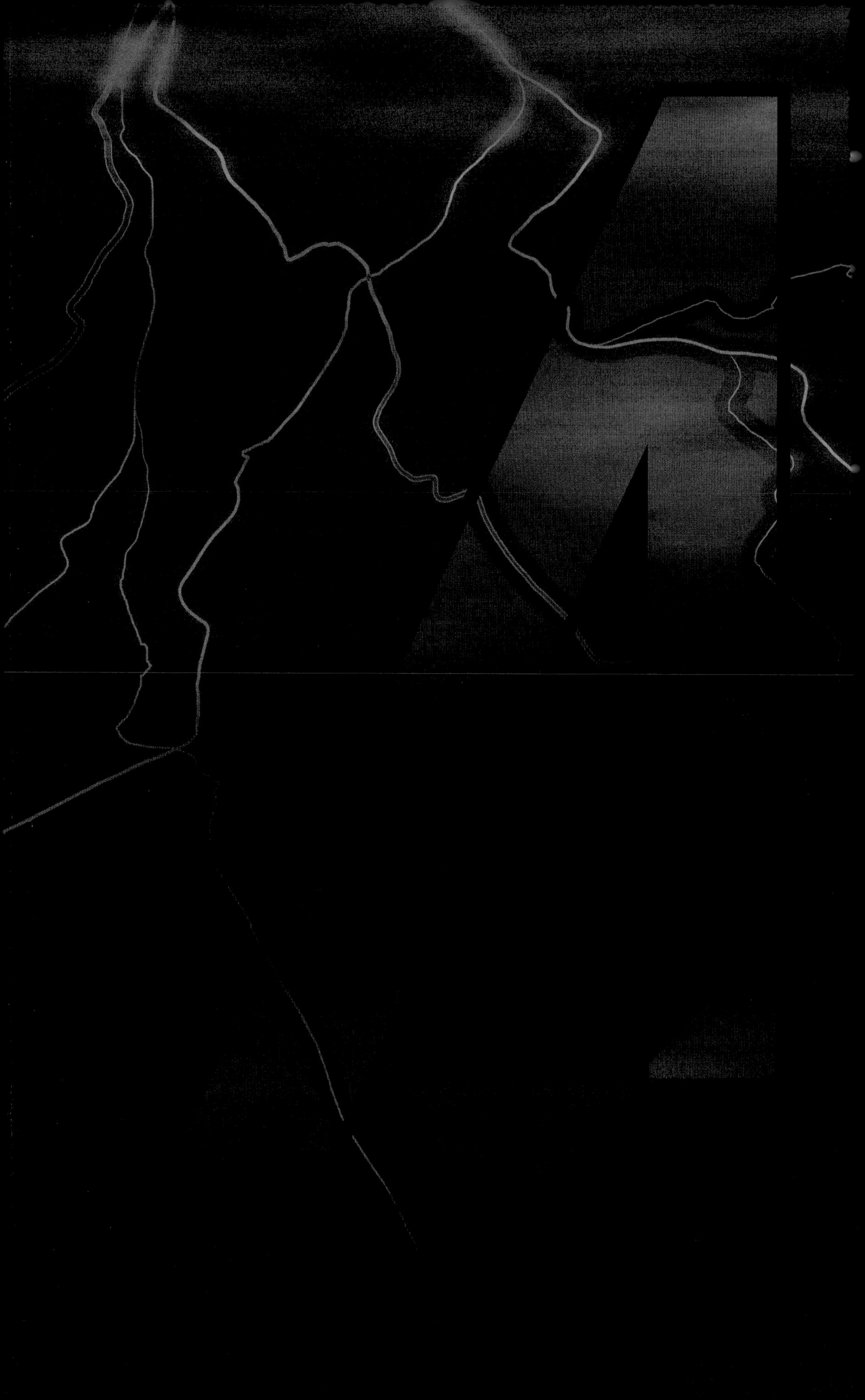

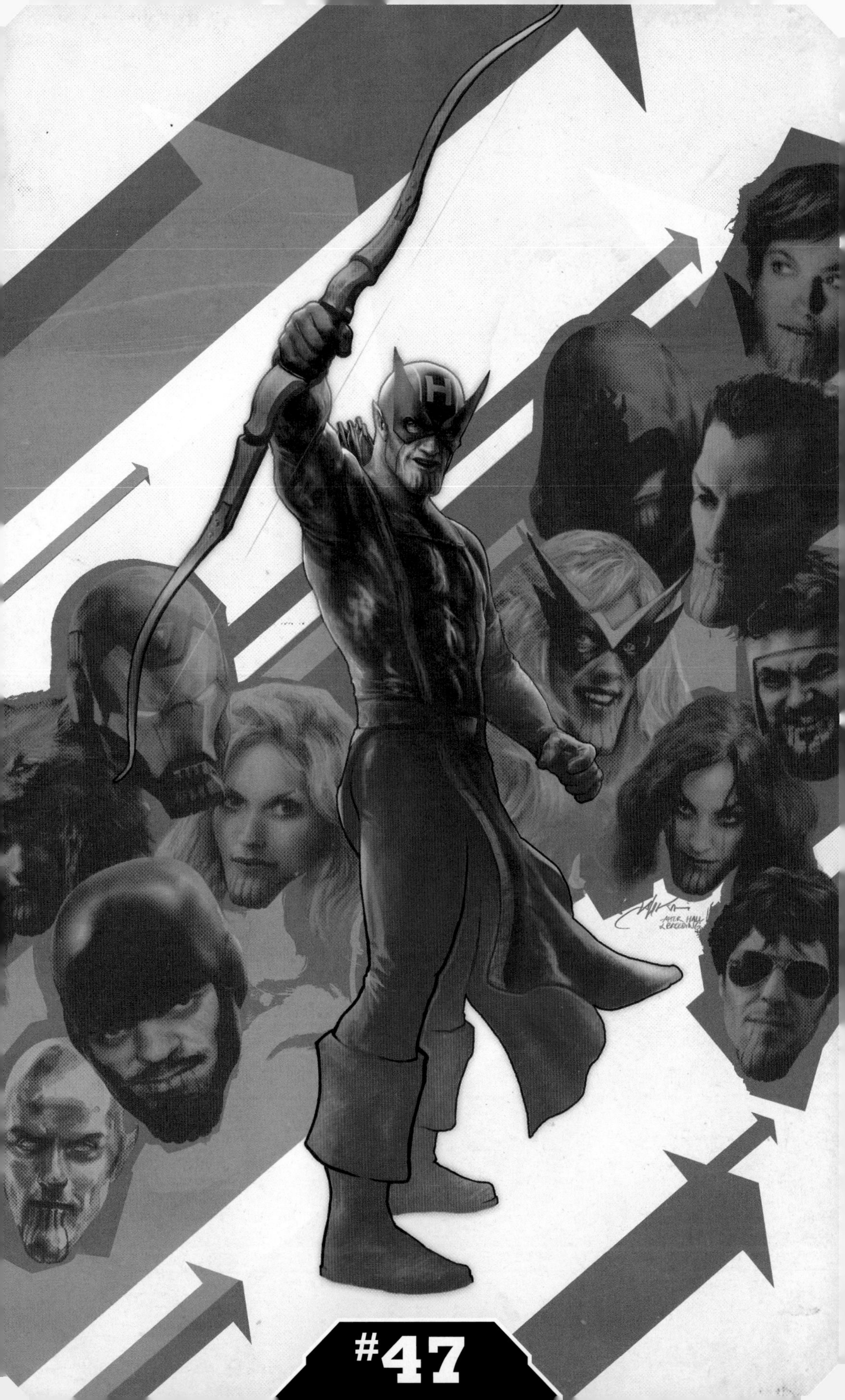
#47

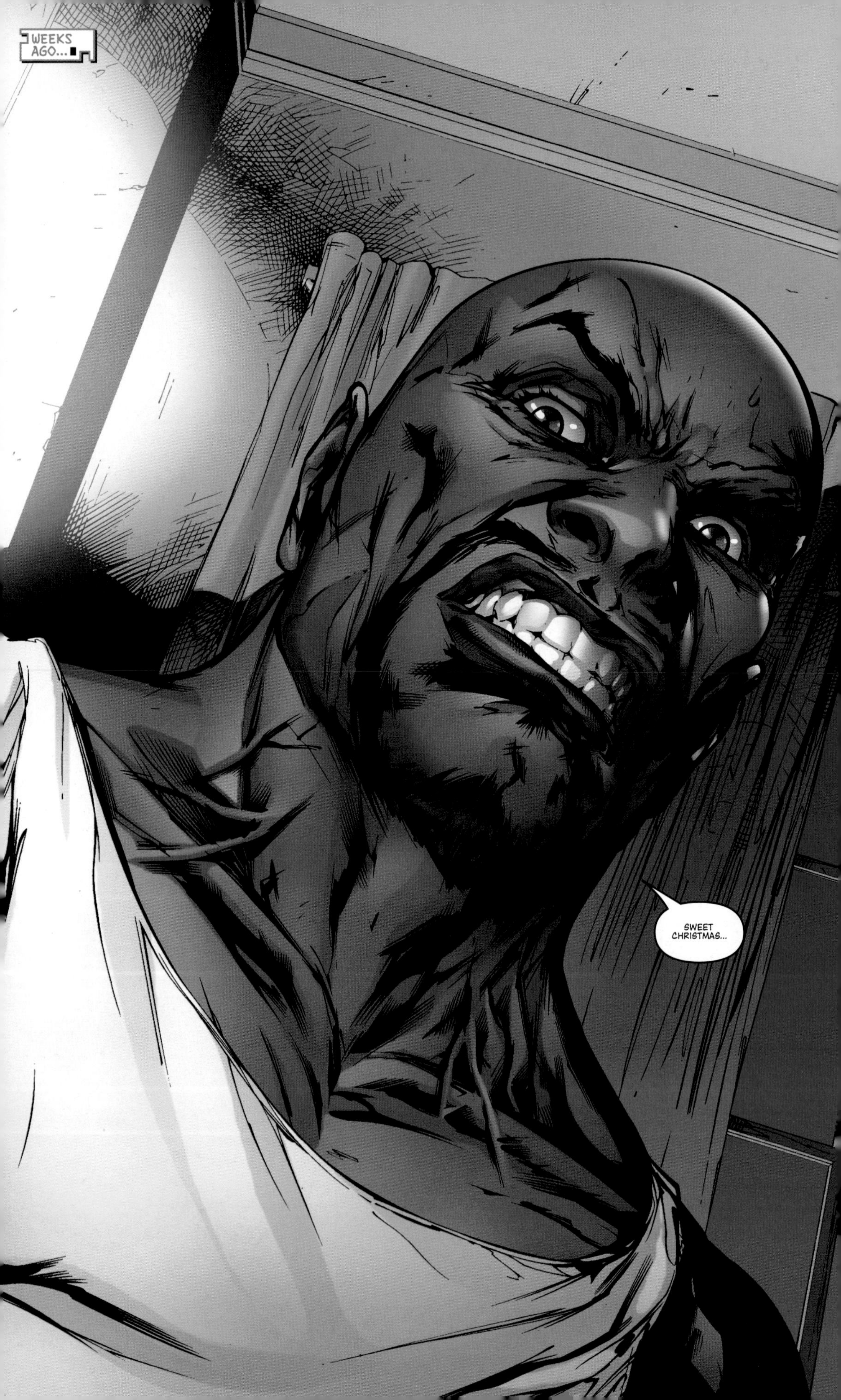
WEEKS AGO...
SWEET CHRISTMAS...

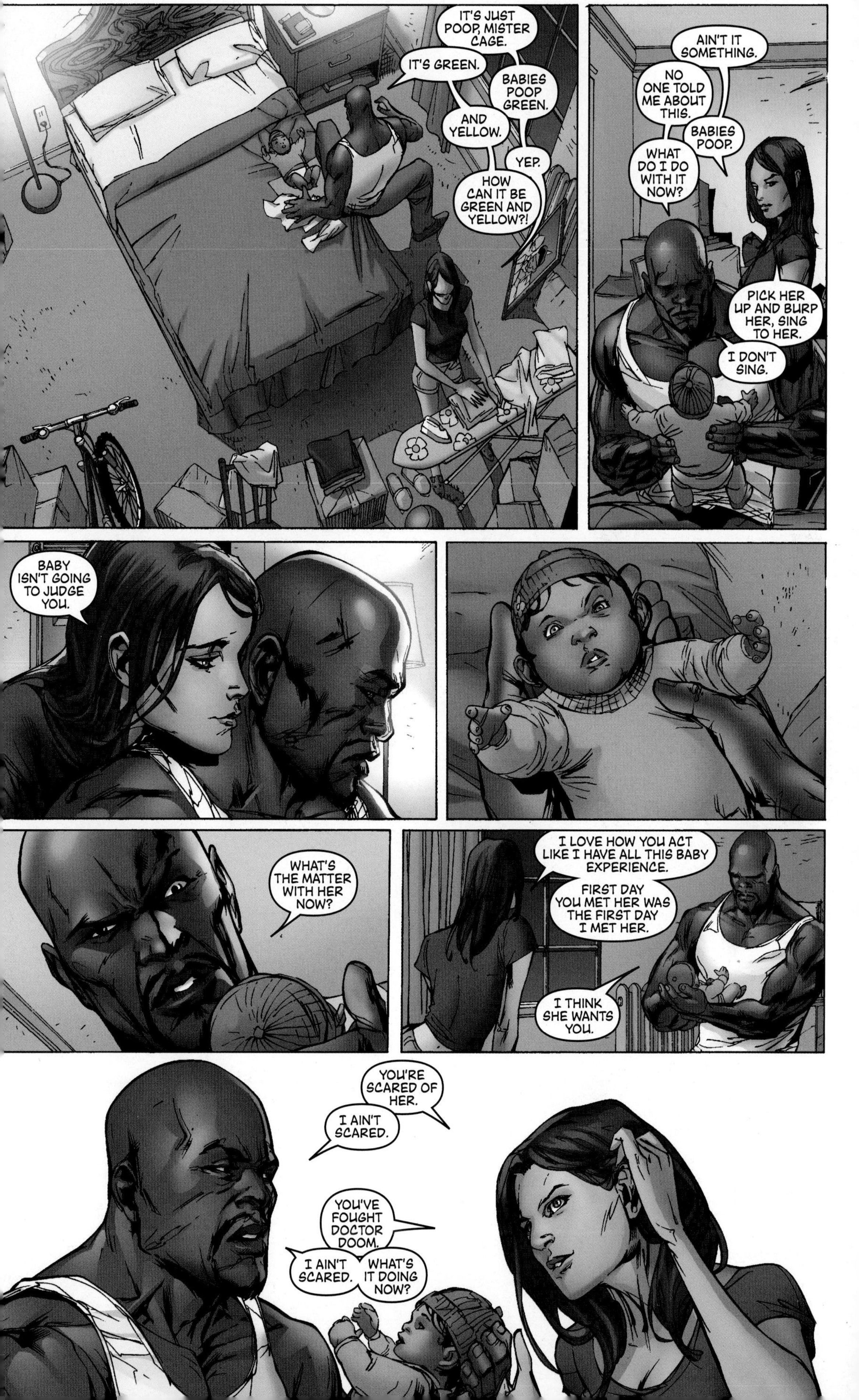
IT'S GREEN.
IT'S JUST POOP, MISTER CAGE.
AND YELLOW.
BABIES POOP GREEN.
YEP.
HOW CAN IT BE GREEN AND YELLOW?!
AIN'T IT SOMETHING.
NO ONE TOLD ME ABOUT THIS.
BABIES POOP.
WHAT DO I DO WITH IT NOW?
PICK HER UP AND BURP HER, SING TO HER.
I DON'T SING.
BABY ISN'T GOING TO JUDGE YOU.
WHAT'S THE MATTER WITH HER NOW?
I LOVE HOW YOU ACT LIKE I HAVE ALL THIS BABY EXPERIENCE.
FIRST DAY YOU MET HER WAS THE FIRST DAY I MET HER.
I THINK SHE WANTS YOU.
YOU'RE SCARED OF HER.
I AIN'T SCARED.
YOU'VE FOUGHT DOCTOR DOOM.
I AIN'T SCARED.
WHAT'S IT DOING NOW?

"IT" HAS FEMALE PRIVATE PARTS SO WE'RE GOING TO CALL IT A SHE FROM NOW ON.

OKAY.

YOU DON'T WANT TO GIVE HER ANY MORE OF A COMPLEX THAN THE ONE SHE'S GOING TO GET WHEN SHE SEES PICTURES OF US IN OUR OLD HERO COSTUMES.

TALK TO HER. BOUNCE HER.

TELL HER A STORY. SHE NEEDS TO HEAR YOUR VOICE.

SHE NEEDS TO KNOW WHO YOU ARE. SHE NEEDS TO FEEL SAFE.

OKAY. HOW ABOUT I TELL YOU ABOUT THE DAY I FELL IN LOVE WITH YOUR MOTHER.

YOU FELL IN LOVE WITH ME THAT FIRST DAY WE MET.

NO, YOU FELL IN LOVE WITH ME THE FIRST WE MET.

I RESERV JUDGEME

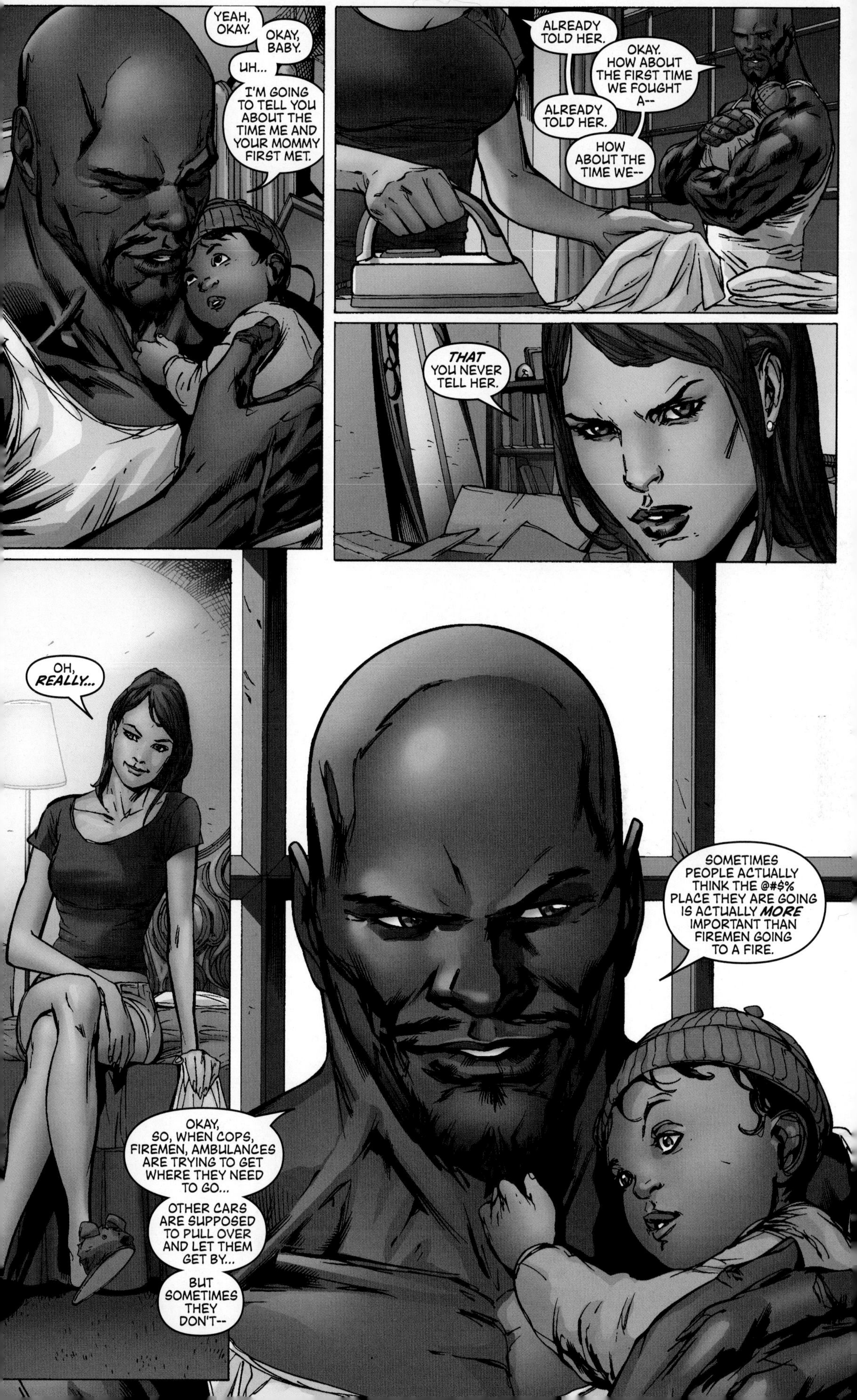
YEAH, OKAY.
OKAY, BABY.
UH...
I'M GOING TO TELL YOU ABOUT THE TIME ME AND YOUR MOMMY FIRST MET.
ALREADY TOLD HER.
OKAY. HOW ABOUT THE FIRST TIME WE FOUGHT A--
ALREADY TOLD HER.
HOW ABOUT THE TIME WE--
THAT YOU NEVER TELL HER.
OH, *REALLY...*
OKAY, SO, WHEN COPS, FIREMEN, AMBULANCES ARE TRYING TO GET WHERE THEY NEED TO GO...
OTHER CARS ARE SUPPOSED TO PULL OVER AND LET THEM GET BY...
BUT SOMETIMES THEY DON'T--
SOMETIMES PEOPLE ACTUALLY THINK THE @#$% PLACE THEY ARE GOING IS ACTUALLY *MORE* IMPORTANT THAN FIREMEN GOING TO A FIRE.

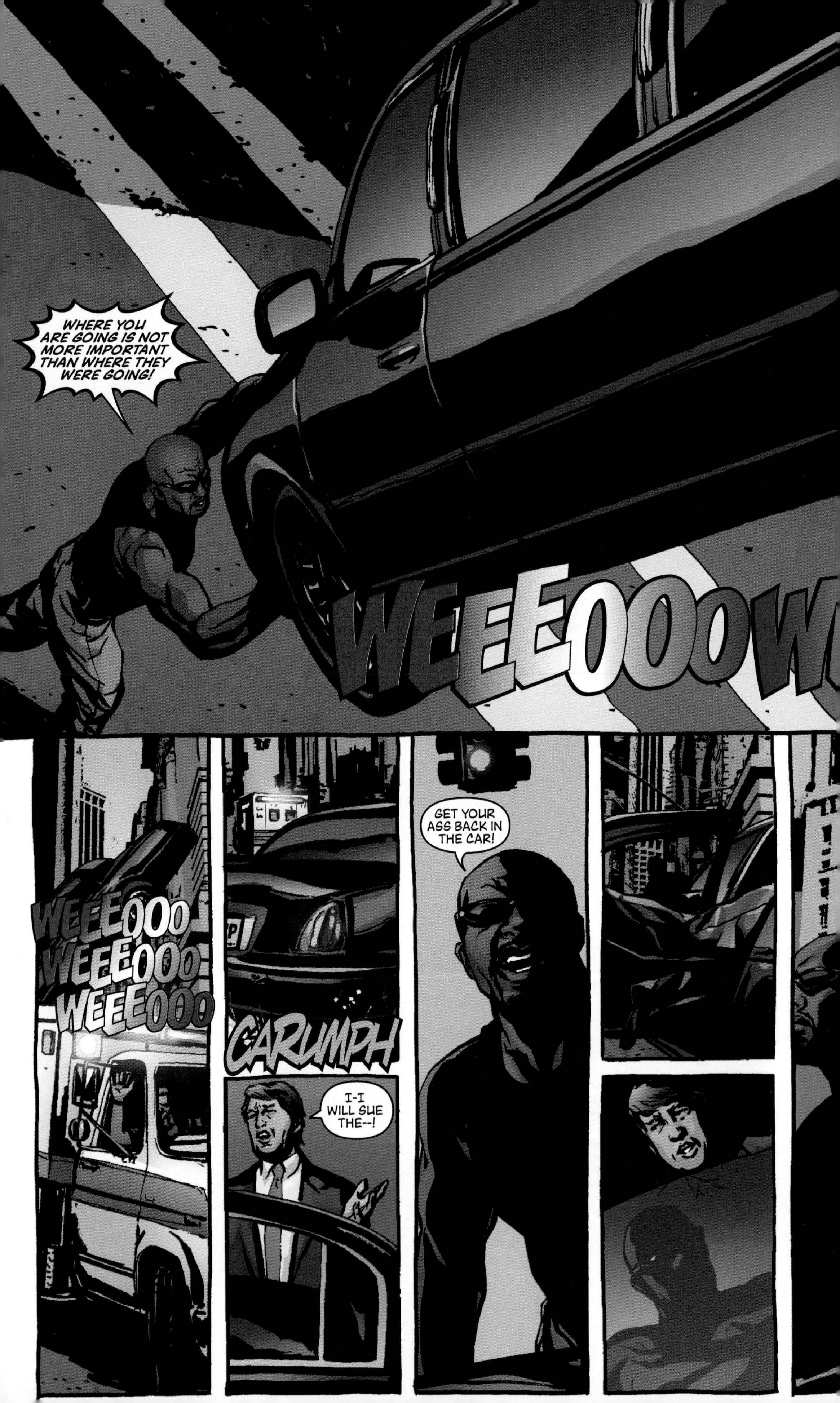
WHERE YOU ARE GOING IS NOT MORE IMPORTANT THAN WHERE THEY WERE GOING!
WEEEOOOW
WEEEOOO
WEEEOOO
WEEEOOO
CARUMPH
I-I WILL SUE THE--!
GET YOUR ASS BACK IN THE CAR!

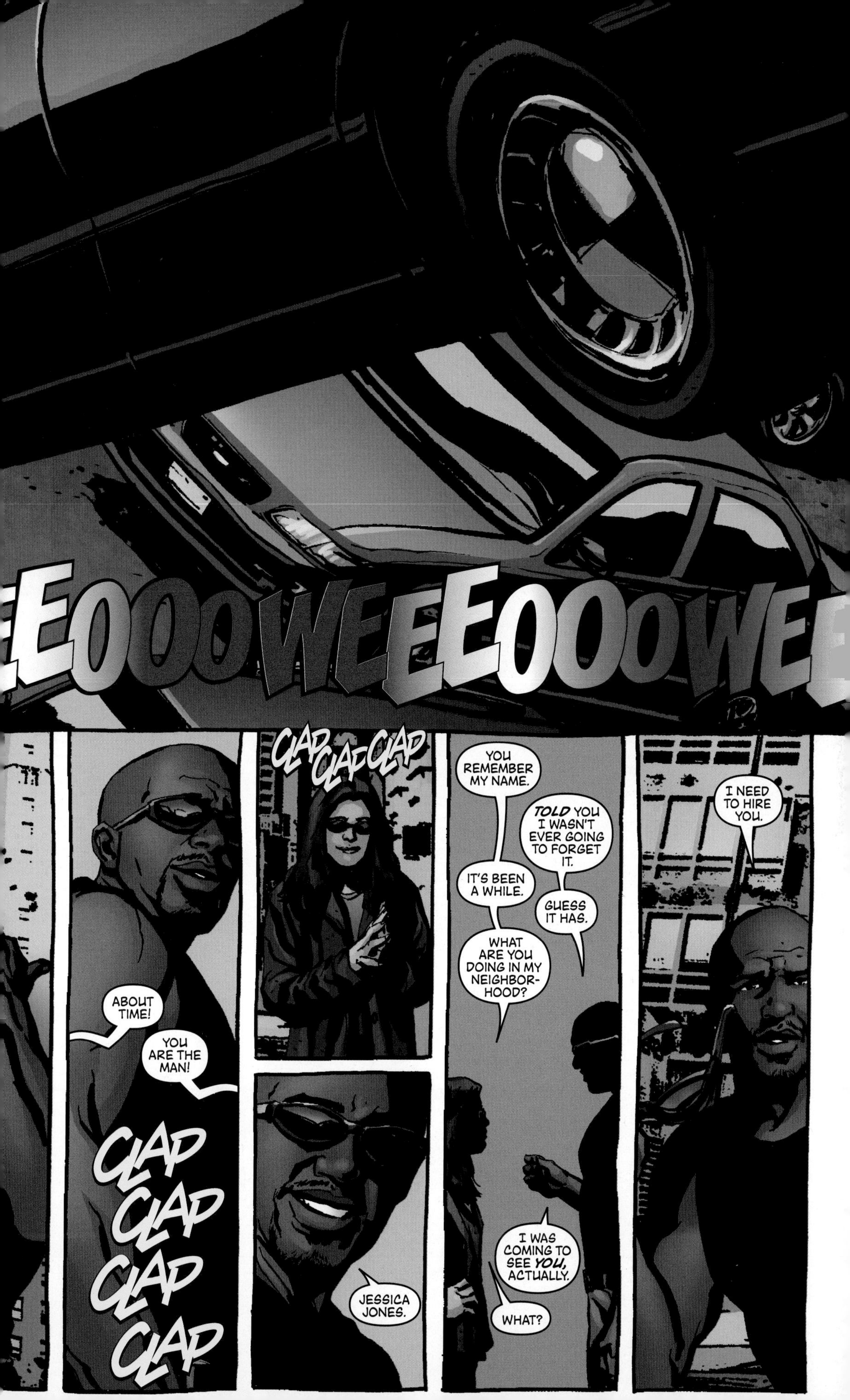
EEOOOWEEEOOOWEE
ABOUT TIME!
YOU ARE THE MAN!
CLAP CLAP CLAP CLAP
CLAP CLAP CLAP
JESSICA JONES.
YOU REMEMBER MY NAME.
TOLD YOU I WASN'T EVER GOING TO FORGET IT.
IT'S BEEN A WHILE.
GUESS IT HAS.
WHAT ARE YOU DOING IN MY NEIGHBOR-HOOD?
I WAS COMING TO SEE YOU, ACTUALLY.
WHAT?
I NEED TO HIRE YOU.

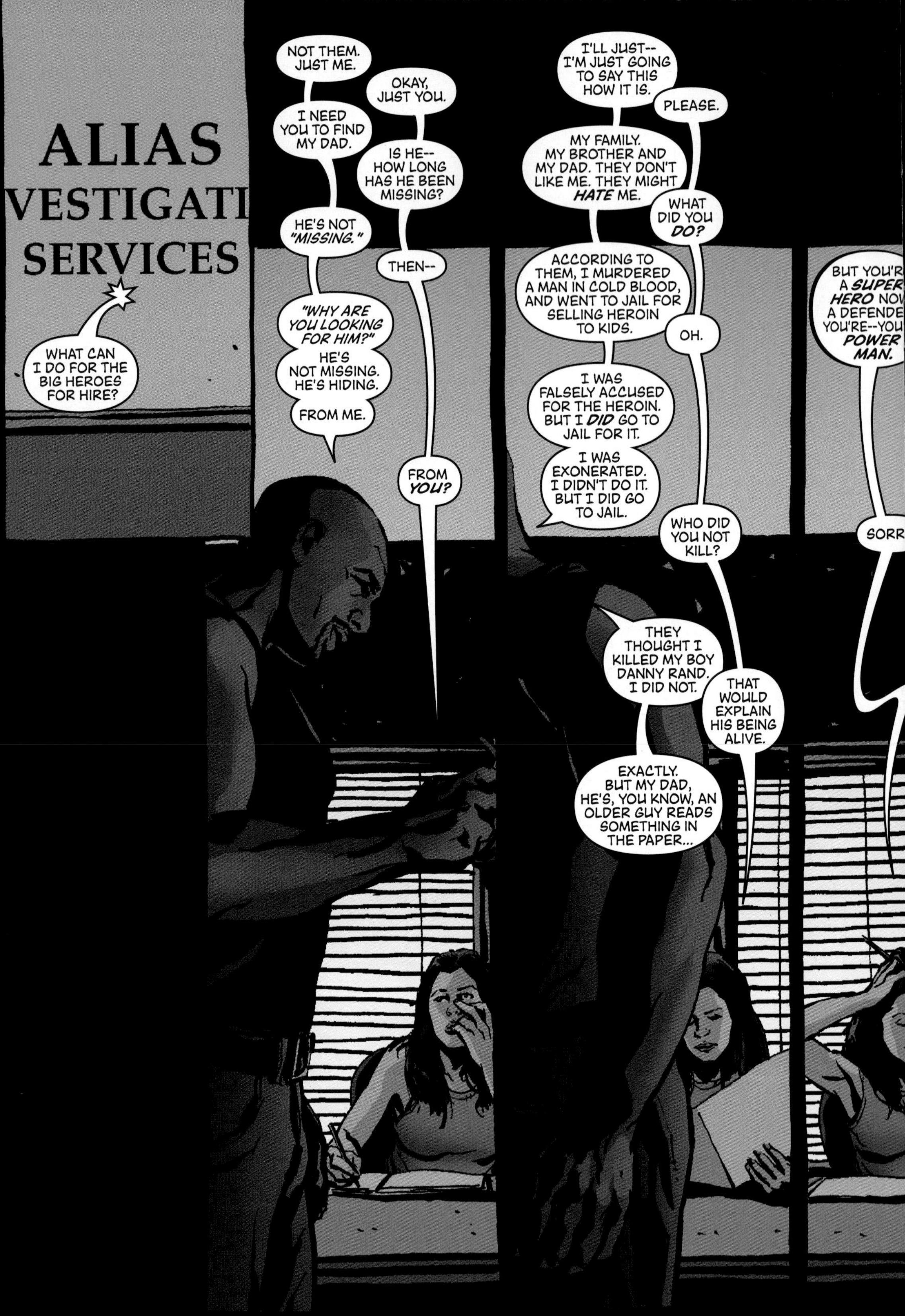
ALIAS
VESTIGATI
SERVICES
WHAT CAN I DO FOR THE BIG HEROES FOR HIRE?
NOT THEM. JUST ME.
OKAY, JUST YOU.
I NEED YOU TO FIND MY DAD.
IS HE-- HOW LONG HAS HE BEEN MISSING?
HE'S NOT "MISSING."
THEN--
"WHY ARE YOU LOOKING FOR HIM?"
HE'S NOT MISSING. HE'S HIDING.
FROM ME.
FROM YOU?
I'LL JUST-- I'M JUST GOING TO SAY THIS HOW IT IS.
PLEASE.
MY FAMILY. MY BROTHER AND MY DAD. THEY DON'T LIKE ME. THEY MIGHT HATE ME.
WHAT DID YOU DO?
ACCORDING TO THEM, I MURDERED A MAN IN COLD BLOOD, AND WENT TO JAIL FOR SELLING HEROIN TO KIDS.
OH.
I WAS FALSELY ACCUSED FOR THE HEROIN. BUT I DID GO TO JAIL FOR IT.
I WAS EXONERATED. I DIDN'T DO IT. BUT I DID GO TO JAIL.
WHO DID YOU NOT KILL?
THEY THOUGHT I KILLED MY BOY DANNY RAND. I DID NOT.
THAT WOULD EXPLAIN HIS BEING ALIVE.
EXACTLY. BUT MY DAD, HE'S, YOU KNOW, AN OLDER GUY READS SOMETHING IN THE PAPER...
BUT YOU'R A SUPER HERO NOW A DEFENDE YOU'RE--YOU POWER MAN.
SORR

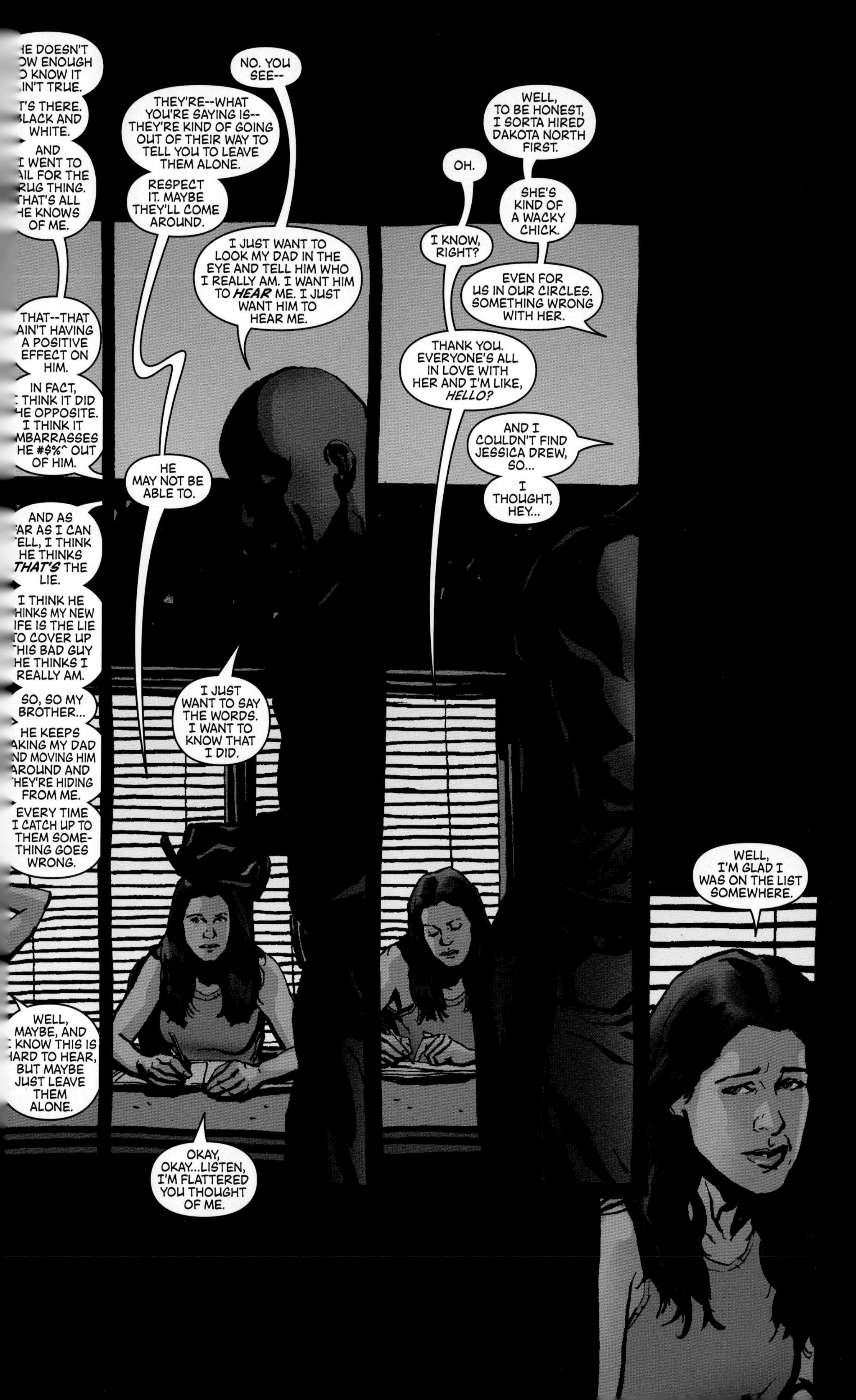

HE DOESN'T OW ENOUGH O KNOW IT AIN'T TRUE.
T'S THERE. BLACK AND WHITE.
AND I WENT TO AIL FOR THE RUG THING. THAT'S ALL HE KNOWS OF ME.
THAT--THAT AIN'T HAVING A POSITIVE EFFECT ON HIM.
IN FACT, I THINK IT DID HE OPPOSITE. I THINK IT MBARRASSES HE #$%^ OUT OF HIM.
AND AS AR AS I CAN ELL, I THINK HE THINKS THAT'S THE LIE.
I THINK HE HINKS MY NEW IFE IS THE LIE O COVER UP THIS BAD GUY HE THINKS I REALLY AM.
SO, SO MY BROTHER...
HE KEEPS AKING MY DAD ND MOVING HIM AROUND AND HEY'RE HIDING FROM ME.
EVERY TIME I CATCH UP TO THEM SOME-THING GOES WRONG.
WELL, MAYBE, AND I KNOW THIS IS HARD TO HEAR, BUT MAYBE JUST LEAVE THEM ALONE.
THEY'RE--WHAT YOU'RE SAYING IS--THEY'RE KIND OF GOING OUT OF THEIR WAY TO TELL YOU TO LEAVE THEM ALONE.
RESPECT IT. MAYBE THEY'LL COME AROUND.
NO. YOU SEE--
I JUST WANT TO LOOK MY DAD IN THE EYE AND TELL HIM WHO I REALLY AM. I WANT HIM TO HEAR ME. I JUST WANT HIM TO HEAR ME.
HE MAY NOT BE ABLE TO.
I JUST WANT TO SAY THE WORDS. I WANT TO KNOW THAT I DID.
OKAY, OKAY...LISTEN, I'M FLATTERED YOU THOUGHT OF ME.
WELL, TO BE HONEST, I SORTA HIRED DAKOTA NORTH FIRST.
OH.
SHE'S KIND OF A WACKY CHICK.
I KNOW, RIGHT?
EVEN FOR US IN OUR CIRCLES. SOMETHING WRONG WITH HER.
THANK YOU. EVERYONE'S ALL IN LOVE WITH HER AND I'M LIKE, HELLO?
AND I COULDN'T FIND JESSICA DREW, SO...
I THOUGHT, HEY...
WELL, I'M GLAD I WAS ON THE LIST SOMEWHERE.

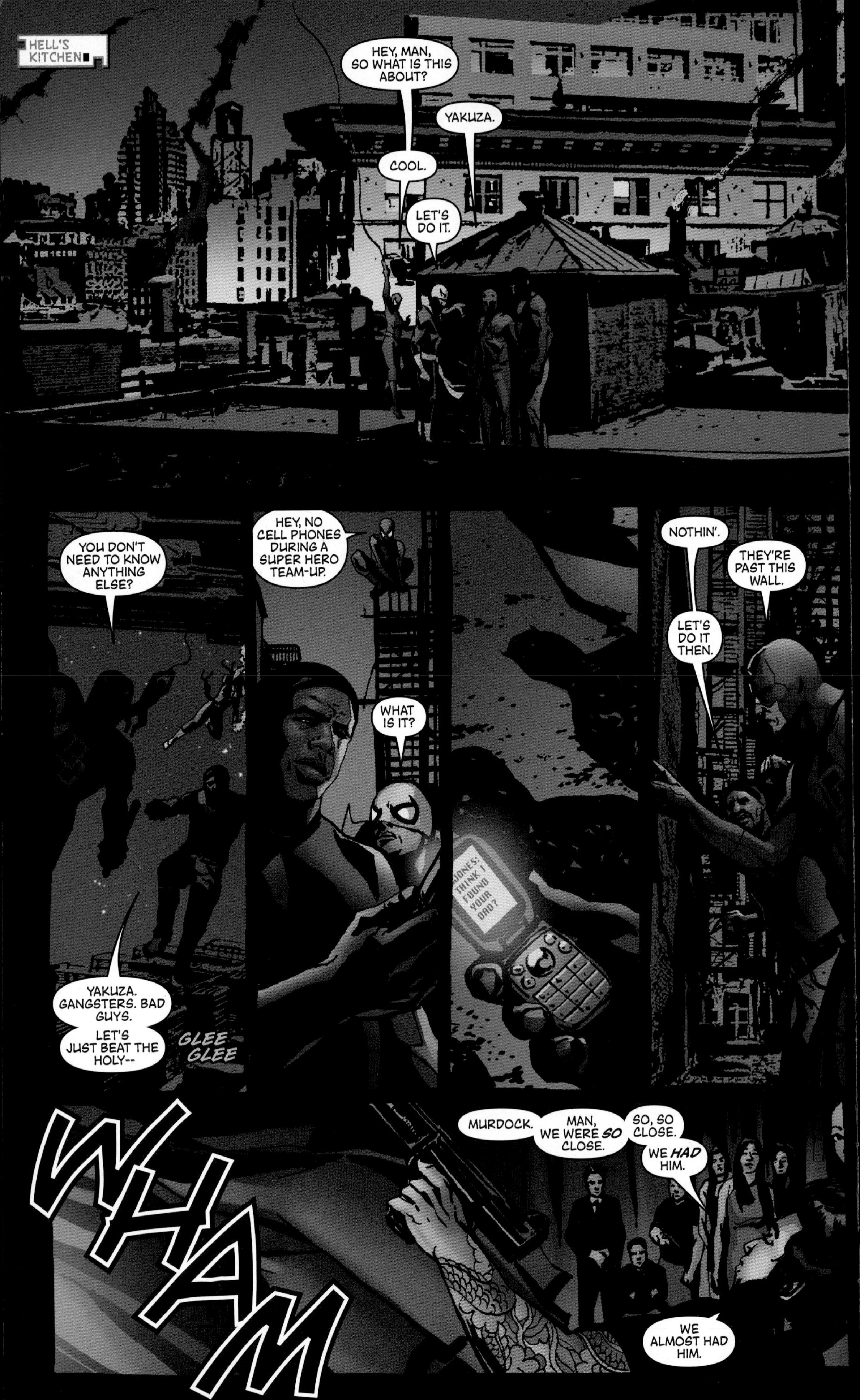
HELL'S KITCHEN
HEY, MAN, SO WHAT IS THIS ABOUT?
YAKUZA.
COOL.
LET'S DO IT.
YOU DON'T NEED TO KNOW ANYTHING ELSE?
YAKUZA. GANGSTERS. BAD GUYS.
LET'S JUST BEAT THE HOLY--
GLEE GLEE
HEY, NO CELL PHONES DURING A SUPER HERO TEAM-UP.
WHAT IS IT?
JONES: THINK I FOUND YOUR DAD?
NOTHIN'.
THEY'RE PAST THIS WALL.
LET'S DO IT THEN.
WHAM
MURDOCK.
MAN, WE WERE SO CLOSE.
SO, SO CLOSE.
WE HAD HIM.
WE ALMOST HAD HIM.

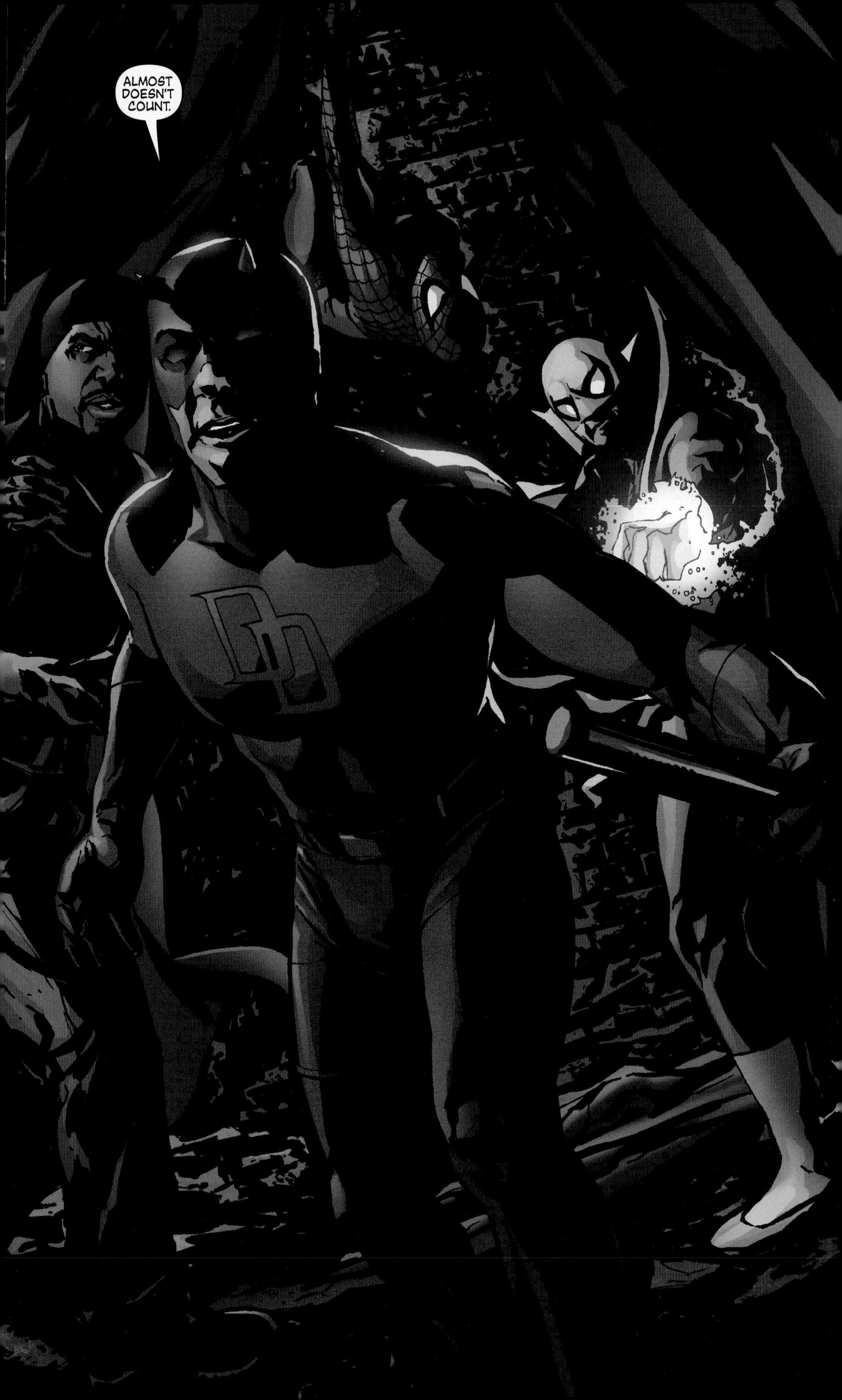
ALMOST DOESN'T COUNT.

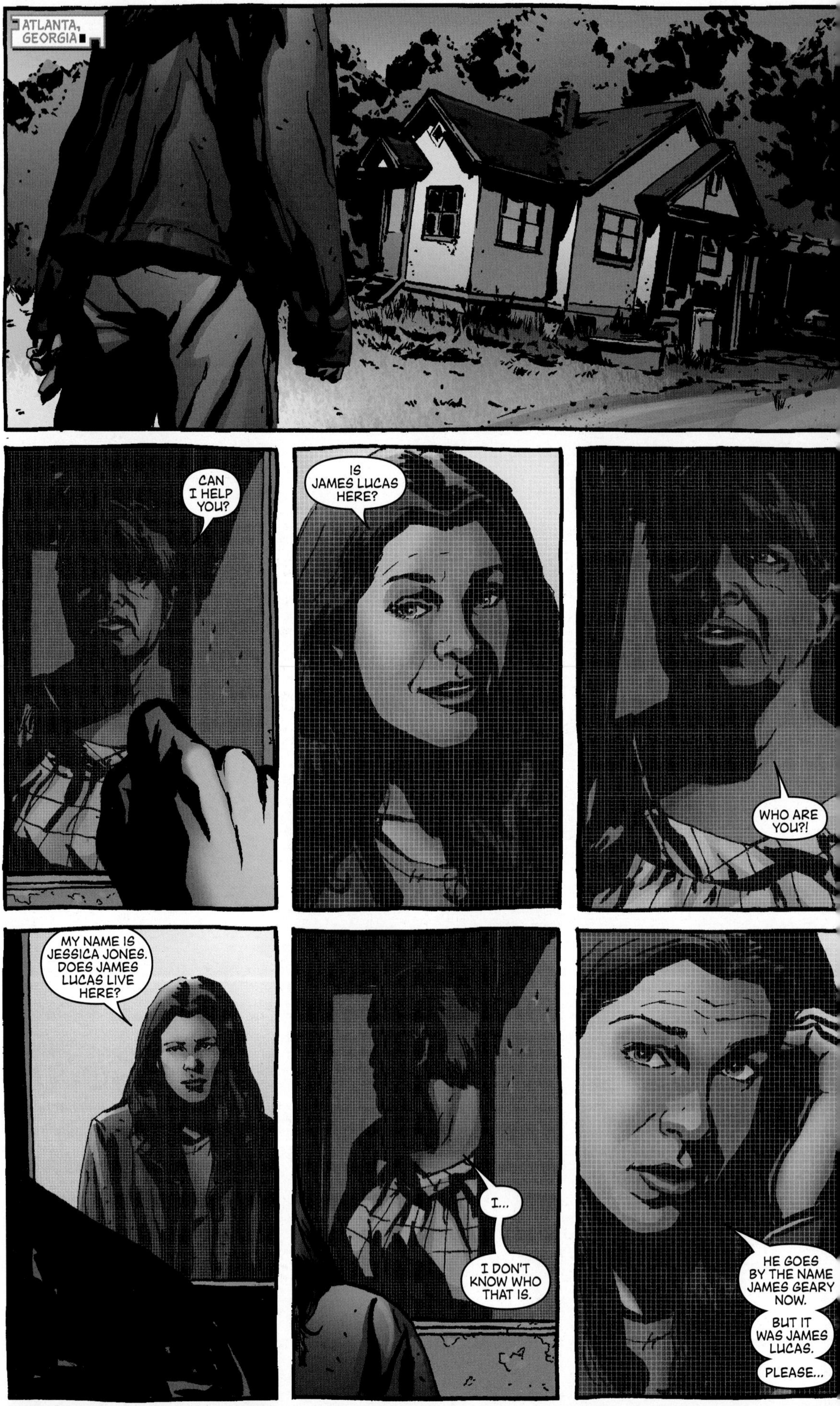
ATLANTA, GEORGIA
CAN I HELP YOU?
IS JAMES LUCAS HERE?
WHO ARE YOU?!
MY NAME IS JESSICA JONES. DOES JAMES LUCAS LIVE HERE?
I...
I DON'T KNOW WHO THAT IS.
HE GOES BY THE NAME JAMES GEARY NOW.
BUT IT WAS JAMES LUCAS.
PLEASE...

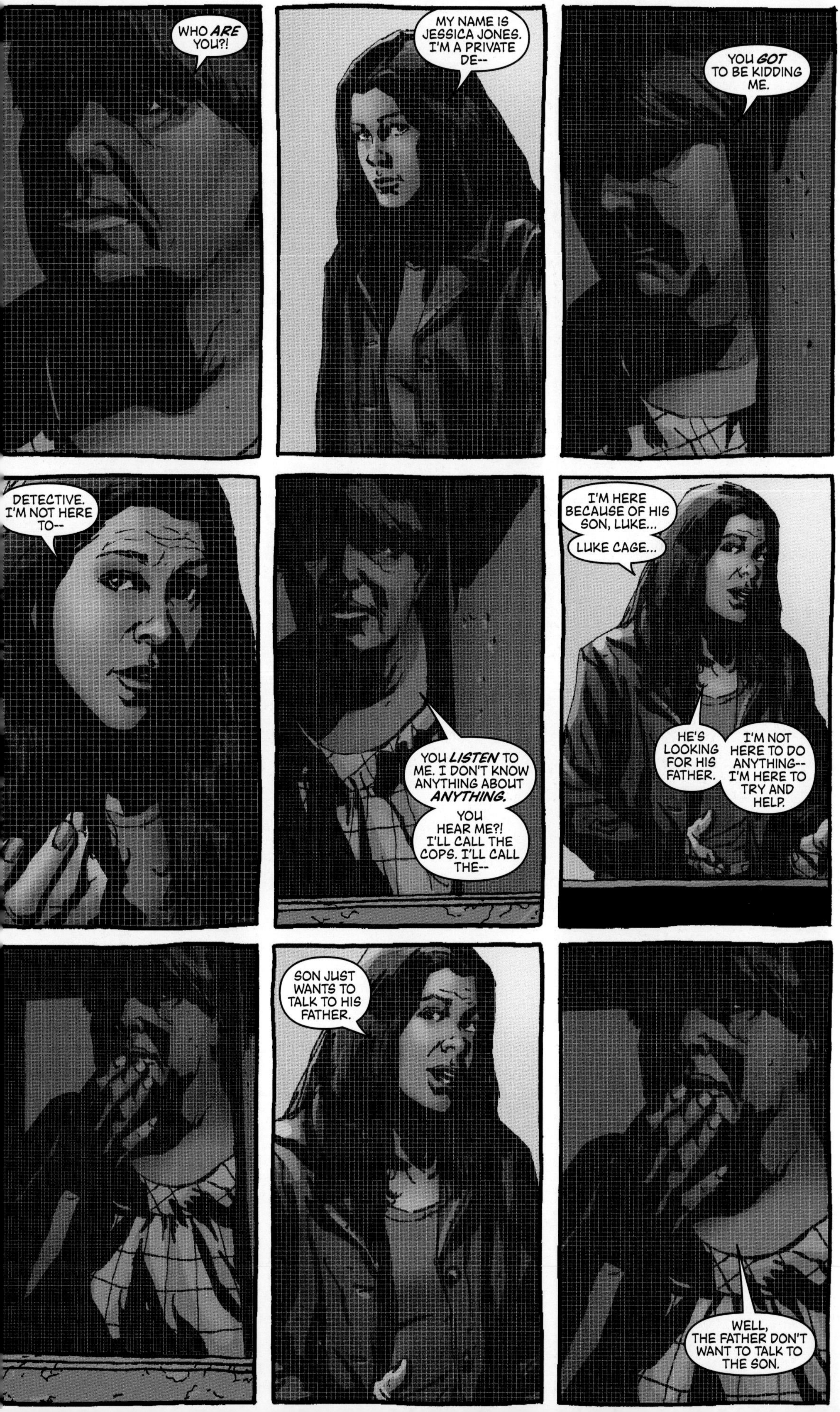
WHO *ARE* YOU?!
MY NAME IS JESSICA JONES. I'M A PRIVATE DE--
YOU *GOT* TO BE KIDDING ME.
DETECTIVE. I'M NOT HERE TO--
YOU *LISTEN* TO ME. I DON'T KNOW ANYTHING ABOUT *ANYTHING.*
YOU HEAR ME?! I'LL CALL THE COPS. I'LL CALL THE--
I'M HERE BECAUSE OF HIS SON, LUKE...
LUKE CAGE...
HE'S LOOKING FOR HIS FATHER.
I'M NOT HERE TO DO ANYTHING-- I'M HERE TO TRY AND HELP.
SON JUST WANTS TO TALK TO HIS FATHER.
WELL, THE FATHER DON'T WANT TO TALK TO THE SON.

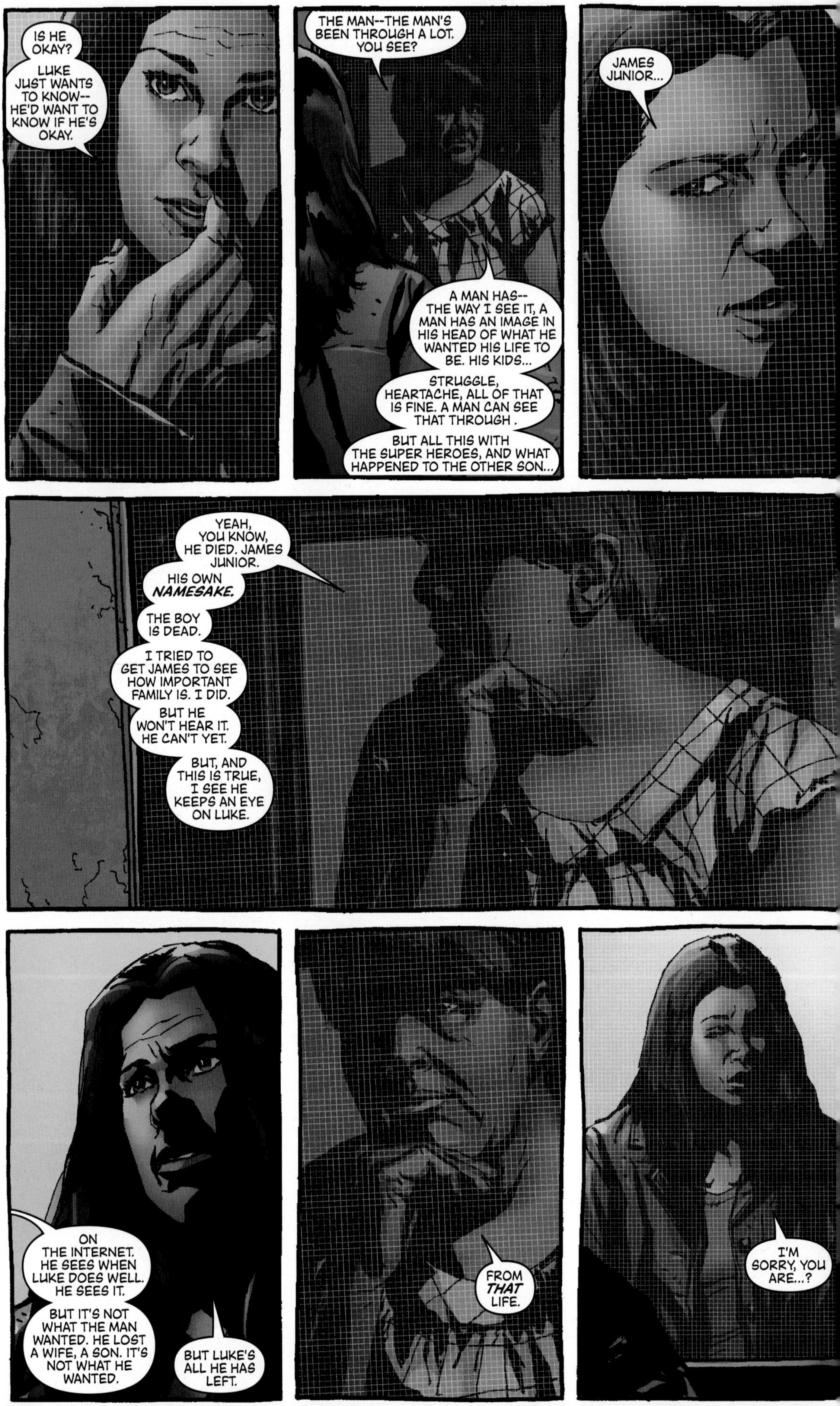
IS HE OKAY?
LUKE JUST WANTS TO KNOW-- HE'D WANT TO KNOW IF HE'S OKAY.
THE MAN--THE MAN'S BEEN THROUGH A LOT. YOU SEE?
A MAN HAS-- THE WAY I SEE IT, A MAN HAS AN IMAGE IN HIS HEAD OF WHAT HE WANTED HIS LIFE TO BE. HIS KIDS...
STRUGGLE, HEARTACHE, ALL OF THAT IS FINE. A MAN CAN SEE THAT THROUGH .
BUT ALL THIS WITH THE SUPER HEROES, AND WHAT HAPPENED TO THE OTHER SON...
JAMES JUNIOR...
YEAH, YOU KNOW, HE DIED. JAMES JUNIOR.
HIS OWN NAMESAKE.
THE BOY IS DEAD.
I TRIED TO GET JAMES TO SEE HOW IMPORTANT FAMILY IS. I DID.
BUT HE WON'T HEAR IT. HE CAN'T YET.
BUT, AND THIS IS TRUE, I SEE HE KEEPS AN EYE ON LUKE.
ON THE INTERNET. HE SEES WHEN LUKE DOES WELL. HE SEES IT.
BUT IT'S NOT WHAT THE MAN WANTED. HE LOST A WIFE, A SON. IT'S NOT WHAT HE WANTED.
BUT LUKE'S ALL HE HAS LEFT.
FROM THAT LIFE.
I'M SORRY, YOU ARE...?

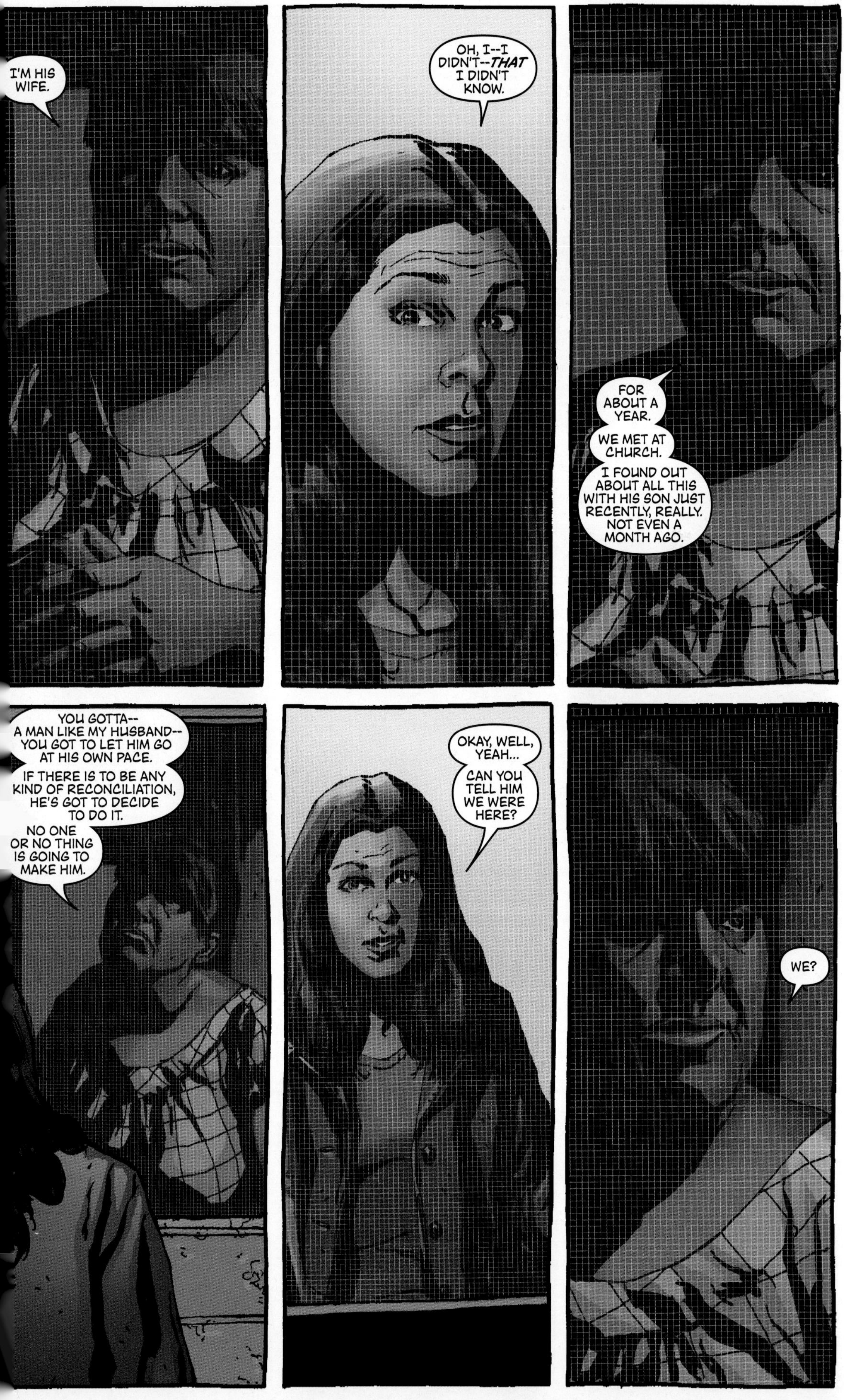
I'M HIS WIFE.
OH, I--I DIDN'T--*THAT* I DIDN'T KNOW.
FOR ABOUT A YEAR.
WE MET AT CHURCH.
I FOUND OUT ABOUT ALL THIS WITH HIS SON JUST RECENTLY, REALLY. NOT EVEN A MONTH AGO.
YOU GOTTA-- A MAN LIKE MY HUSBAND-- YOU GOT TO LET HIM GO AT HIS OWN PACE.
IF THERE IS TO BE ANY KIND OF RECONCILIATION, HE'S GOT TO DECIDE TO DO IT.
NO ONE OR NO THING IS GOING TO MAKE HIM.
OKAY, WELL, YEAH...
CAN YOU TELL HIM WE WERE HERE?
WE?

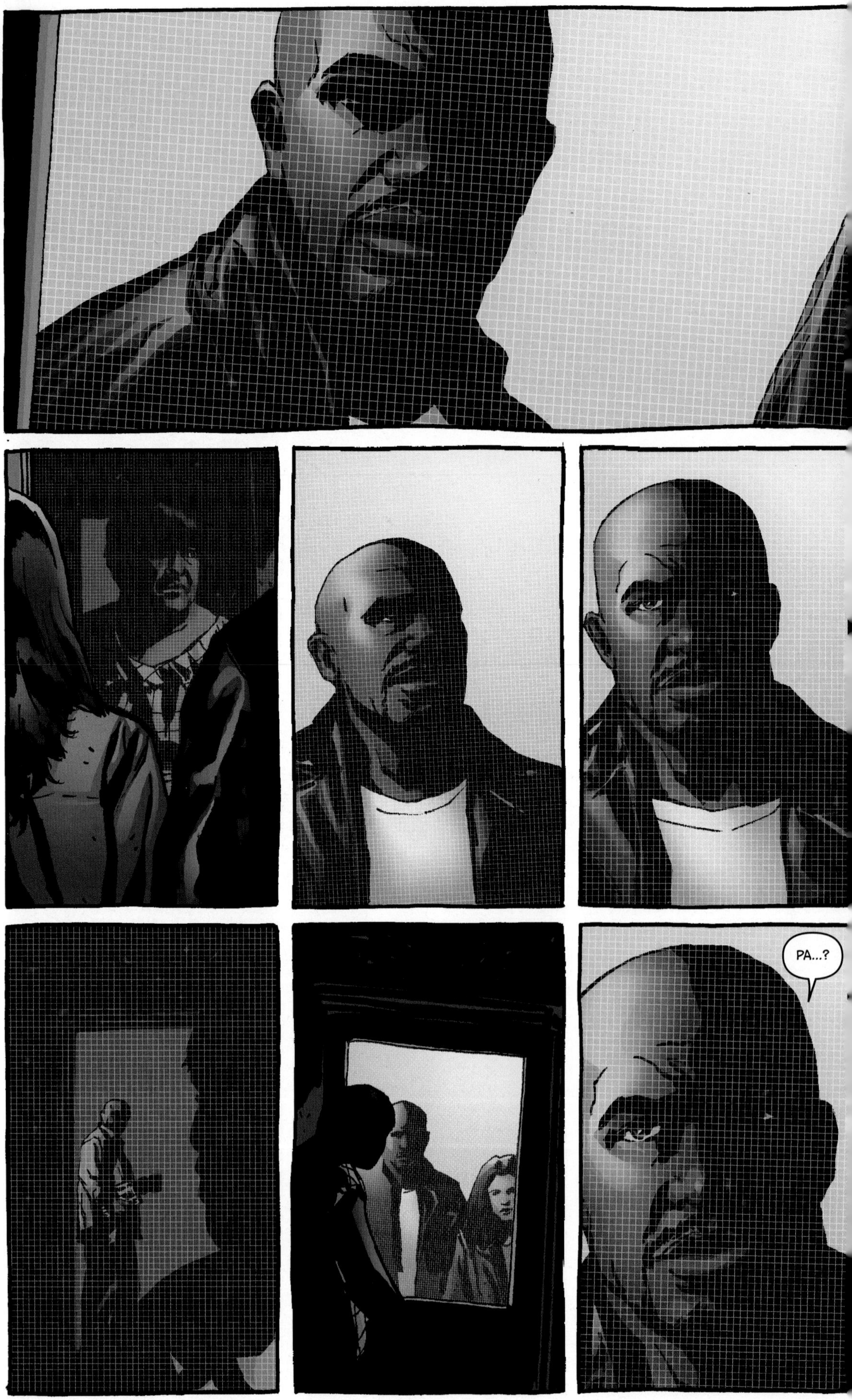
PA...?

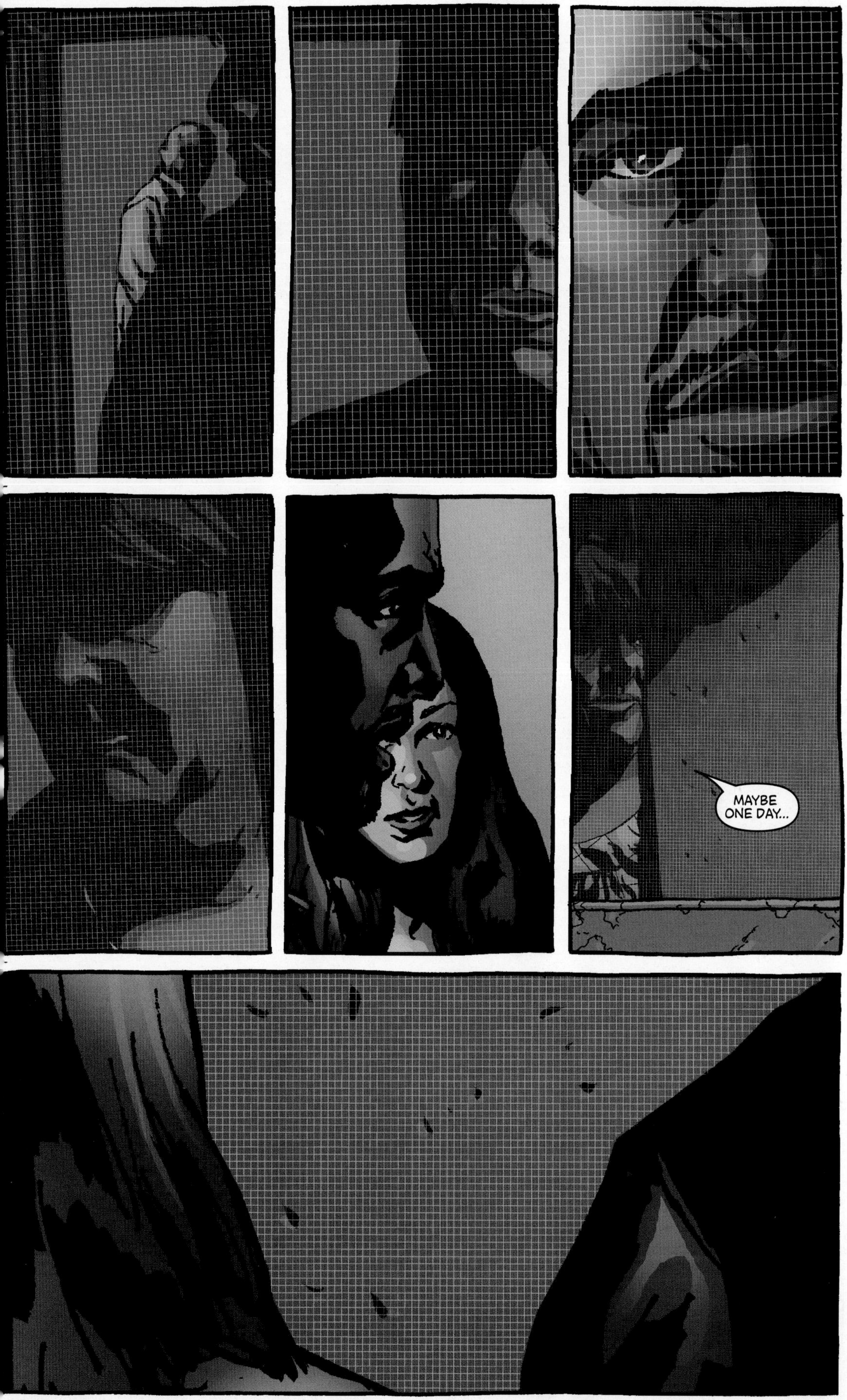
MAYBE ONE DAY...

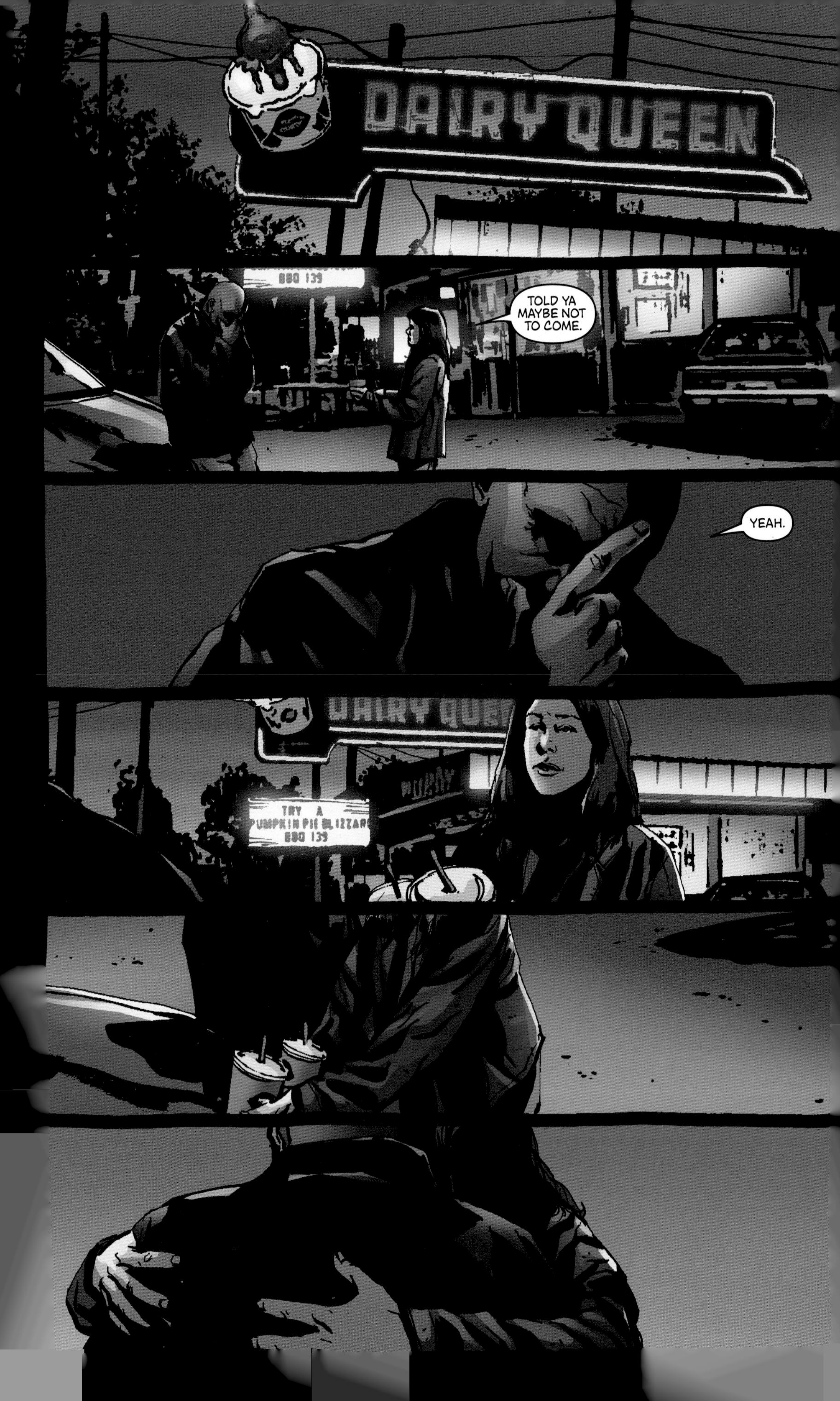
DAIRY QUEEN
TOLD YA MAYBE NOT TO COME.
YEAH.
TRY A PUMPKIN PIE BLIZZARD
880 139

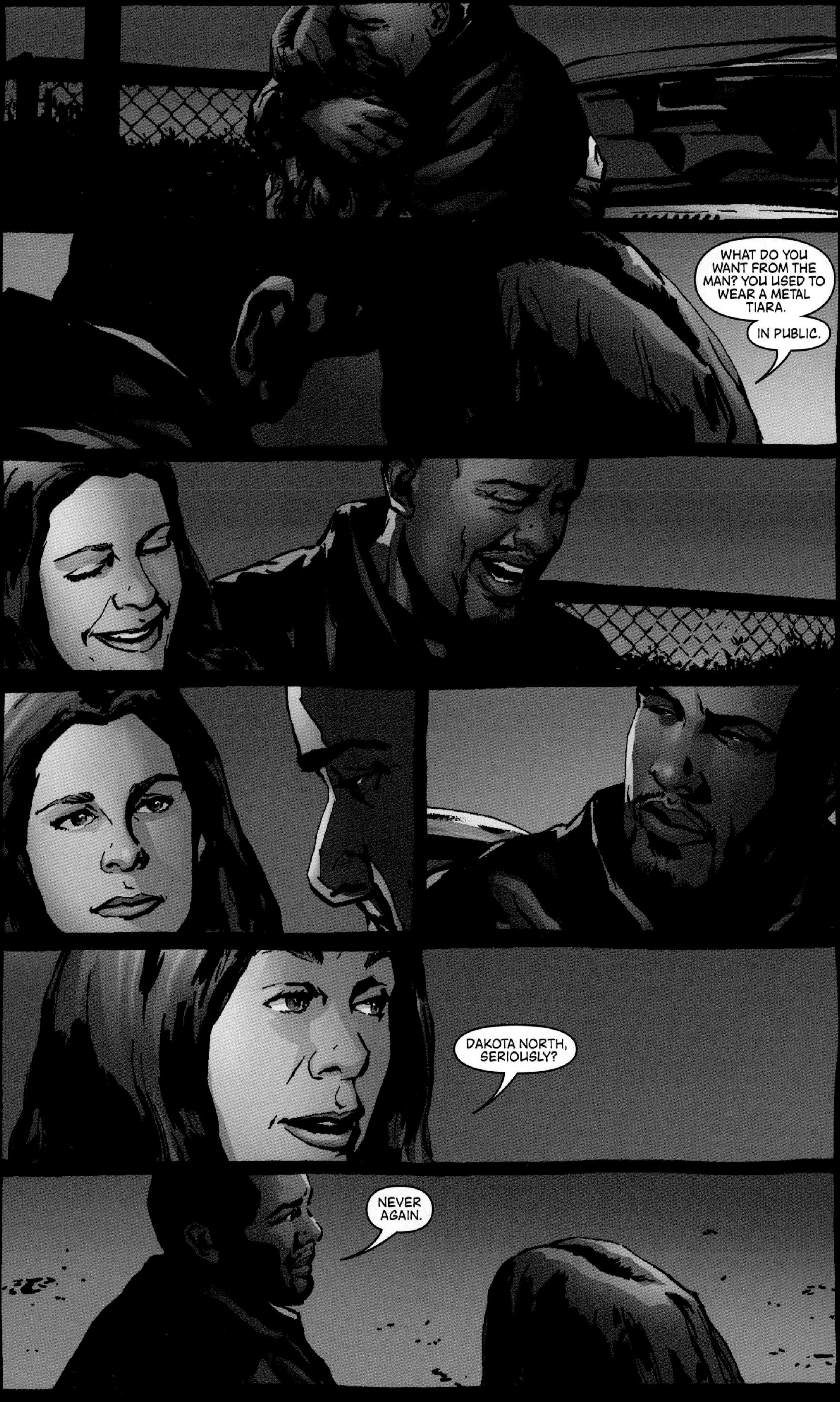
WHAT DO YOU WANT FROM THE MAN? YOU USED TO WEAR A METAL TIARA.
IN PUBLIC.
DAKOTA NORTH, SERIOUSLY?
NEVER AGAIN.

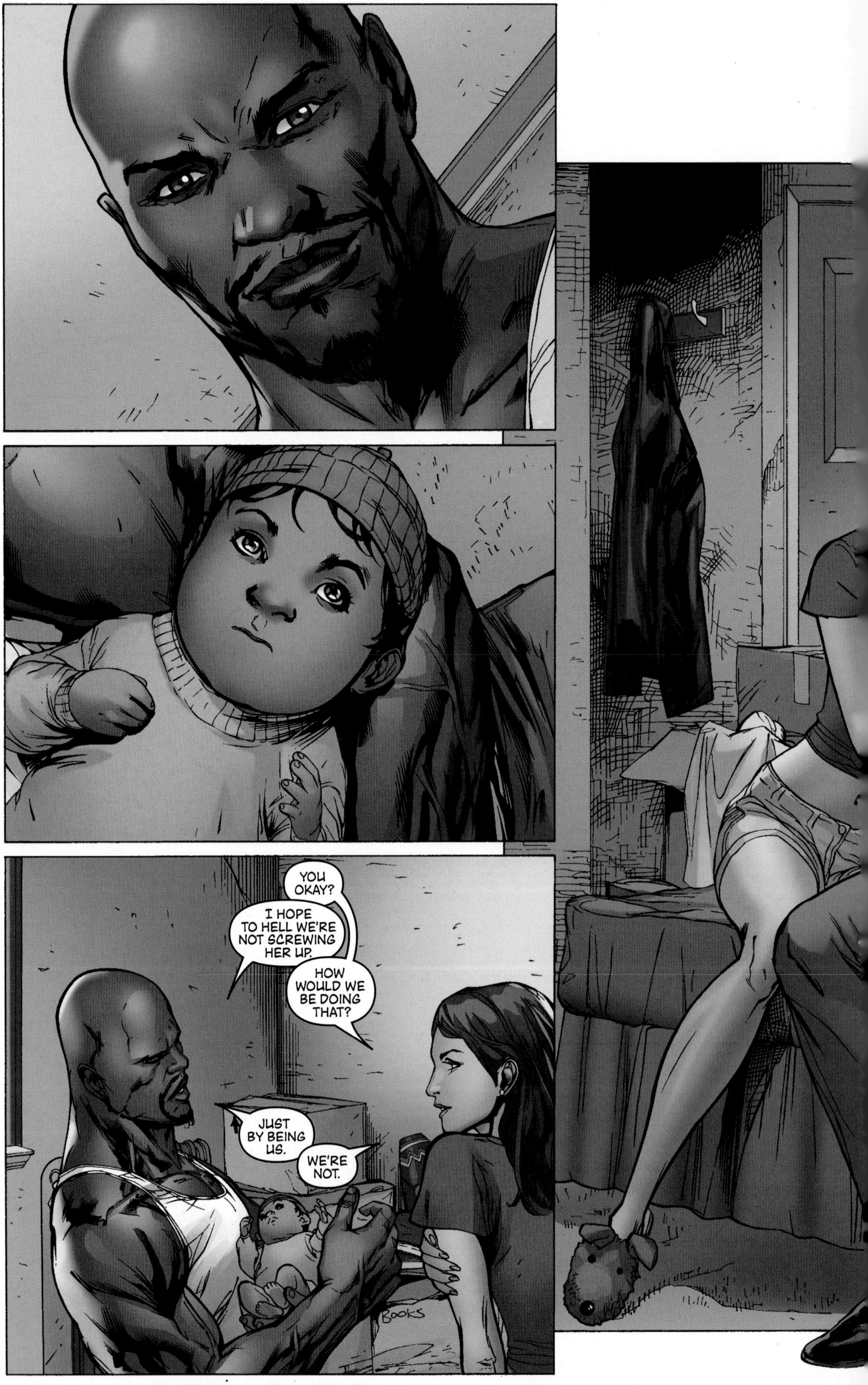
YOU OKAY?
I HOPE TO HELL WE'RE NOT SCREWING HER UP.
HOW WOULD WE BE DOING THAT?
JUST BY BEING US.
WE'RE NOT.
BOOKS

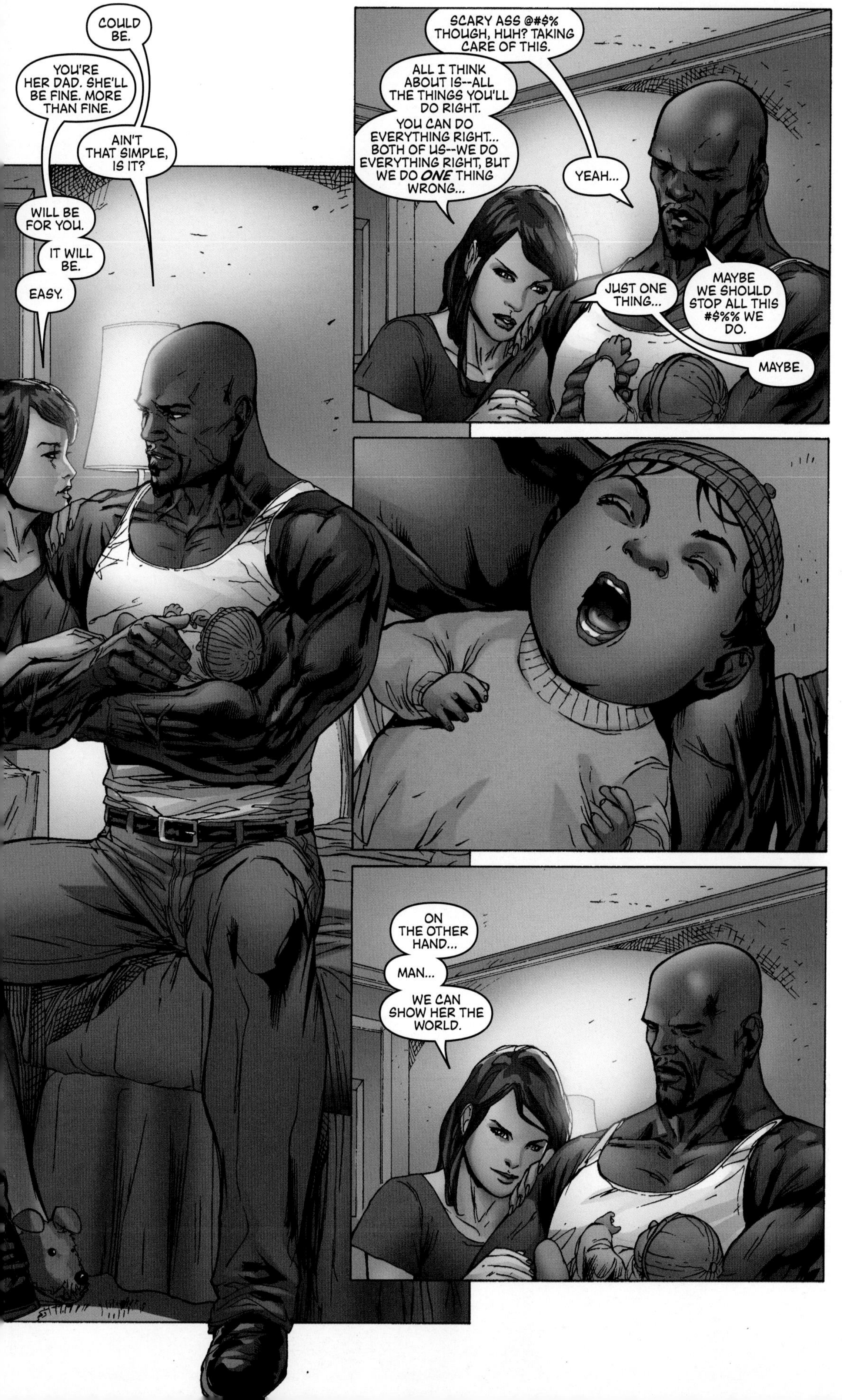
COULD BE.
YOU'RE HER DAD. SHE'LL BE FINE. MORE THAN FINE.
AIN'T THAT SIMPLE, IS IT?
WILL BE FOR YOU.
IT WILL BE.
EASY.
SCARY ASS @#$% THOUGH, HUH? TAKING CARE OF THIS.
ALL I THINK ABOUT IS--ALL THE THINGS YOU'LL DO RIGHT.
YOU CAN DO EVERYTHING RIGHT... BOTH OF US--WE DO EVERYTHING RIGHT, BUT WE DO *ONE* THING WRONG...
YEAH...
JUST ONE THING...
MAYBE WE SHOULD STOP ALL THIS #$%% WE DO.
MAYBE.
ON THE OTHER HAND...
MAN...
WE CAN SHOW HER THE WORLD.

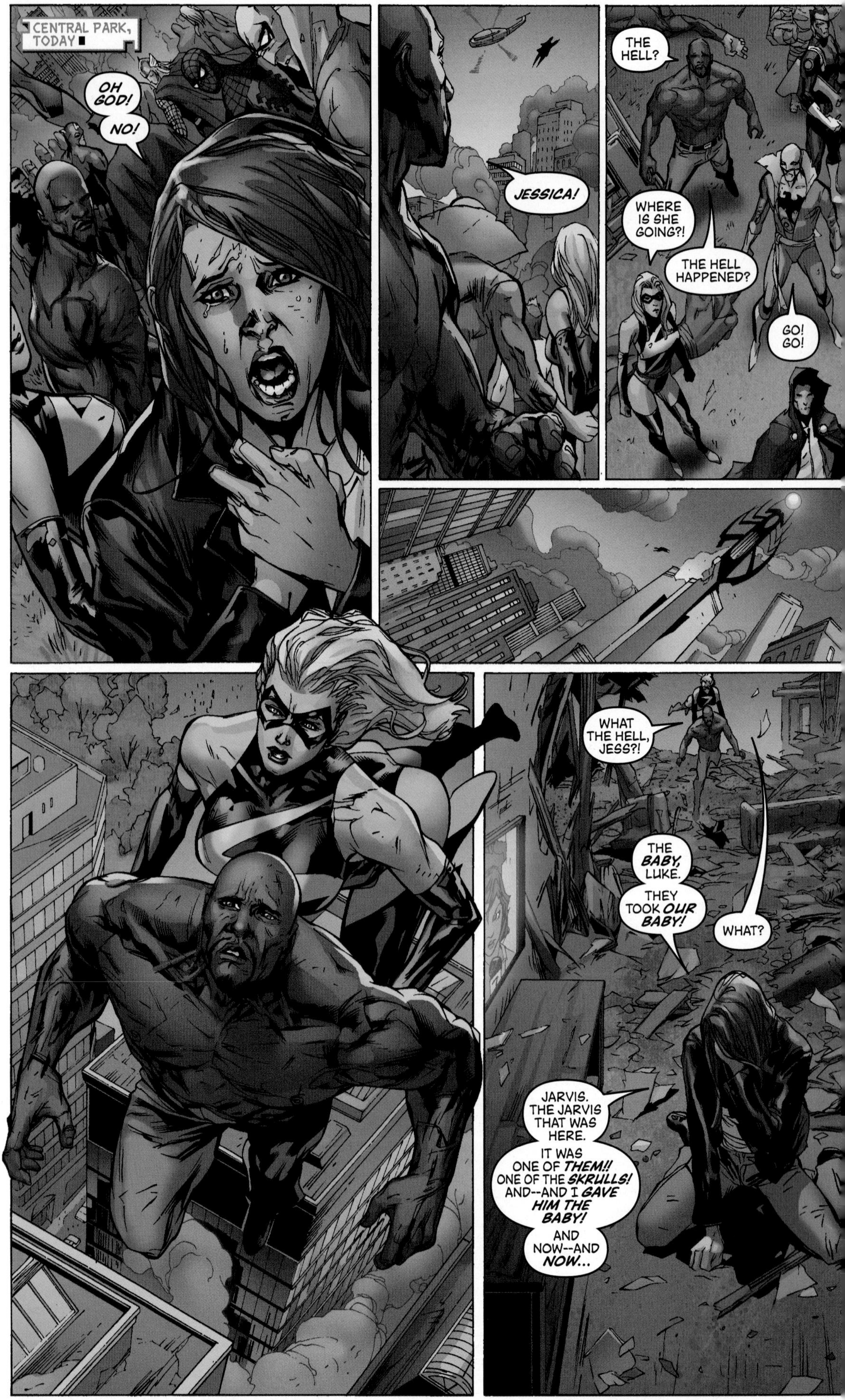
CENTRAL PARK, TODAY
OH GOD!
NO!
JESSICA!
THE HELL?
WHERE IS SHE GOING?!
THE HELL HAPPENED?
GO! GO!
WHAT THE HELL, JESS?!
THE BABY, LUKE.
THEY TOOK OUR BABY!
WHAT?
JARVIS. THE JARVIS THAT WAS HERE.
IT WAS ONE OF THEM!! ONE OF THE SKRULLS! AND--AND I GAVE HIM THE BABY!
AND NOW--AND NOW...

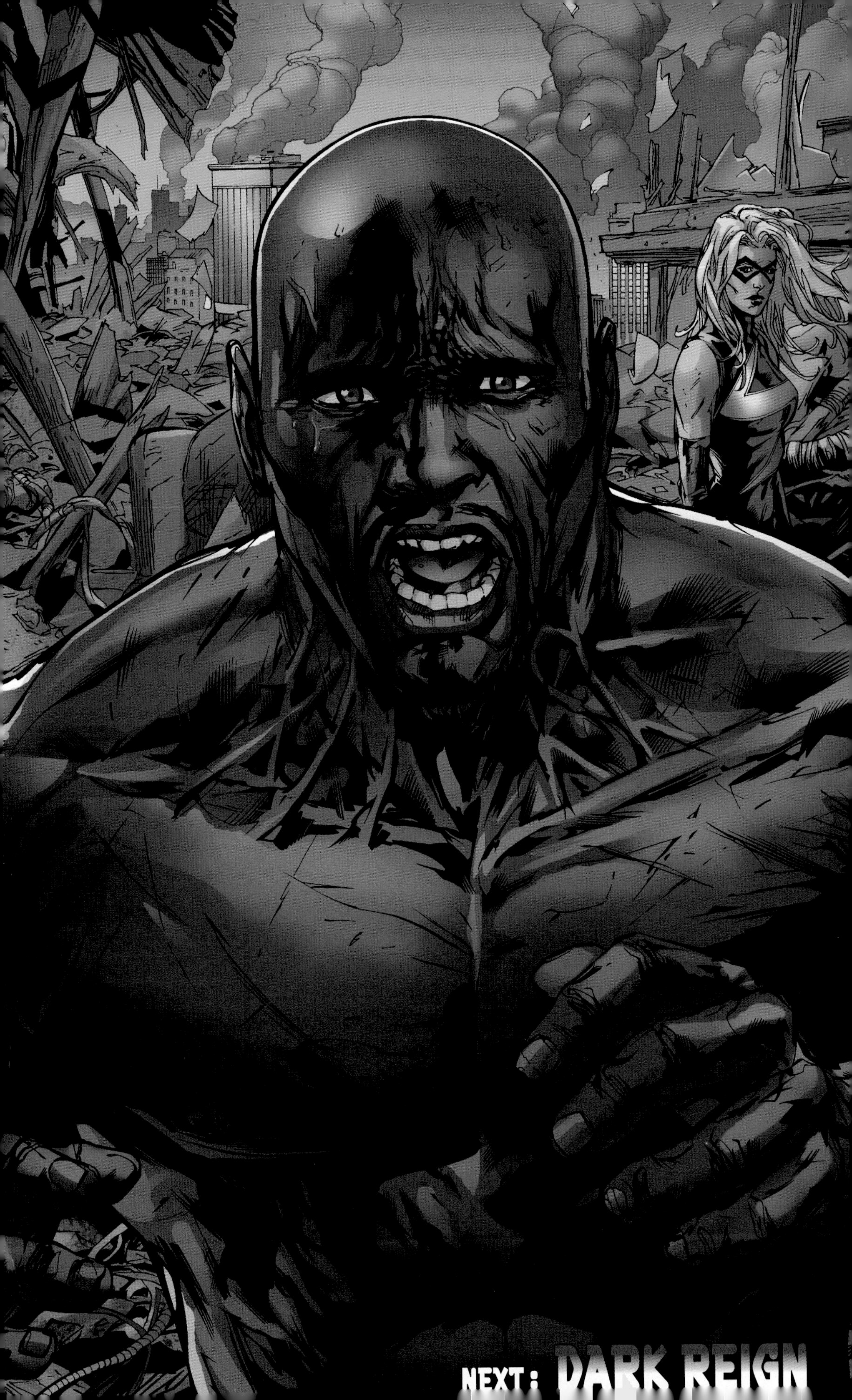
NEXT: DARK REIGN

COVER HOMAGES
BY ALEKSI BRICLOT

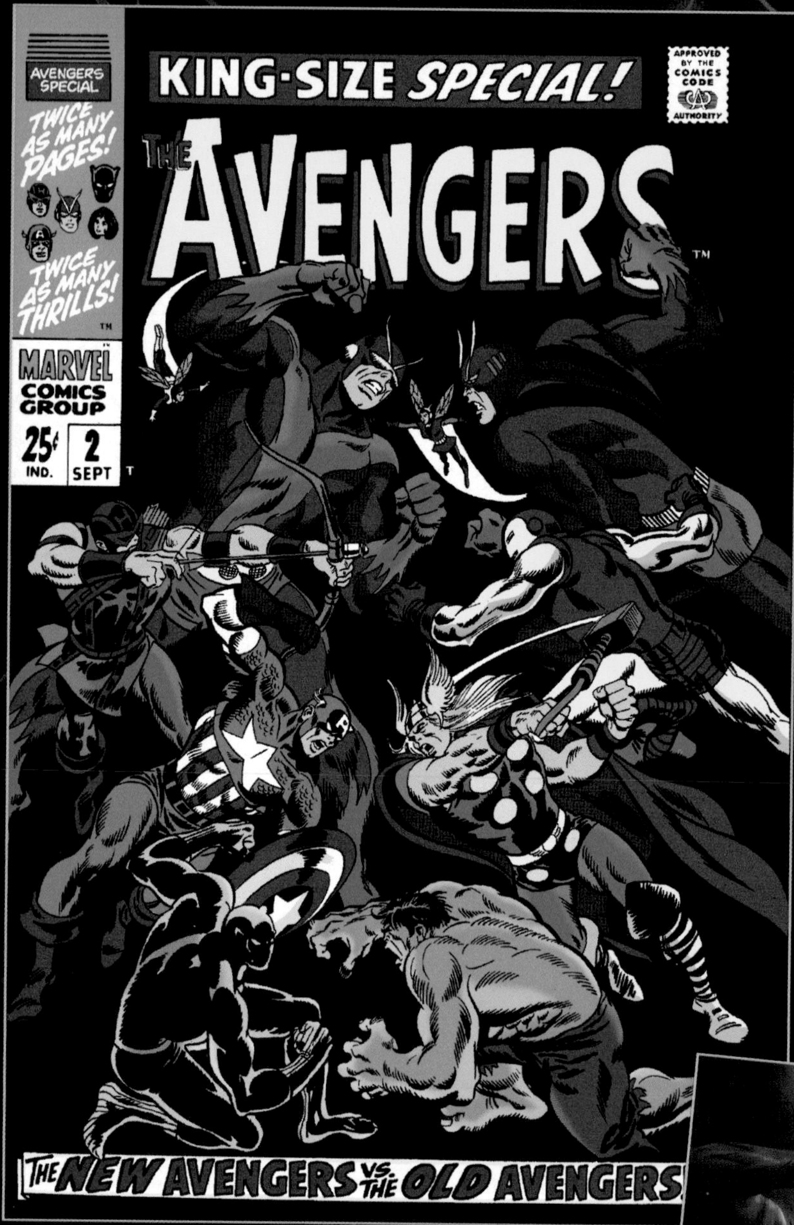
AVENGERS SPECIAL
TWICE AS MANY PAGES!
TWICE AS MANY THRILLS!
MARVEL COMICS GROUP
25¢ IND.
2 SEPT
KING-SIZE SPECIAL!
APPROVED BY THE COMICS CODE AUTHORITY
THE AVENGERS
THE NEW AVENGERS VS. THE OLD AVENGERS!

BY JOHN BUSCEMA

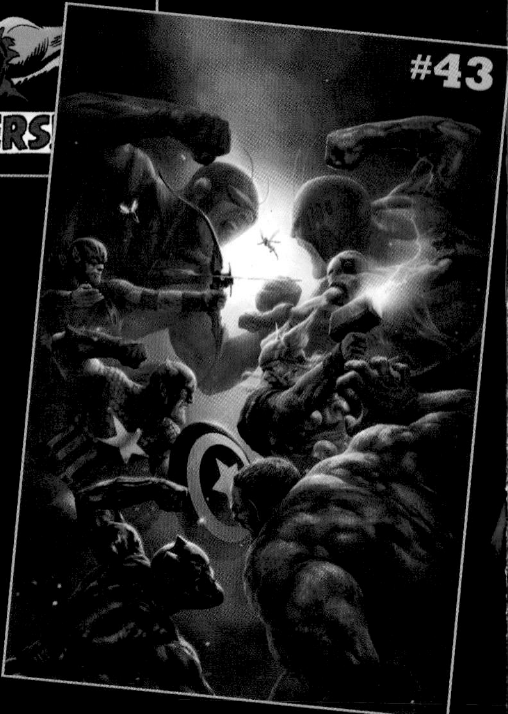
#43

NEW AVENGERS: ILLUMINATI #1
BY JIM CHEUNG

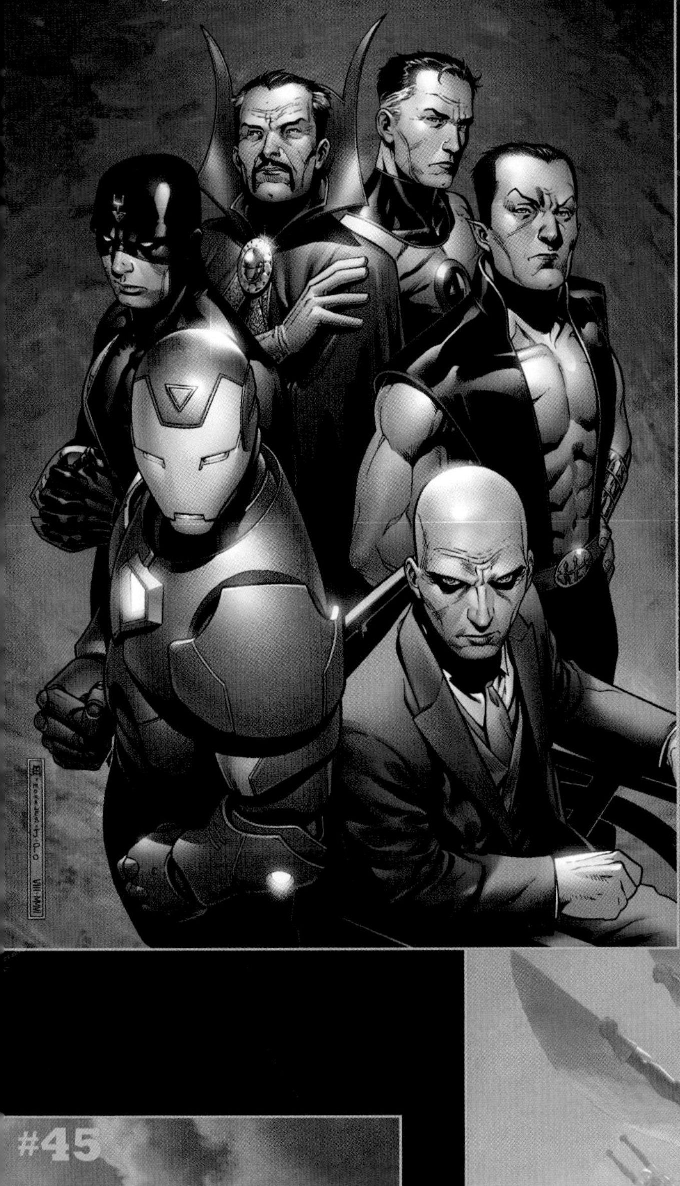

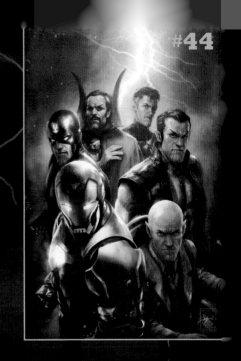

#44

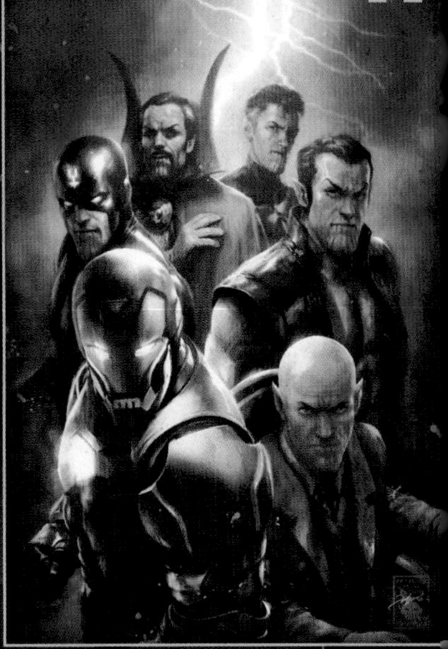

HOUSE OF M #1
BY ESAD RIBIC

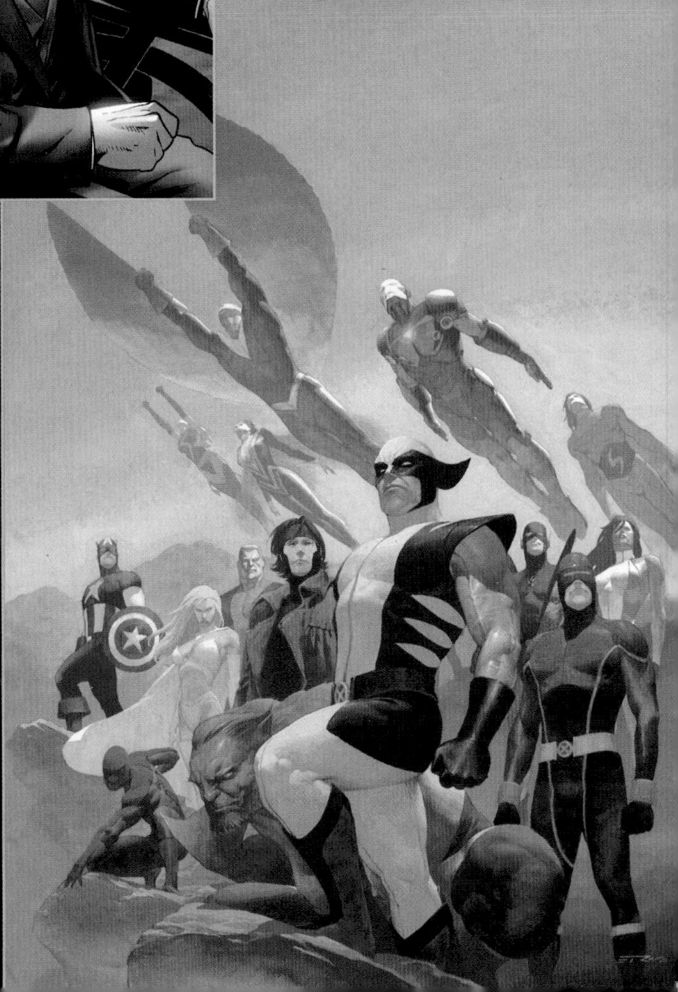

#45

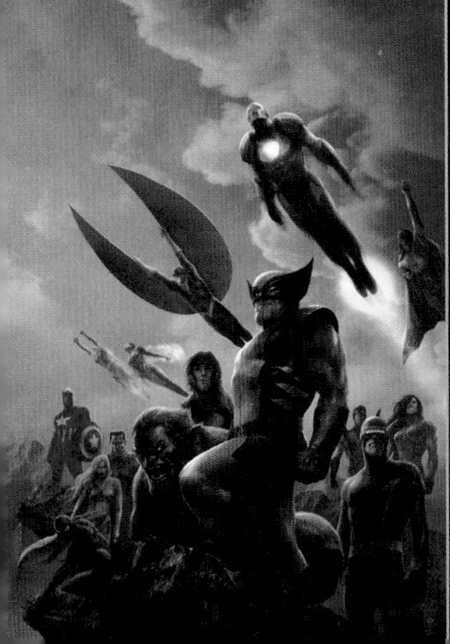

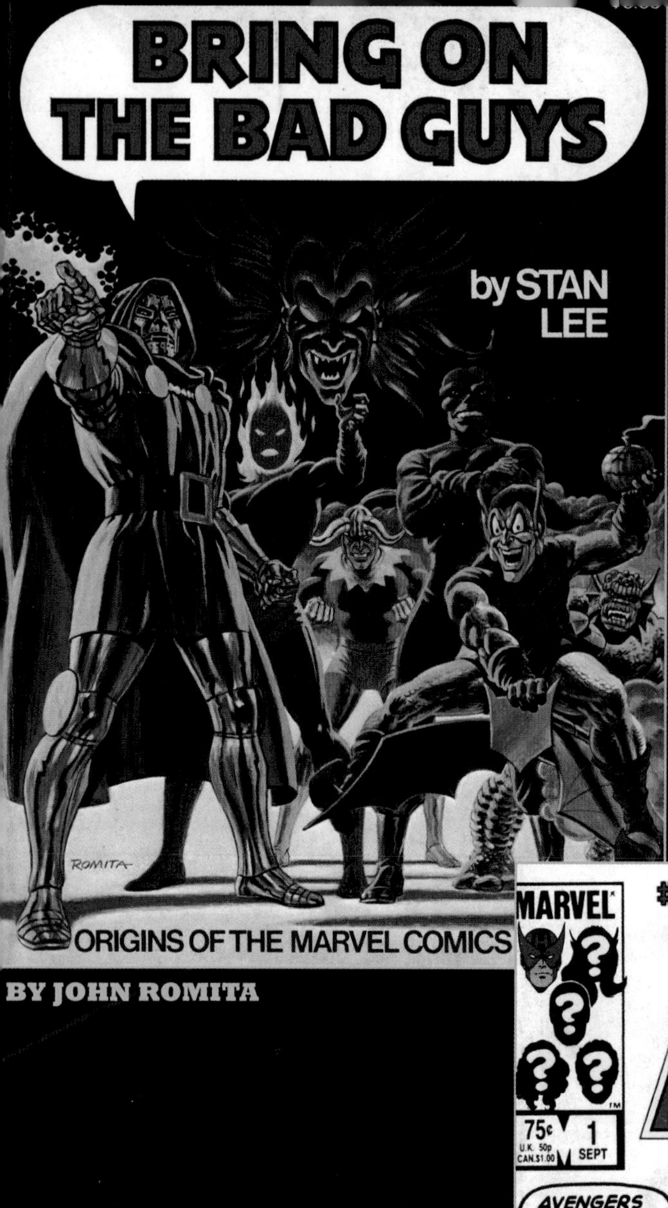
BRING ON THE BAD GUYS
by STAN LEE
ROMITA
ORIGINS OF THE MARVEL COMICS

BY JOHN ROMITA

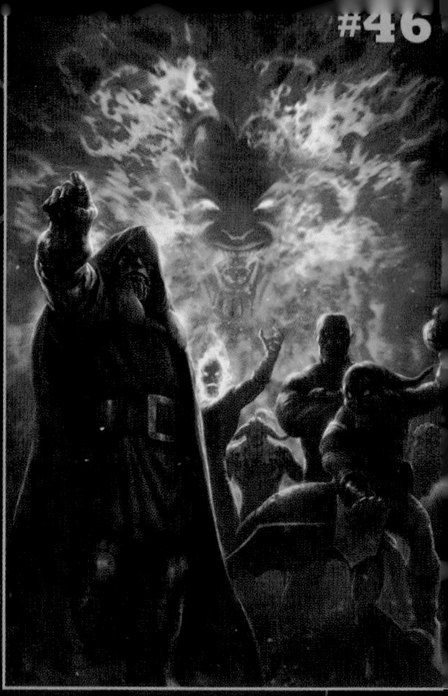
#46

BY BOB HALL

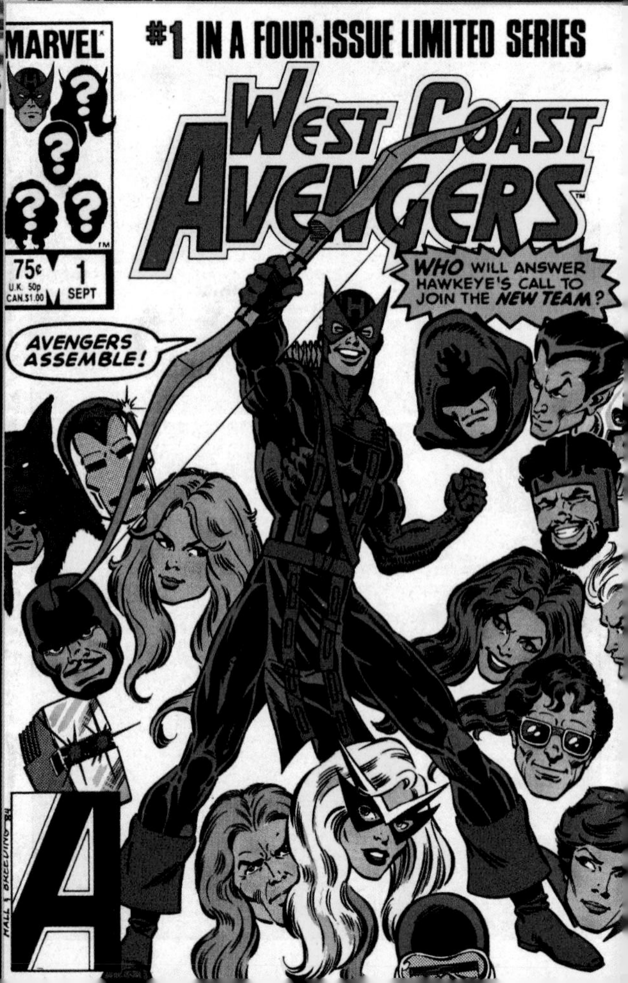
#1 IN A FOUR-ISSUE LIMITED SERIES
MARVEL
WEST COAST AVENGERS
75¢ 1 SEPT
U.K. 50p
CAN.$1.00
WHO WILL ANSWER HAWKEYE'S CALL TO JOIN THE NEW TEAM?
AVENGERS ASSEMBLE!

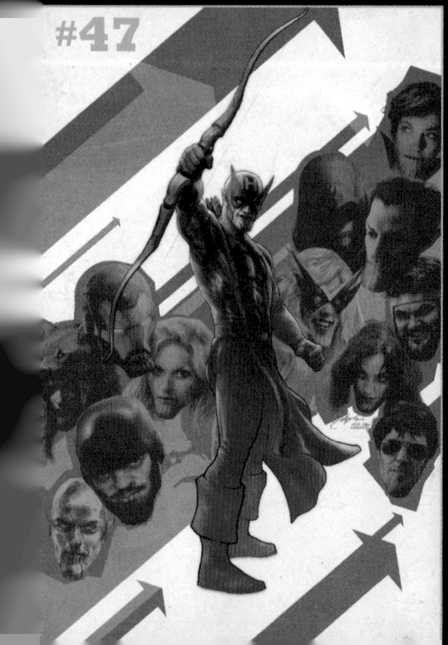
#47